Age *of*
Opportunity

Resources for Changing Lives

A series published in cooperation with
THE CHRISTIAN COUNSELING AND EDUCATIONAL FOUNDATION
Glenside, Pennsylvania

Susan Lutz, Series Editor

Available in the series:

Edward T. Welch, *When People Are Big and God Is Small: Overcoming Peer Pressure, Codependency, and the Fear of Man*

Paul David Tripp, *Age of Opportunity: A Biblical Guide to Parenting Teens*

Edward T. Welch, *Blame It on the Brain? Distinguishing Chemical Imbalances, Brain Disorders, and Disobedience*

James C. Petty, *Step by Step: Divine Guidance for Ordinary Christians*

Paul David Tripp, *War of Words: Getting to the Heart of Your Communication Struggles*

Edward T. Welch, *Addictions—A Banquet in the Grave: Finding Hope in the Power of the Gospel*

Paul David Tripp, *Instruments in the Redeemer's Hands: People in Need of Change Helping People in Need of Change*

David Powlison, *Seeing with New Eyes: Counseling and the Human Condition through the Lens of Scripture*

Age *of* Opportunity

A Biblical Guide to Parenting Teens

PAUL DAVID TRIPP

P&R PUBLISHING
P.O. BOX 817 • PHILLIPSBURG • NEW JERSEY 08865-0817

Unless otherwise indicated, Scripture quotations are from the HOLY BIBLE, NEW INTERNATIONAL VERSION. Copyright © 1973, 1978, 1984 International Bible Society. Used by permission of Zondervan Bible Publishers. Italics indicate emphasis added.

Printed in the United States of America

Library of Congress Cataloging-in-Publication Data

Tripp, Paul David, 1950–
    Age of opportunity : a biblical guide to parenting teens / Paul David Tripp.—2nd ed.
        p.   cm. — (Resources for changing lives)
    ISBN-10: 0-87552-605-5 (pbk.)
    ISBN-13: 978-0-87552-605-8 (pbk.)
    1. Parenting—Religious aspects—Christianity. 2. Parent and teenager—
Religious aspects—Christianity. 3. Christian teenagers—Religious life. I. Title.
II. Series.

BV4529.T75 2001
248.8'45—dc21

                                        2001034350

To Luella

For twenty-six years you have been

my best friend, teacher, and example.

In many ways you have taught me

what parenting is all about.

Thank you; your contribution

is greater than you will ever know.

CONTENTS

PREFACE

IT was in August of 1971 that I took my first pastoral position as the Youth Director of Whaley Street United Methodist Church in Columbia, South Carolina. I was three months away from my twenty-first birthday. Those days at Whaley Street seem so distant, almost like part of someone else's life. Yet there is one thing that remains with me: a desire to see the Gospel applied to those difficult years when a person passes from childhood into adulthood.

I couldn't have written this book in 1971. In many ways I was one of the youth that I am writing about here. But more than that, there was much work that God needed to do in me through many people that he would raise up. It would be impossible to list all the people who have contributed to the thinking that is reflected here. This book represents the loving ministry of pastors, teachers, friends, fellow elders, and family; all who have contributed to my understanding of what it means to live biblically.

I would like to thank some people who have been significant contributors to my life, my ministry, and this book. First my children, Justin (9/76), Ethan (9/78), Nicole (9/81), and Darnay (10/85). You have given me room to learn and taught me so much about what it means to parent God's way. Thank you for the gift of forgiveness you have given me again and again. Thank you for helping me to see that the teen years are really years of huge opportunity. Thank you also for not accusing me of loving my laptop more than I loved you as I spent those many nights in the bedroom typing away. Finally, thanks for letting me tell the stories of our struggles. They help give this book integrity.

Tedd, I am sure that you have no idea how much you have mentored me over the years. I seldom teach without your name coming up in an illustration or a quote. Thanks for encouraging me to write this book.

Ed, Dave, and John (faculty members at the Christian Counseling and Educational Foundation), thank you for helping me take scriptural theology and make it work where the rubber meets the road. Thanks, too, for your continuing influence as we minister together.

Sue, I cannot thank you enough for the hours of editorial work that have simply made this a much better book. Your ability to capture my thoughts with an economy and clarity of words is greatly appreciated.

Ruth, thank you for the many hours of transcription. Your willing labor gave me the "jump start" I needed.

Jayne, thank you for being committed to making the things that have been planned actually happen. This book is one of the fruits of that commitment.

My prayer is that this book would give hope, courage, and insight to thousands of parents who are entering or are in the midst of the teen years with their children. May the truths of God's Word turn a time of anxious survival into a time of expectation and opportunity!

PART ONE *Clearing the Debris*

CHAPTER

AGE OF OPPORTUNITY OR SEASON FOR SURVIVAL?

IT is everywhere around us—on the television sitcom, in the magazine on the supermarket rack, on the shelves of the local bookstore, on television and radio talk shows, and yes, even in a number of Christian books on the family. Parents are afraid of their teenagers. Even as they are enjoying the early years of a child's life, they are looking over their shoulders with dread, expecting the worst, knowing that in a few short years this precious little one will turn into a monster overnight. They've heard enough stories from parents who have gone through the dark valley of the teen years to know the dangers that lie ahead. They are told to expect the worst and to be thankful if they come out of the valley sane, with their teenager alive and their family intact.

I encountered this view of the teen years recently at a marriage conference. It had been a great weekend in all ways. The teaching had been engaging, convicting, and encouraging. The food and accommodations had been superb, and the conference had been held in a beautiful seaside location. Near the end of the weekend, I was looking out at the sun glistening on the waters of the bay when I noticed a couple sitting nearby. They looked very unhappy.

I was curious, so I asked them if they had enjoyed the weekend. Everything had been great, they replied. I commented that they didn't look very happy. The women responded, "We have two teenagers and we are dreading going home. We wish this weekend would last forever!" "You just have to expect your teenager to be rebellious; all of us were," her husband added. "You just have to ride it out." "Besides," she moaned, "you can't argue with hormones!"

I walked away impressed that something is fundamentally wrong with the way we think about this time in a child's life. Something is inherently wrong with the cultural epidemic of fear and cynicism about our teenagers. Something is wrong when a parent's highest goal is survival. We need to take another look: Is this a biblical view of this period in a child's life? Does this view lead to biblical strategies of parenting and biblical hope?

We need to examine what is wrong with the cynicism about teenagers that is endemic in our culture.

A Biological View of Teens

We often talk about our teenagers as if they were nothing more than collections of raging, rebel hormones encased in developing skin. We see our goal as somehow holding these hormones back so that we can survive until the teen has reached twenty. A parent recently rejoiced to me that her son had turned twenty, as if he had passed through some magic portal from danger into safety. "We made it!" she said.

This survival mentality exposes the poverty of this view of teenagers. Many parents who talk to me about their teenagers talk without hope; they see them as victims of hormones that drive them to do crazy things. Although they would never say this, the working theology that hides behind this view is that the truths of Scripture, the power of the Gospel, biblical communication, and godly relationship are no match for the teen years. Yes, we believe that God's Word is powerful and effective—except if some poor soul is trying to apply it to a child between the years of thirteen and nineteen! We now even have a category of children called "pre-teen." These are the years when the monsterish characteristics of the teenagers begin to develop and rear their ugly heads.

Are we comfortable with a view of teenagers that says that because of the significant biological changes going on inside them, they are essentially unreachable? Are we comfortable with a hormonal view of teens that reduces them to victims of biological forces, freeing them from responsibility for their own choices and actions? Do we really want a view of teens that would have us believe that the truths that give life and hope to anyone who believes cannot reach a teenager? We cannot hold onto a robust belief in the power of the Gospel if we continue to buy into our culture's cynicism about the teen years.

Particular Sacrifice and Suffering?

In 2 Timothy 2:22, Paul exhorts Timothy to "flee the evil desires [lusts] of youth." This interesting little phrase calls us to be balanced in the way we think about teenagers and the way we define this time of life. On the one hand, the Bible challenges us not to be naive about this period of life. There are lusts that uniquely plague young people, temptations that are particularly powerful. These must to be faced. Scripture enjoins us to be strategic, to ask the question, "What are the evil desires that grip a person during this phase of life?"

At the same time Paul uses the qualifier, "youthful," because each phase of life has its own set of temptations. The temptations of the little boy, the young man, and the old man are not identical. The temptations of the teenager are not particularly savage and severe. Each person at each time in his life, if he seeks to please the Lord, must watch, pray, stand fast, and fight lest he fall into temptation. The teenager is called to guard against the temptations that are unique to youth, while the older person is called to guard against the temptations unique to that age. Each person, whatever his or her age, must accept each stage of warfare as a Christian living in this fallen world.

Battle of Biology or Battle of the Heart?

The 2 Timothy passage is also helpful in the way it locates and defines the battle of youth. There *is* a battle raging in the lives of young people, but it is not the battle of biology. It is an intensely spiritual battle, a battle for the heart. This is exactly what Paul wants us to be aware of as he exhorts Timothy not to let his heart be controlled by evil desires. This battle is not unique to teens. It takes a certain shape during the teen years, but it is the battle of every sinner.

The tendency of every sinner, no matter what his age, is captured well by Paul in Romans 1:25, that is, the tendency to exchange worship and service of the Creator for the worship and service of the created thing. Yes, it's there in the life of the teenager who forsakes his convictions for the approval of his peers, but it is just as powerfully present in the adult who compromises family and spiritual priorities for professional success. The battle, as Paul understands it, is a heart battle, and it is dramatically important because what controls the heart will direct the life.

There are significant temptations of the heart that greet teenagers, calling them to believe that they cannot live without some aspect of the creation. These voices call them to believe that identity, meaning, and purpose can be found in the creature rather than the Creator. These are the life-altering conflicts of the teen years. We dare not miss them because of our biologically oriented fears and our survival mentality. We must believe that Jesus came so that each of us would be freed from the desires of our sinful nature so that we may serve him and him alone. This includes our teenagers.

The Struggles of Parents

The tumult of the teen years is not only about the attitudes and actions of teens, but the thoughts, desires, attitudes, and actions of parents as well. The teen years are hard for us because they tend to bring out the worst in us. It is in these years that parents hear themselves saying things that they never thought they would say. Parents find themselves reacting with accusations, guilt manipulation, and ultimatums, responding with a level of anger that they would not have thought possible. It is in these years that parents struggle with embarrassment at being related to the teen who was once, as a child, a great source of pride and joy.

It is vital for us to confess that the struggle of the teen years is not only about teen biology and teen rebellion. These years are hard for us because they expose the wrong thoughts and desires of our *own* hearts. There is a principle here that we need to recognize. My mother put it this way: "There is nothing that comes out of a drunk that was not in there in the beginning." These years are hard for us because they rip back the curtain and expose us. This is why trials are so difficult, yet so useful in God's hands. We don't radically change in a moment of trial. No, trials expose what we have always been. Trials bare things to which we would have otherwise been blind. So, too, the teen years expose our self-righteousness, our impatience, our unforgiving spirit, our lack of servant love, the weakness of our faith, and our craving for comfort and ease.

Why We Miss the Opportunities

I sat recently in my office with a father who was so angry at his son that it was all he could do to be civil. He did not see the tremendous spiritual needs in his son that he had been uniquely positioned by God to meet. There was no tenderness in their relationship; there wasn't even cordiality. There was tense distance. At one point the father rose to speak to his son about his report card. He walked to his son's chair and stuck the failing report card in his face and said, "How dare you do this to me after all I have done for you!" To him, the bad grades were a personal affront. This was not the way he thought it was supposed to work. He had done his job; now the son was supposed to do his. He was angry at his son, but not because of his sin against God. He was angry because his son had taken things away from *him* as a father that he valued very much: his reputation as a successful Christian father, the respect he thought he deserved, and the ease he thought he would finally achieve with older children.

There was no attitude of ministry, no sense of opportunity, no quest to be part of what God was doing in the life of his son. Instead, he was filled with the anger described in James 4:2: "You want something, but you don't get it."

The cultural cynicism we have been discussing is based on who we think teenagers are and what we think they are going through. We tend to believe that there is little we can do to make these years more productive. Rather, the culture would say, we need to come up with positive strategies of survival that preserve the sanity of the parents and the stability of the marriage, and that keep the teenager out of as much self-inflicted danger as possible.

However, it is my experience that when parents begin to recognize, own, confess, and turn from their own wrong heart attitudes and the wrong actions that flow from them, the result is a marked difference in their relationship to their teen and in the way they view the struggles of the teen years. When we look with concerned eyes toward the teen years, we need to look not only at our children, but also at ourselves. Parents who are humbly willing to change, position themselves to be God's instruments of change.

A Better Way

It is time for us to reject the wholesale cynicism of our culture regarding adolescence. Rather than years of undirected and unproductive struggle, these are years of unprecedented opportunity. They are the golden age of parenting, when you begin to reap all the seeds you have sown in their lives, when you can help your teenager to internalize truth, preparing him or her for a productive, God-honoring life as an adult.

These are the years of penetrating questions, the years of wonderful discussions never before possible. These are the years of failure and struggle that put the teen's true heart on the table. These are the years of daily ministry and of great opportunity.

These are not years merely to be survived! They are to be approached with a sense of hope and a sense of mission. Almost every day brings a new opportunity to enter the life of your teen with help, hope, and truth. We should not resign ourselves to an increasingly distant relationship. This is the time to connect with our children as never before. These are years of great opportunity.

That is what this book is about. It is a book of opportunity and hope. It is time for us to come out of the bunkers of cynicism and fear and into the light, examining the plan God has for us as we parent our teenagers. This is a book about activity, goals, and practical strategies. This is a book that believes that the truths of Scripture apply as powerfully to teens as they do to anyone else.

At the same time, this book will not be naive. The teen years are often cataclysmic years of conflict, struggle, and grief. They are years of new temptations, of trial and testing. Yet these very struggles, conflicts, trials, and tests are what produce such wonderful parental opportunities.

Recognizing God's Moments of Change

It was a wintry Tuesday night. I had had counseling appointments all day and had taught for three hours in the evening. I was driving home at about ten o'clock, dreaming about an hour or so of relaxation before I hit the bed. I silently hoped that for some inexplicable reason, the whole family had gone to sleep at nine o'clock. Or if they had not gone to bed, I hoped that they would instinctively know that I was tired and not to be disturbed. I reasoned that I had served God faithfully that day. Surely, God would agree that I had the right to punch out from life! I dreamed of an empty family room, a well-iced Diet Coke, the newspaper, and the remote control. I was totally exhausted and I had a right to relax. (You can see that I was approaching the house with a selfless attitude of ministry!)

I quietly opened the door in the vain hope that I could sneak in unnoticed. The living room lights were out and the house was quiet. I was filled with hope. Maybe my dreams had come true; an evening of relaxation all to myself! I had only put one foot in the door when I heard an angry voice. My heart sank! I wanted to act as if I hadn't heard it. It was the voice of Ethan, my teenage son. My disappointment soon gave way to anger. I wanted to grab him and say, "Don't you know what my day has been like? Don't you know how tired I am? The last thing I need right now is to deal with your problems. You're going to have to solve this one yourself. I wish for once you'd think of somebody besides yourself. I do and do for you and this is the thanks I get. You can't leave me alone one night?"

All these thoughts raged within me, but I didn't say a word. I listened to Ethan as he poured out his complaint. He was as angry as he had ever been at his older brother. He was cursing the fact that he had an older brother who seemed to do nothing but "trash his life." It was after ten. The issue that started this thing was petty. I was tempted to tell him to get a grip and deal with it, but another agenda gripped me. Here was one of those unexpected moments of opportunity, one of those mundane moments ordained by a loving and sovereign God where the heart of my teenager was being exposed. It was more than an Ethan and Dad moment. This was God's moment, a dynamic moment of redemption where God was continuing the work of rescue he had begun years ago in my son. The only question in the moment was whether I would pursue God's agenda or my own. Would I believe the Gospel in that moment, trusting God to give me what I needed so that I could do what he was calling me to do in the life of my son?

I asked Ethan to sit down at the dining room table and tell me what was going on. He was hurt and angry. His heart was on the table. We talked through his anger and he became ready to listen. A petty argument with his brother opened the door to discussing things that were far from petty. God gave me strength and patience. He filled my mouth with the right things to say. Ethan saw himself in new ways that night and confessed to things that he had never before recognized.

It was approaching midnight when I said goodnight to Ethan. We hugged and went to bed. What first appeared to be an irritating moment over an obviously petty issue had in fact been a wonderful opportunity of ministry, ordained by a God of love. It became very clear that God wasn't only working to change Ethan; he was working to change me as well. The selfishness of *my* heart had been revealed that evening, the same selfishness that causes parents to lash out in anger at the very teens who need them. My need of Christ, too, had been exposed. There was no way I could function as his instrument without his strength.

Little Moments, High Calling

I chose to write about this moment because it was one of those unremarkable moments that not only happen daily, but many times a day. Each of these moments is loaded with opportunity. There are many, many more of these moments than the dramatic moments of adolescence—like pregnancy, drugs, and violence—that get so much press. None of us lives constantly in the grand moments of significant decision; there aren't many of them in life. No, we live in the world of the incredibly mundane. This is where we need to see our teenagers with the eyes of opportunity rather than eyes of dread and fear.

The argument over the last pop tart, the cry of nothing to wear a half hour before school, the report card crumpled in the pocket of jeans heading for the wash, the pouting expression in the face of a parent's "No," the third fender-bender in a month, the constant words of discontent, the "everybody else does," and the "I'm the only one whose parents make them . . ." all must be seen as something more than hassles that get in the way of an otherwise enjoyable life. These are the moments God made parents for. You are God's agents on the watch. You have been given an incredibly high calling. You are God's instrument of help and preparation as this child makes his final steps out of the home and into God's world. These moments make your life worthwhile. Here you will make a contribution that is worth infinitely more than any career or financial accomplishment.

Recognizing the Opportunities

The more I have lived with my own teenage children, watched their peers, and interacted with other parents of teenagers, the more

I am convinced that this is a time of unbridled opportunity. There are issues that get exposed in this delicate, scary, awkward, and volatile period of development that make it so full of opportunity. It is not a time to head for the bunkers! It is not a time to dread worst-case scenarios of total domestic chaos. This is not a time to accept a culturally dictated "generation gap." This is a time to jump into the battle and move toward your teenager. It is a time for engagement, interaction, discussion, and committed relationship. This is not a time to let a teenager hide his doubts, fears, and failures, but a time to pursue, love, encourage, teach, forgive, confess, and accept. It is a wonderful time.

As I write this, my wife and I have three teenagers. We have never had more of a sense of calling. We have laughed, cried, discussed, and prayed with our teens. We have struggled for them and with them. We have seen failure and trial as opportunity. We have not always responded in faith, and we have needed to confess our own sin, but we have commented to one another that this is a wonderful period of family life. We are so happy to be doing what we are doing. We see the glory of God being revealed even in the midst of our own feeble efforts and weak faith.

There are three fundamental doors of opportunity that every teenage parent can walk through. Each of these problems becomes a means of helping the teenager to internalize the truths to which he has been exposed for years. The problems of teenage insecurity, teenage rebellion, and the teenager's widening world are actually God's doors of opportunity where parents have unique access to the central issues in their teenagers' lives.

Teenage Insecurity

Teenagers are not secure people! The teenager who seems secure at breakfast can easily fall apart by supper. The teenager who goes to bed thinking she looks okay, awakes, looks in the mirror before breakfast, and becomes convinced that her head is too large for her body. The teenager who is secure because he thinks he finally understands enough of the rules to be thought of as a quasi-normal humanoid will be convinced he is a terminal social misfit because of an embarrassing moment at a party.

Our son Ethan was about fifteen when he came in one afternoon obviously discouraged. I asked him what was wrong. He told me that every day, people made fun of him on the way to or from school. He said, "I see them looking at me and talking and laughing." It was a tough period for him. He was rapidly growing. He was unsure of himself, his body, and his looks. He was in that limbo-land between boy and man, and he projected his insecurity to everyone around him. This time of physical insecurity provided many opportunities for listening, love, encouragement, and the Gospel.

This is a period when the teenager is flooded with questions. Who am I? Do I look okay? Why is life so confusing? Will I ever remember all of the rules? What is right and what is wrong? Who is right and who is wrong? What is happening to my body? What am I going to do with my life? Will I be a success or a failure? Do people really like me? Am I normal? Is my family normal? Is God for real?

The world of physical appearance, the world of relationships, the world of ideas, the world of responsibilities, and the world of the future all are scary and uncertain to the teenager. It is this reality that makes this time such an age of opportunity. In the midst of these questions, significant biblical themes can be discussed, such as the doctrine of creation, the fear of man, the sovereignty of God, the nature of truth, identity in Christ, and spiritual warfare and temptation, to mention a few. In the context of daily insecurities we have an opportunity to help the teen make conceptual theology become functional, life-shaping theology. Each of these questions provides an opportunity to discuss, test, experience, apply, and internalize important biblical truths.

Teenage Rebellion

The stories of gross and flagrant rebellion are one of the reasons that parents fear the teen years. The thought that the once-precious child will turn into the leader of the violent neighborhood gang is the parent's worst nightmare. We have to re-evaluate our expectation of automatic teen rebellion. At the same time, we have to recognize that this is an age when children push at the boundaries, when temptation abounds, and when peer relationships do not always encourage right behavior.

We received one of those dreaded calls one Sunday afternoon. It was a mother in our church telling us that our son had not stayed at her house overnight as we had thought. She told us that our son had asked her son to cover for him, but he was conscience-stricken and went to his mother for help. She called us. We were afraid and disappointed. For a moment we gave in to worst-case scenarios. How many more lies had there been? Were we living with a son we did not know? At the same time, we were so deeply thankful for the Lord's rescuing mercy. We questioned our son and he confessed. It was a watershed moment of choosing whom he would serve. We left the room so thankful that an event that we hoped would never happen had, in God's plan of mercy, taken place.

There are desires that make the teenager susceptible to the temptation to rebel: the desire to be an individual and think for oneself, the desire for freedom, the desire to try new things, the desire to test the boundaries, the desire for control, the desire to make one's own decisions, the desire to be different, the desire to fit in, and the desire to be accepted. These, with a host of other desires, all fueled by the autonomy and self-centeredness of the sin nature, can surely lead the teenager astray.

At the same time, these struggles of rebellion and submission become the context in which another set of critical biblical issues can be discussed, applied, and internalized. Biblical truths having to do with authority, sowing and reaping, the nature of truth and falsehood, wisdom and foolishness, law and grace, confession, repentance, forgiveness, and the nature and function of the heart all get put on the table in the midst of these crucial moments of submission and rebellion. Parents with eyes toward opportunity will have many, many openings to deal with central issues of biblical faith in the life of their teenager.

A Teenager's Widening World

One of the frightening things for parents and a source of insecurity for their teenagers is the sudden explosion of the teen's world. All of a sudden, it seems as if the world gets bigger. That little boy or girl who played for hours on the backyard swing set now drives miles away to new locations, new experiences, and new friends.

This world is not always exciting to the teenager. Sometimes it seems scary and overwhelming. There are moments when the teen is alive with the joy of discovery, and there are other times when he is shy and avoiding. Sometime he enjoys being a teenager, while at other times he seems afraid of the new expectations laid upon him.

There is no stopping the widening of his world. It is a world of new friends, new locations, new opportunities and responsibilities, new thoughts, new plans, new freedoms, new temptations, new feelings, new experiences, and new discoveries. All of the joys and insecurities of this widening world provide opportunities to help your teenager really understand and personally internalize fundamental truths. These include the sovereignty and providence of God, the ever-present help of the Lord, the nature of biblical relationships, spiritual warfare, discipline, self-control, contentment, faithfulness, trust-worthiness, the nature of the body of Christ, the world, the flesh, and the Devil, the principles of responsibility and accountability, biblical priorities, discovery and stewardship of gifts, and many other biblical truths and principles. That's quite a list! But this widening world provides wonderful opportunities for parents to prepare their teenager for an effective and productive life in God's world.

Rejecting the Cynicism

The place to begin as we build a biblical understanding of parenting our teenagers is to reject the dark, foreboding cynicism of our culture. Yes, the teen years are years of change, insecurity, and tumult, yet these are the very things that God uses to bring truth to light in the eyes of our children. If we are to be his instruments, we must deal with our own idolatry and bring a robust biblical faith to each rocky moment, a faith that believes that God rules over all things for our sake, that he is an ever-present help in trouble, that he is at work in every situation accomplishing his redemptive purpose, and that his Word is powerful, active, and effective.

We do not want to be driven into bunkers of survival by teenage insecurity, rebellion, and widening world. Rather, we want to take Paul's call to Timothy as God's agenda for our work with our teens. "Preach the Word; be prepared in season and out of season; correct, rebuke, and encourage—with great patience and careful instruction" (2 Tim. 4:2). We want to approach these important years with hope; not hope in our teenagers or hope in ourselves, but hope in God who is able to do more than anything we could ever ask or imagine as we seize the opportunities he places in our path. We want to approach these years with a sense of purpose and a sense of calling.

When people ask you what you do, say, "I am the parent of a

teenager. It is the most important job I have ever had. Everything else I do for a living is secondary." Then say, "You know, I have never had a job that is so exciting! I have never had a job that is so full of opportunities. Every day I am needed. Every day I do things that are important, worthwhile, and lasting. I wouldn't give up this job for anything!"

CHAPTER 2

WHOSE IDOLS
ARE IN THE WAY?

IF we are ever to be effective for Christ in the lives of our teenagers, it is important to be honest about our own idols—the places where *we* have tended to exchange worship and service of the Creator for worship and service of created things. Too often when we seek to understand the struggles of adolescence, we only look at teenagers and their problems. In reality, it is time for us to take a look inside and ask, "What really rules *our* hearts?" Now, surely, every Christian parent would spontaneously give the correct theological answer. We are God's children. He rules our hearts. Or does he? This is not about a theological affirmation, but about our day-to-day worship. At the level where the rubber meets the road—in the bedrooms, living rooms, kitchens, and hallways of life—what really controls our hearts?

Start with Your Heart

It is a waste of time for us as parents to think about strategies for parenting our teens without first examining ourselves. If our hearts are controlled by something other than God, we will not view the golden parenting opportunities of the teen years as opportunities at all. Instead they will be a constant stream of irritating hassles brought on by an incredibly self-centered person who is neither adult nor child, but who has the uncanny ability to make even the most unimportant moments of our lives chaotic. The cynicism of our culture toward teenagers not only reveals something about who teenagers are, but it also reveals what we as parents are serving. Our hearts blind us to the opportunities all around us during the teen years.

There is an important principle here that is taught all through Scripture, but enunciated most clearly in Ezekiel 14:4: "This is what the Sovereign LORD says: When any Israelite sets up idols in his heart and puts a wicked stumbling block before his face and then goes to a prophet, I the LORD will answer him in keeping with his great idolatry."

Let me put this passage in my own words. The leaders of Israel have come to God to hear his words to them, but as they come, God recognizes that their hearts have been captured by idols. So, God says, "Because there are idols in your hearts, the only thing that I am interested in talking about is your idolatry." Why? There is a little phrase here that clues us in. God says that when a person sets up an idol in his heart, he also puts "a wicked stumbling block before his face." The principle revealed here is the principle of inescapable influence. What controls my heart will control my life. An idol of the heart will always put a wicked stumbling block before my face.

Imagine that you have placed your hand, with fingers narrowly separated, in front of your face. When you attempt to look through your fingers, your vision is obstructed. As long as your hand is in front of your face, no matter where you turn to look, your vision will be altered by your fingers. So it is with an idol in my heart. It will exercise inescapable influence over my life. Wherever I go, whatever I am doing, the idol will influence what I do and how I do it. This is the reason God says, "It makes no sense for me to talk about anything else, because whatever I say somehow, some way, will be used to serve the idol that rules your heart. Therefore, I want to deal with your idolatry. That is my priority."

We cannot ignore this central issue. I am deeply persuaded that our idols have caused us to see opportunity as trial and caused us to strike back at our teenagers with bitter words of judgment, accusation, and condemnation, behaving toward them with intolerance and anger. While God is calling us to love, accept, forgive, and serve, we are often barely able to be nice.

Let's consider some typical parental idols and the way they shape our responses to our teens.

The Idol of Comfort

Secretly in our hearts, many of us want life to be a resort. A resort is a place where you are the one who is served. Your needs come first, and you only do what you want to do when you want to do it. The only demands you deal with in a resort are the demands you put on yourself. At a resort, you live with a sense of entitlement. You've paid your money, and you have the right to expect certain things. I am afraid that many of us live for comfort and bring this entitlement mentality to our parenting. We reason that we have the right to quiet, harmony, peace, and respect, and we respond in anger when we do not get it.

Scripture warns us that life is far from being a resort. Life is war. This is clearly demonstrated in the teen years. I have said to my teenagers many times as they are leaving home, "There is a war out there; it is being fought on the turf of your heart. It is being fought for the control of your soul." The tumult, chaos, and unrest of the teen years are not only the result of significant biological changes taking place, but because of a dramatic spiritual war going on as well.

Parents who demand comfort, ease, regularity, peace, space, quiet, and harmony will be ill-equipped for this war. They will begin to see their teenager as the enemy. They will begin to fight *with* him rather than for him, and even worse, they will tend to forget the true nature of the battle and the identity of the real enemy. They will act out of frustrated desire, doing and saying regrettable things, and they will fail to be effective and productive in those strategic moments of ministry in which God has placed them.

The Idol of Respect

The father had stomped on every one of his daughter's CDs. He had locked her in her room every night, and had publicly shared her sins with the whole church at a prayer meeting. He had slapped her in the face in front of her friends, and tried to goad and belittle her into submission. He never failed to remind her that he had been a model teen. In my office, he told me with great energy and resolve, "I will get her to respect me if it is the last thing I ever do!"

Respect is what ruled his heart. He was convinced that he was entitled to it. Thus, every issue became an issue of respect. He saw disrespect where there was none. Life became a series of final exams in which he never gave his daughter better than an "F." He viewed all of the development, insecurity, and awkwardness of his daughter as a personal affront. There was no vertical, spiritual dimension to his thinking. He saw his daughter not in terms of her relationship to God, but only in relation to himself. He did not see himself as an agent to lead her to a life-saving fear of God. His heart was driven by the goal that she would fear *him* and give him the respect he thought he deserved.

Is respect a good thing? Of course! Is it something that parents should seek to instill in their children? Yes! But it must not be the thing that controls my heart or I will personalize what is not personal,

I will lose sight of my role as God's representative, and I will fight for and demand what only God can produce.

Sadly, the father's eyes were blind to the god that ruled him and to the fact that in his quest to get respect, he encouraged the exact opposite response.

The Idol of Appreciation

We've been there when the calls have come from school. We've been there in the wee hours of the morning when the nightmares have hit. We've changed the bed that had been wet once again. We've gone out in pajamas and slippers to the all-night drugstore for medicine. We've made the special skateboard-shaped birthday cakes. We've cleaned up vomit from the bedroom carpet. We've sat in on meetings with the principal. We've spent hours making the papier-mâché volcano. We've provided transportation to thousands of events. We've sat through scores of painful recitals, spent thousands on memorable vacations. We've walked miles and miles in the aisles of the supermarket so mouths would be fed and stomachs filled. We've trudged hours through malls looking for "cool" clothes. We've washed enough clothes to fill the Grand Canyon! We've given up our dreams to pay for musical instruments and braces. Isn't it about time that we get some credit?

I cannot tell you how many times I've heard parts of this list recited to me by parents, always with that same, final punch line. It seems so logical, so harmless, so right. Children *should* appreciate their parents. Yet being appreciated cannot be our goal. When it becomes the thing we live for, we will unwittingly look with hyper-vigilant eyes for appreciation in every situation.

Teenagers don't often burst in the door at the end of the day and say, "Do you know what I was thinking about on the bus ride home today, Mom? I was thinking about how much you and Dad have done for me over the years. You have been with me and for me from the very first moment of my life until now. On the bus I was flooded with gratitude and I just couldn't wait to get home and say thank you!" If this happens to you, erect stones as a lasting memorial, or light an eternal flame!

Very few parents have headed to bed only to hear sobbing coming from their teenage daughter's bedroom and had this conversation. "What's wrong, Dear?" "Oh, I was just thinking about you and Mom and how unthankful I've been. I feel so guilty that I haven't appreciated you more, and I've committed myself to demonstrating that I appreciate you every day!" On the contrary, the trend for teenagers is to be much more filled with self-orientation and self-interest than to be filled with an awareness and appreciation of others.

If parents have forgotten their own vertical relationship with God as they've ministered to their teens, if they think of it all as an "I serve, you appreciate" contract between parent and child, they will struggle with lots of discouragement and anger during the teen years. Just when parents expect their almost-grown child to give a little something back, they seem to be more selfish and lacking in gratitude than ever before. Again, every parent needs to ask, "Why am I doing what I am doing? Who am I serving? What are the things that I have come to expect and demand? Whose desires rule the moments of opportunity with my teenager—God's or mine?"

The Idol of Success

I listened as the father said to me in the presence of his teenage son, "Do you know what it's like to go to church and know that everyone there has been talking about and praying for your rebellious son? Do you know what it's like to enter a service with all eyes on you, knowing that people are wondering how it is going and how you and your wife are coping? This is not the way it is supposed to be. We tried to faithfully do everything God called us to do as parents, and look what we ended up with! I ask myself, if I knew that this was the way it would all turn out, would we have ever chosen to have children? I cannot describe how disappointed and embarrassed I am."

That afternoon, with his son listening, that father spoke what many parents have felt but never verbalized. We tend to approach parenting with expectations as if we had hard-and-fast guarantees. We think that if we do our part, our children will be model citizens. Yet in a fallen world, this is not the way it works. We tend to approach parenting with a sense of ownership, that these are our children and their obedience is our right.

These assumptions pave the way for our identity to get wrapped up in our children. We begin to need them to be what they should be so that we can feel a sense of achievement and success. We begin to look at our children as our trophies rather than God's creatures. We secretly want to display them on the mantels of our lives as visible testimonies to a job well done. When they fail to live up to our expectations, we find ourselves not grieving for them and fighting for them, but angry at them, fighting against them, and, in fact, grieving for ourselves and our loss. We are angry because they have taken something valuable away from us, something we have come to treasure, something that has come to rule our hearts: a reputation for success.

It is so easy to lose sight of the fact that these are God's children. They do not belong to us. They are given not to bring *us* glory, but *him*. Our teenagers are from him, they exist through him, and the glory of their lives points to him. We are but agents to accomplish his plan. We are but instruments in his hands. Our identity is rooted in him and his call to us, not in our children and their performance. The ultimate rejection that should make us weep is not that they have rejected us, but him.

As parents, we are in trouble whenever we lose sight of these "vertical realities," when we lose sight of God, his ownership of our children, and his call to us to be faithful parents no matter what the outcome. Whenever parenting is reduced to our hard work, the teen's performance, and the reputation of the family, it will be very hard for us to respond with selfless faithfulness in the face of our child's failure. God-ordained moments of ministry will become moments of angry confrontation filled with words of judgment. Instead of leading the needy teen once again to Christ, we will beat him with words. Instead of loving, we will reject. Instead of speaking words of hope, we will condemn. Our feelings will be flooded much more with our own embarrassment, anger, and hurt than with grief over our wayward child's standing before God.

We need to start with an examination of our own hearts. Do we have an attitude of ownership and entitlement? Have we subtly become ruled by reputation? Is there within us a struggle to love our teenager? Is there distance between us that is the result of that struggle? Are we oppressed by thoughts of what others think? Have we even doubted the principles of the Word and why they haven't "worked" for us? These questions need to be faced if we are ever to be what God has commanded us to be in the lives of our teenagers, who are sinners living in a fallen world.

The Idol of Control

I am increasingly persuaded that there are only two ways of living: (1) trusting God and living in submission to his will and his rule, or (2) trying to be God. There is little in between. As sinners we seem to be better at the latter than we are at the former!

This spiritual dynamic hits right at the heart of parenting. Successful parenting is the rightful, God-ordained loss of control. The goal of parenting is to work ourselves out of a job. The goal of parenting is to raise children who were once totally dependent on us to be independent, mature people who, with reliance on God and proper connectedness to the Christian community, are able to stand on their own two feet.

In the early years of parenting, we were in control of everything, and although we complained about the stress of it all, we liked having the power! There is little that an infant chooses to do, other than spontaneous bodily functions. We chose their food, times of rest, manner of physical exercise, what they saw and heard, where they went, who their friends were, and the list could go on and on. However, the truth is that from day one our children are growing independent. The baby who once was unable to roll over without assistance now can crawl into the bathroom without our permission and unravel the entire roll of toilet paper! This same child will soon be driving away from the house to places well out of our parental reach.

It creeps up on us. We expect our kids to turn out just like us. I love sports, played sports in school, and like to watch them. I remember the first time my oldest son Justin said that he did not want to watch a football game with me. What? No love for football? I wanted to say, "It's not right! I raised you to be a fan of organized sports! Don't you want to be like me?"

Or I remember when my daughter Nicole first announced that she did not like peanut butter. It was almost like saying that she didn't like Christmas or summer vacation. There almost seemed to be something theologically wrong with it! I determined that I would convince her that peanut butter was great. Before she left this home she would have a deep and abiding commitment to spreadable crushed peanuts!

How many parents have struggled with the friends that their children have chosen? Yes, the choice of companions is a very serious matter, but it is also a place where we surrender control to a maturing child. The goal of parenting is not to retain tight-fisted control over our children in an attempt to guarantee their safety and our sanity. Only God is able to exercise that kind of control. The goal is to be used of him to instill in our children an ever-maturing self-control through the principles of the Word and to allow them to exercise ever-widening circles of choice, control, and independence.

I regularly work with parents who want to turn back the clock. They think that the only hope is to go back to the former days of total control. They try to treat their teenager like a little child. They end up more like jailers than parents, and they forget to minister the Gospel that is the only hope in those crucial moments of struggle.

It is vital that we remember the truths of the Gospel: First, there is no situation that is not "under control," for Christ "rules over all things for the sake of his body, the church" (Eph. 1:22). Second, not only is the situation under control, but God is at work in it doing the good that he has promised to do (Rom. 8:28). So I do not need to control my teenager's every desire, thought, and action. In every situation he is under the sovereign control of Christ, who is accomplishing what I cannot. Third, I need to remember that the goal of my parenting is not to conform my children to my image, but to work so that they are conformed to the image of Christ! My goal is not to clone my tastes, my opinions, and my habits in my children. I am not looking for my image in them; I long to see Christ's.

We cannot consider the teenage years, with their tumult and struggle, without honestly looking at what we, as parents, bring to the struggle. If our hearts are ruled by comfort, respect, appreciation, success, and control, we will unwittingly hunger for our teens to meet our expectations instead of ministering to their spiritual needs. Instead of seeing moments of struggle as God-given doors of opportunity, we will view them as frustrating, disappointing irritants, and we will experience growing anger against the very children to whom we have been called to minister.

CHAPTER

WHAT IS A FAMILY?
A DEFINITION

THE question "What is a family?" has been debated throughout human history and will be the subject of debate for generations to come. Each generation recognizes the significance of the family and the fact that it has changed from what it was in previous generations. The nature of the family is a raging debate in our culture today under the politically hot title of "family values."

Our purpose here is not to enter into this cultural debate by trying to give a biblically comprehensive definition to the family. Our goal is to define the family in a very different way, that is, to answer the question "What is a family?" functionally. What we are really asking is, "What did God intend the family to do?" This is important because our functional definition of the family will shape our goals for our children and our actions toward them. The question "What did God intend the family to do?" is the basis for asking "What does God want us to do with our teenagers?" You will never get a proper biblical sense of your job description as the parent of a teen unless you have first understood your job description as a parent more generally.

I have listened to many of my Christian brothers and sisters tell stories of their vacations and the elaborate plans they made for many months to ensure that their family would have a good time. It hit me one day, as I was listening to yet another account of the well-researched vacation package to Orlando, that many parents are more organized, more intentional, better researched, and more goal-oriented when planning their vacations than they are in raising their children.

Imagine how a vacation would go if I "sort of" understood what a vacation was supposed to be, but I really wasn't completely sure. Imagine how it would go if I "sort of" knew where I wanted to go with my family on vacation, but I wasn't really committed to one destination. What if I had a bit of a sense of direction, but had taken no time to really study the maps? What if I knew that vacations tended to be costly, but I hadn't really prepared financially? What possibility would there be that my family would, in fact, have any vacation, let alone a successful one? So it is with family life. It is vital that we are biblically informed, biblically prepared, and biblically intentional.

The Family: God's Primary Learning Community

Judges 2:6–15 describes one of the saddest situations in all of Scripture. It is a description that trumpets the importance of the family in what God is doing on earth. In this account we are told that the very first generation of Israelites who grew up in the Promised Land "knew neither the LORD nor what he had done for Israel" (v. 10). Let the words sink in. They ought to shock us! The *first* generation of children who grew up in Palestine did not know who God was and did not know about the amazing things he did to deliver and sustain his people!

What happened? How could this have happened? How could Israelite children not know about God? How could they not know about the plagues, the Red Sea, Mount Sinai, water from rocks and manna from heaven? What went wrong? How could Israelite children grow up comfortably worshiping other gods?

Did the prophets of Israel fail to do their job? Were the priests negligent? No, the failure was not there. The fundamental failure was a failure of the family to do what God intended it to do.

As Israel was preparing to enter the land of promise, God took time to talk about his purposes for the family. Deuteronomy 6 records God's plan. God essentially says this: "I have designed the family to be my primary learning community. There is no better context to teach the truths that need to be taught so that my people would live the way they should live." God says, "You live with your children. You are there when they are lying down, you are there when they are rising up. You are there during the many days of a child's life. Teach your children; the family is your classroom."

Parents have unique opportunities to instruct their children, opportunities no one else will have, because parents live with them. God commands us to make the most of the opportunities. Capitalize on the searching question that is asked just as you are tucking your child into bed. Make the most of the morning complaint that you feel you don't have time to deal with. Ask your school-age children what their day was like, but do it at the kitchen table over the afternoon snack so that it is a conversation, not just a quick greeting as the child comes through the door. Turn off the car radio and engage your children in conversation. The family is God's primary learning community. Parents have a platform for instruction that no one else has.

You see, the family is radically different from the classroom as a setting for learning. The classroom is a vacuum, separate from life. In classrooms we go to elaborate lengths to recreate life so that we can study it. But family life *is* life! In the family, life is brought not only to our doorstep, but into our kitchens, bedrooms, and dens. In the family, life is happening all around us, and it begs to be questioned, evaluated, interpreted, and discussed. There is no more consistent, pregnant, dynamic forum for instruction about life than the family, because that is exactly what God designed the family to be, a learning community.

The Creator God who rules over all things, in whom are hidden all the treasures of wisdom and knowledge, who reveals himself in the world he made and the Word he inspired, has called parents to be his primary teachers. It is our responsibility to make sure that the family, no matter what else it does, is functioning as an effective learning community. This means that every moment of problem, conflict, doubt, question, confusion, difficulty, unity, division, joy, sorrow, work, leisure, relationship, obedience, rebellion, hope, fear, laughter, authority, and submission that makes up the multicolored moments of family life must be seen as a teaching moment. Here it is—every moment of family life is a teaching moment! This is what makes the family a vital tool for the work the Redeemer is doing on earth.

Unlike the classroom, teaching in the family happens spontaneously. There are no lesson plans, workbooks, or rows of desks. You have to live prepared, with eyes open. The moment may come on the way to the hardware store when the little boy asks if God made telephone poles. Or it may come unexpectedly as the teenager mutters in the bathroom that she hates her face so much that she is embarrassed to leave the house. God calls us to grab the opportunities and teach, teach, teach.

Getting to Know the Students

If you are going to function as God's instrument in the life of your teen, you need to know that God intended the family to be his primary learning community, parents to be his primary teachers, and family life to be just the right context for life instruction to take place. Once you understand that you are one of God's teachers, the next question to ask is, "Who are the students?" It is not enough to say that the students are our children. We need to have a biblical description of who those children are. A good teacher not only knows his material well, but he knows his students well too. So it is with parenting. The more accurate our understanding of our children, the more successful we will be at doing what God has called us to do.

There are a host of ways in which the Bible describes our children, but four things the Bible says about them are most essential. Once I understand these as a parent, my teaching task will begin to take shape.

Children Are Covenantal Beings

Maybe you are thinking, *What in the world does that mean, and how will knowing this help me to be a better parent of my teenager?* Let me explain. When the Bible declares that children are covenantal beings, it means that children were made for a relationship with God. They were made to know, love, serve, and obey him. Children were not made to live autonomous, self-oriented, self-directed, and self-sufficient lives. Everything a child thinks, does, and says was purposed by God to be done in loving submission to him. This is the first and greatest commandment according to Christ (Matt. 22:37–38). This is the most foundational thing that can be said about the identity of children.

The Bible says something further. It says that if children are not living in joyful submission to God, they will live in submission to someone or something else. Children will serve and worship God, or they will serve and worship something else. You cannot divide children into two groups, those who worship and those who do not. *Every* child is a worshiper. The question is, What does he worship (see Rom. 1:18–32)? Everything that a child does, everything a child desires, every thought he thinks and every choice he makes, every relationship he pursues, and every action he takes is somehow an expression of worship. When brother and sister fight aggressively over who gets the telephone, or when a teenager wants to die because of the lack of peer acceptance, it is important to remember that worship is being expressed. There is a vertical, Godward dimension to every horizontal, interpersonal action.

Children are worshipers, and their lives are shaped and controlled by whatever they worship. That means that every moment is a God moment. In every moment, a child is accepting his role as a creature and living in worshipful obedience to God, or he is exchanging God for some aspect of the created world he is living to get. Children don't typically think of themselves this way (nor do their parents!), so they need us to faithfully point out to them the covenantal nature of their actions. There is no more important piece of the Bible's job description for parents.

Children Are Social Beings

Children were not only created for relationship with God; they were created for relationships with other people. This is the second great commandment (Matt. 22:39). Children were made for community. God always talks of people as people in relationship. The self-sufficient, self-made individualism of Western culture is foreign to Scripture. The goal of a person's life is not to be a healthy individual; the goal is to be a person living in community with other people who are living in community with God!

From the very first moment of his life, a child has a moral responsibility for the people around him. He is called to love others as he does himself. Everything the child does will either express a submission to God's call to community or a rejection of it. Sinners don't do community well. By their very nature they are self-oriented. Sin flows out of self-worship. So sinful children living in a fallen world will struggle with God's design for community.

I have never seen one of my children eye the last chocolate donut and say to a sibling, "You know, I love chocolate donuts, but there is something that would give me more pleasure than eating it myself. I would enjoy it so much to know that you got the last donut and that it brought you pleasure." No, I observe my children getting nervous as they watch the donut pile dwindle. I listen to them ask, "Is anybody still hungry?" "Who had the other chocolate donut?" "How many of you have had three donuts already?" Each question is born out of self-interest, out of the fear that someone else may get what they want.

Finally, the last donut arrives on someone's plate and the tumult begins. There is the self-pitying child who cries that nobody loves him and that it is not fair. There is the lawyer child who argues the injustice of the situation, given what has happened the last four times we had donuts. (Who remembers?!) There is the fatalistic child who says that he hates having donuts because this always happens. Sinners struggle with God's call to love, so community must be a consistent emphasis in our homes.

Children were created by God for community, but because of their sin, it is one of their greatest struggles. Loving neighbor as oneself seems like a radical command to the sinner. (And it is!) It argues against everything within him. Children's self-orientation is as natural as respiration. I remember this hitting me years ago as a kindergarten teacher. I never had to teach my children to hit one another, to be jealous, to speak unkindly, to push to the front of the line, to announce that their lunch was better than their neighbor's, to brag about their achievements, and to turn everything into a competition. But I spent hours trying to turn that room of selfish sinners into a loving community where learning could thrive. Such is the life of a parent. Much of your work will be the result of recognizing also that children were created by God to be social beings, to live in loving community with one another, and recognizing that sin replaces their love for others with an idolatrous love of self.

Children Are Interpreters

The Bible has so much to say about the way we think because it is such an important part of who we are as creatures made in God's image. Let me propose something that may shock you: all children think. Some of them show it more than others, but all children think, and the thoughts of their hearts shape the way they live their lives. For that reason, the Bible highlights the importance of what we are thinking. The Bible talks about truth and falsehood, about wisdom and foolishness, about belief and unbelief, about revelation and human tradition, about light and darkness, and about good and evil. God says that there is a right way and a wrong way to think about life, and whatever you think about life shapes the way you act.

What does it mean to say that children think? It means that children will seek to make sense out of life. They will try to organize, interpret, and explain the things that go on around them and inside of them. Children are incessant interpreters, and they respond to life not on the basis of the facts, but on the basis of the sense they have made out of those facts.

Recently, my teenage daughter yelled from the door of her bedroom, "Someone stole my book bag!" Now, the first thing that you need to know is that this is not a statement of fact, but an interpretation of the facts. In this case it was a wonderfully self-serving interpretation of the facts. It was easier for her to believe that there was some book-bag-snatching plot in our house than for her to face the possibility that she was responsible for its disappearance. I helped her understand that she was interpreting and explained how that interpretation served her. Then we found the book bag about three feet from where she was standing, under the clothes of yesteryear.

The Bible not only says that human beings are interpreters but that, in order to interpret life correctly, we need God's revelation, his truth. That is why he gave us his Word. Immediately after creating Adam and Eve, the very first thing God did was talk to them, explaining to them the meaning and purpose for their lives. Why did God do this? Because even though he knew that they were perfect people living in a perfect world in perfect relationship with him, they would not figure life out on their own. Adam and Eve needed God's words to make sense out of their world. The same is true for our children.

In Genesis 3 another interpreter comes on the scene, the Serpent. It is important to understand what is happening there. What the Serpent did was take the very same set of facts about which God spoke to Adam and Eve, and give them a very different interpretation. If Adam and Eve decided to believe the interpretation of the Serpent, they would be stupid to continue to obey God! They did listen, they did believe, and the result was the fall of the world into sin. Like their first parents, children are incessantly interpreting. The sense they are making out of life is always important. It is based on truth or falsehood, and it will shape everything they do.

Parents who understand that their children are interpreters do everything they can to get them to think out loud and instill in them a distinctively biblical view of life. They will realize that this is usually not done in formal times of instruction like family worship, but spontaneously as issues come up in the course of family life. You don't accomplish this by having daily family devotions. As important as that is, it is not enough. It is vital that as we live in the mundane moments of life with our children, we teach them to see life from God's perspective. Parents who understand that their children are not simply reacting to the facts, but are interpreting the facts in a way that gives them a particular shape and meaning, will ask good questions and be good listeners. For them, family conversation will take on a whole new meaning and purpose.

Children Behave Out of the Heart

Most of the parents I have worked with have this goal: to get their children to do what is right. Their goal is to control, direct, or guide the behavior of their children. To them, this is the heart of Christian parenting. So John, who has gotten poor grades, is forbidden to watch television until his grades are better, and Sue, who didn't return her sister's blouse after she borrowed it without asking, is told that she cannot borrow anyone's clothes for six weeks. Solutions? Yes, outwardly, but no change of heart.

We need to ask why Sue thinks it is her right to take the possessions of others without permission and with no sense of obligation to return them. What is it about the way she thinks about herself and others that makes this acceptable to her conscience? It is not enough to place behavioral boundaries around her. Our goal is to be used of God to expose and nurture the hearts of our children so that they want to behave in ways that please the Lord.

On the surface, emphasizing behavior seems right and biblical. Isn't behavior important? Doesn't God call us to be holy as he is holy? Aren't we called to obey? The obvious answer to each of these questions is yes, but more needs to be said. Scripture not only calls us to obey, but also tells us what it is that controls our behavior—the heart.

Luke 6:43–45 says,

No good tree bears bad fruit, nor does a bad tree bear good fruit. Each tree is recognized by its own fruit. People do not pick figs from thornbushes, or grapes from briers. The good man brings good things out of the good stored up in his heart, and the evil man brings evil things out of the evil stored up in his heart. For out of the overflow of his heart his mouth speaks.

Like all of us, children behave out of the heart. The particular behavior discussed in Luke 6 is a person's communication, but the principle applies to all human behavior, even to the behavior of a child. The thoughts and motives of the heart shape the way a child responds. If the child is believing things that are not true and desiring what is wrong, there is no way that he will do what is right. So the goal of parenting is not to focus on getting the right behavior, but to shepherd the hearts of our children. We must always seek to be used of God to expose the heart. Why is John, a bright teenager, getting such poor grades? We need to realize that his grades are a window into the thoughts and motives of his heart. We need to consider what desires of heart lead him to use the time he needs for study on things of much less importance. We need to examine how he justifies his irresponsibility to himself. Heart response and heart change are our focus because we know that what controls the heart will control the life.

Let me use Christ's metaphor, the tree, to draw out the importance of this truth in understanding our task with our teenagers.

Pretend with me that I have a big apple tree in my backyard and that every year it buds and grows apples. But just as the apples are ready to be picked, they rot and fall to the ground. After several seasons of this, my wife comes to me and says, "You know, Paul, it doesn't make much sense to have an apple tree and never be able to eat the apples. All we ever end up with is brown mush on our lawn. Can't you do something with our apple tree?" So I think and ponder and come up with an idea. I tell my wife that I am going to fix our tree and that I will be gone for about an hour, picking up the things that I need.

Before long I return to the yard carrying a step ladder, a pair of branch cutters, an industrial grade stapler, and two bushels of apples. I carefully cut all of the rotten apples off the tree and staple bright red Delicious apples to it. Delighted that I have fixed the problem, I call my wife out to the yard to look at the tree.

Ridiculous? Yes! Ridiculous because I have not solved the problem. The problem was more than a fruit problem. There is something fundamentally wrong with the tree itself, even to the level of its roots, that needs to change. I have exchanged good fruit for bad fruit, but the tree itself is still unable to produce healthy fruit. What's more, the fruit I have artificially attached to the tree cannot last because it has nothing to give it life, healthy roots that can nourish it.

I am convinced that much of what we have called Christian parenting is nothing more or less than "fruit stapling." It is an artificial attempt to replace fruit with fruit. It focuses only on ways of changing behavior. It doesn't hunger to know and shepherd the hearts of our children. This "sin is bad, don't do it" brand of parenting forgets that sin is not only a matter of behavior, but a matter of the thoughts and motives of the heart as well. It fails to recognize that if the heart does not change, any behavioral changes that take place will be temporary and cosmetic, because they will not be attached to roots in the heart.

Christ recognized this when he discussed the nature of adultery in the Sermon on the Mount, recorded in Matthew 5:27–28. Christ gave thoughts and desires the moral value of actions as he declared that adultery was not only the physical act of sexual unfaithfulness, but included the lusts of the heart as well. Christ put the boundaries not at the level of behavior, but at the level of the heart. As parents we must do the same. Our ultimate goal is that God would effectively and functionally rule the hearts of our children. We are working in every parental encounter as his instruments to make this happen. We cannot be satisfied with the fruit-stapling agenda of controlling behavior.

The successful parent understands that the family is God's primary learning community. It is uniquely positioned by God to consistently and effectively communicate truth. Parents are God's primary teachers. If you want to do your God-given job well, then you'll want to know your students, your children. You are going to take the biblical description of your children seriously and seek to understand how that description shapes the way you approach your teaching task. This is what we will do in the next chapter.

C H A P T E R

WHAT IS A FAMILY?
A JOB DESCRIPTION

IF you are going to take a long trip, you need to know more than where you are going and how you're going to get there. You need to know a lot about the vehicle that will transport you. If for some strange reason you knew you were to travel to California, but you did not know how to start or stop your car, nor the fact that it needed fuel, there is no way that you would reach your destination. The same is true with parenting teens. If we are ever going to reach God's goals for us as we parent our teenagers, we need an accurate understanding of his vehicle for doing that, the family.

In the previous chapter we defined the family as God's primary learning community. We recognized that the family provides the most consistent, comprehensive context to teach children a distinctively biblical perspective on life. As parents we must understand the implications of accepting our role as God's primary educators.

Perhaps you're thinking that you understand the concept of the family as a learning community, but you're not sure how to teach God's truth in everyday life. When Joey is mocked because of his "bobo" sneakers, how do you make that a teaching moment? When

Sarah tells you at 9:45 P.M. that she needs poster board for a project that is due the next morning, how do you make the most of this teaching opportunity? When Josh stands in front of the open doors of a well-stocked refrigerator and says that there is nothing to eat, how do you capitalize on that moment? When Pete walks in with green hair that he has just dyed with lime Jell-O at his friend's house, what truths do you teach?

I am convinced that we miss these dynamic moments because we don't know what to talk about. Our Christianity often becomes fuzzier the closer it gets to real-life, everyday experience. So we clumsily throw out-of-context Bible passages at our children in the hope that they will somehow motivate them to do what is right. There are, however, three fundamental themes that are present in some way in every human situation. The Bible has much to say about them, and these themes should form the content of our teaching interactions with our children.

The Family as a Theological Community

What is theology? It is the study of God, his existence, his nature, and his works. It is God's plan that the family function as a theological community. What this means is that the ultimate fact of family life is the fact that God exists and that we are his creatures. Everything we do, think, and say is attached to that reality. We must never allow ourselves to view life horizontally, that is, only in terms of earthly relationships and circumstances. We must always ask questions about God, his will, and his work no matter what the subject or situation being discussed.

The goal of all of this is to root our children's identity in the existence and glory of God. We want them to understand that they were made by him, that they belong to him, and that they are called to live for his glory. We are called by God to *do* theology, that is, to live our lives with a moment-by-moment consciousness of God. He is the reality that gives sense and shape to every other fact we discuss and consider.

In Deuteronomy 6:20–25, the task of rooting our children's identity in the existence and work of God is placed in an everyday life context. The son comes to his father and says, "Dad, why do we have to obey all of these rules?" Many parents have answered that question this way: "Just do it because I told you to do it!" Or "Do it or else!" Moses calls us to something very different. He calls us to see the opportunity within the question. He instructs us to tell the child that he is a child of a God of redemption. Tell him how God harnessed the forces of nature in order to fulfill his promises to his people. Tell him that God gave us his rules for our good, that his way is a pathway of blessing. Root his identity in the soil of the glory and goodness of God.

The Teacher in Ecclesiastes says it this way: "Meaningless! Meaningless! Utterly meaningless! Everything is meaningless under the sun." Powerful words that every parent needs to consider. If you cut off the heavens, if you act as if God doesn't exist, everything loses its meaning. If you only look at life horizontally, all things lose their meaning. The Teacher in Ecclesiastes says that all labor, all wisdom, all achievement, all pleasure, all success, and all toil are utterly meaningless unless connected to God. If there is no God who is glorious and good, who rules the earth, who has a plan, and whose will is to be done, there is no reason for anything. Why think, work, obey, love, study, discuss, serve, or give? Why? Why? All of life blows into a chaotic mass of meaningless choices unless it is rooted in the one fact that makes every other fact make sense—GOD. This truth must dye every encounter with our children as red dye permeates every fiber of a white cloth dipped into it.

To say that the family is a theological community means that we are always theologizing. We are always viewing everything in reference to God: who he is, what he is doing, and what he wants us to be and do. There are no unattached moments. All the stuff of our life has cords that attach it to him. Let's talk about what to say as we are theologizing with our children.

Every Moment Is God's Moment

We must never allow our children to believe in a God who is distant and uninvolved, who comes to the rescue only when he hears our cries in prayer. The Bible presents God as someone who is near and active in our lives. The psalmist says that he is an "ever-present help in trouble" (Ps. 46:1). There is no divine 911 telephone line because God is already here and already active. There is never a moment in which God is absent or inactive. There is never a situation, location, or relationship that he does not rule.

Paul told the Athenians that God ruled his world in such a way that "he is not far from each one of us" and that he did this so that we would "seek him and perhaps reach out for him and find him" (Acts 17:27). God is near. God is involved. This moment is his moment, where he is actively accomplishing his will. The thing that is most important in this moment is not what we desire, but what he is doing. Teenagers will mistakenly believe that what they desire is most important. They will see their desires as needs and express these "needs" as demands, questioning our love if we fail to meet them. We must be faithful to turn their eyes from what they desire to what God requires.

Paul says to the Romans that "in all things God works for the good of those who love him" (Rom. 8:28). In every situation, in every problem, in every location, in every relationship, every time, God is at work. Every moment is God's moment.

My son stood in front of the store window and said, "I just have to have those shoes! Dad, I need them!" I looked at his feet to make sure he wasn't barefoot. I knew that he had more shoes at home. What did he mean when he said that he needed those shoes?

Teenagers don't tend to live with a functional God-consciousness. They are filled with a sense of self. They know quite well what they want out of the moments of life, and they tend to wallow in self-pity, grumble and complain, or burst out in anger when their will is not done. They tend to forget God and his will. They tend to reduce life to this moment of desire. Teenagers don't tend to deal with disappointment well; they tend to live with a sense of entitlement. What all of this means is that teenagers tend to be incredibly focused on the horizontal and the present. They need us to direct them toward God, his existence, his character, and his will.

Always a Higher Agenda

In every situation of family life, there is always something more important than what we plan, what we desire, what we want, or what we are working for. There is always a higher purpose and a higher agenda. The higher purpose is the will of God and the higher agenda is that we would live to please him. This means that he is to be the focus and reason for all we do, rather than ourselves and our happiness.

If you would ask most teenagers what they want out of life, most of them would tell you that they just want to be happy. What is scary about this is not only that their definition of happiness changes almost hourly, but that there is no higher focus than their own pleasure. The "whose pleasure" question needs to be asked by parents in every situation until it is the instinctive heart response of the teenager.

My son came in one day from school with his head hanging. I asked him what was wrong and he said, "Nothing." I told him that he was not very convincing, that obviously something was bothering him. I expressed my love for him and told him that I would love to talk with him when he was ready. Later that evening I approached him. I asked him how he was doing and told him that he had really looked discouraged earlier. He blurted out, "No one wants to be friends with a kid who has character! All of the popular kids at school, all of the kids who are leaders, are jerks. They are the center of attention, they get all the girls and here I am, a nice guy who can be trusted, and I have no friends! I'd be better off being a jerk! What sense does it make to be good if nobody notices?"

What a great moment to talk about a higher agenda! We talked about living to please God. We looked at Psalm 73, where the psalmist, too, was convinced that the wrong guys were winning. We talked about the fact that Somebody noticed. We talked of the fallenness of our world and how wrong gets applauded and right gets mocked or ignored. We made connections between the existence, glory, and plan of God and my son's high school experience. We talked about God's purpose in putting him through that trial. We've had that same talk, in different situations, over and over again. We need to call our teenagers away from their own glory to a concrete understanding of what it means to live for God's glory.

Their Story in God's Story

Modern Christians have wrongly attempted to handle the Bible as if it were an encyclopedia of religious thought. We tend to have a "where can I find a verse on . . ." approach to Scripture. This approach robs the Bible of its vitality, its genius. The Bible is not put together like an encyclopedia, organized by topic. For instance, you would not understand what the Bible has to say if you separated out all of the verses on marriage, government, sex, parenting, communication, work, money, the church, etc. Whatever you would learn from these verses would be distorted and out of context because they would be understood separate from what the Bible is really all about. The Bible is not a topical index, a dictionary, or an encyclopedia. The

Bible is a *storybook*. It is God's story, the story of his character, his creation, his redemption of this fallen world, and his sovereign plan for the ages. It is the one true and unalterable story. It is *the* story. All other stories of people and nations find their life, meaning, and hope in this story. This grand, universal story is what gives all of us a reason to get up in the morning and do what we have been called to do.

To theologize with your teenagers does not mean you are to throw in an occasional Scripture verse that relates to the topic at hand. Rather, it means that every day, in every way possible, to embed the story of your teenager in the larger story of God. Teens live overwhelmed by their own story. They tend to live with such *angst*. The drama of the particular moment seems like the most significant thing in history! When we seek to help them see that it is not as significant as they think, they fire back the quintessential, "You just don't understand!"

It is the present power of their story that often gets teenagers into so much trouble. They lose focus. They live only for what they can get out of this moment. They tend to live driven by their own desires and enslaved to a quest for personal happiness. In this quest for satisfied desire and personal pleasure, they often make decisions they live to regret. Teenagers desperately need to see the larger story. They need to see their lives as part of something that is bigger and more important than their own happiness. They need a glory to hook into and live for that is bigger than their own glory. They need their story embedded every day in the story of God. This will give them a reason to do what is right. This will give them hope. This will give them strength to endure what God calls them to endure.

The Bible has much to say about all the topics mentioned earlier, but what it has to say only makes sense when seen from the vantage point of the glorious story of God and his work. We have to be very careful that we do not "de-God" the commands and principles of

Scripture. He stands in power and glory behind every one. Every command looks to him for strength to obey, every principle looks to him for wisdom, and every promise looks to him for its fulfillment. The whole system depends on the truthfulness of the story.

This is what teenagers need to understand about life. There is a God. He is alive and active! His story and his work are recorded in the Bible. The most important thing in life is to live in tune with what he is doing. As God's child I become part of his grand, universal plan. I become part of what he is doing on earth. This is what gives meaning and purpose to whatever drama I may be living right now! As parents, we need to be faithful every day, to embed the stories of our teenagers in the story of God. We must teach them always to ask, "Who is God?" "What is he doing?" "What has he promised?" "What does he command?" "How will these facts shape the way I think about and respond to the daily situations of life?"

Trust and Obey

Finally, approaching the family as a theological community means getting very practical about what it means to follow God in the mundane, everyday situations of life. We don't do very many grand and significant things in our life. Most of us will not be written up in history books. Most of us will only be remembered by family and perhaps a few friends. Most of us will be forgotten in two or three generations after our deaths. There simply are not many grand moments of life, and we surely don't live life in those moments. No, we live life in the utterly mundane. We exist in the bathrooms, bedrooms, living rooms, and hallways of life. This where the character of our life is set. This is where we live the life of faith. Thus we need to teach our children to take this Godward focus into the most mundane moments of life.

We need to teach our teenagers what it means to live for God where they live every day, in all those unspectacular moments at home, at school, or with friends. There are two questions that, if regularly asked, will bring God into every one of those moments. We want to ask them of our teenagers until they learn to ask them of themselves. They are summarized by these two words: *trust* and *obey.*

Let me start with the second word. In every situation we want our teenagers to have a heart for God. We want them to have the goal of living to please him. So we must encourage them in every situation to ask, *"What, in this situation, are the things that God calls me to do that I cannot pass on to anyone else?"*

This question requires them to be concrete and specific in the way they think about their calling from God. Once the teenager has biblically clarified those responsibilities, the only proper response is to obey.

The word *trust* points the teenager to the fact that he has limits. There are important things in every situation that need to change, yet are outside of the teenager's control. They are not his responsibility because they are beyond his ability to produce. These areas must be entrusted to God. So we need to get our teens to ask this question: *"What, in this situation, are the things I need to entrust into God's capable and loving hands?"*

Teenagers tend to get these areas confused (and so do adults). They try to do things that are God's job and they forget to do the things that he has called them to do. The daughter said to her mom, "If it's the last thing I ever do, I am going to teach him (her younger brother) that he had better stay out of my room. I'll get him to respect me and my stuff one way or the other." Although she didn't realize it, here was a teenager dead set on doing God's work and forgetting to do the simple things that God had called her to do during times of mistreatment. She would reap the disaster of attempting to do what only God can do.

The family is a theological community, so we need to teach our children that every moment is God's moment. There is always a higher agenda than personal happiness, there is a bigger, more significant story than their story of the moment, and in every situation, they are called to trust and obey God. The Christian family doesn't just think theologically on Sundays; it *does* theology from Sunday to Sunday.

The Family as a Sociological Community

Just as teenagers need us to root their identity in the character and existence of God, they also need us to root their identity in community. Sinners are rugged individualists. Sinners want to sing with Frank Sinatra, "I did it my way!" They are filled with a sense of self. Their thoughts are dominated by what they need and what they want. Sinners, according to Paul in Ephesians, are people who are led around by the cravings of their sinful nature (Eph. 2:3). Sinners want their will to be done, and they will fight with whoever gets in their way. Consequently, sinners are much better at making war than they are at making peace (see James 4:1–10), much better at hatred than they are at love. They are much better at causing division than they are at creating unity.

We have all experienced this in our homes. It has been said that if you have more than one person in a room, you will probably have conflict at some point, and sometimes even if you only have one person in the room! Sadly, because of sin, conflict is the norm in our homes. No, I don't mean those knock-down, drag-out fights, but people struggling to get along. We see competition going on where it shouldn't, unkind words being spoken, selfish acts being done, and anger being expressed. Conflict infects many of our family moments. The conflict exists because, as sinners, we tend to live for ourselves. Our own good becomes our highest good and the people around us seem always to be in our way.

How different life looks when we approach it biblically! You see, God's story is not just the story of his character and his work to redeem; it is also the story of his calling together a people to be the people of God. It is the story of his forming a community of love where all the old dividing lines of race, gender, nation, and economic class are broken down and God's people live as "one new man in Christ" (Eph. 2:11–22). A successful person in God's eyes is not just a person who loves him, but someone who also really does love his neighbor as himself.

There is no more fundamental, readily available, consistent context in which to teach what it means to live in community than the family. The family *is* a community, and it will model a view of community whether it realizes it or not. The family will teach and model what it means to love your neighbor as yourself or it will violate that standard at every point and teach a self-centered individualism. Powerful messages about the nature of relationships will be taught in the way Mom and Dad talk to one another, serve one another, make decisions, and deal with their differences. It is impossible for a family to escape teaching and modeling some functional philosophy of relationship for its children.

The family is called to be the context in which what it means to love your neighbor as yourself is self-consciously taught at every turn. There are daily opportunities not only to do first-great-command instruction, but second-great-command instruction as well. At the same time, in the rush of our frenetic schedules it is very easy for us to rush by the opportunities, enforcing surface solutions rather than dealing with issues of the heart.

A mom and dad were telling me how their two teenage sons were constantly fighting over the stereo in the family room. These fights had gotten so ugly that they had even broken a piece of furniture as they tussled over who was going play his CD. The parents' solution, which they proudly shared with me, was to devise a weekly schedule of stereo time for each son. They no longer had any conflict, and in that way the problem had been solved. But they had missed a God-given opportunity to talk about the significant issue of the heart, loving your neighbor as yourself. In arriving at a human, second-best solution, these parents missed a God-given opportunity to shine the light of the second great command on the moment.

This is what Christ called one of the weightier issues of the law in Matthew 23. He rebuked the Pharisees for emphasizing the doable issues of behavior while neglecting the more fundamental issues of the heart, like justice, mercy, and faithfulness. Yet parents will often respond to a situation caused by heart problems by enforcing some doable standard. This creates an instant situational fix, yet leaves the more important heart issues unexposed and unchanged.

Proverbs 20:5 says, "The purposes of a man's heart are deep waters, but a man of understanding draws them out." This is what we must be committed to in our relationships. When selfishness, individualism, and demandingness create conflict, strife, and tension in our homes, we must thank God for the opportunity to deal with something that he has said is second in importance only to our relationship to him. If we are truly thankful, we will not opt for quick, surface solutions, but we will work to uncover the issues of the heart that are the real reason for the conflict.

There is no better place to do this than the family. Here children are called by God to love people with whom they did not choose to live. Here they cannot escape the daily responsibilities to give, to love, and to serve. Almost everything around them must be shared. Here their desires will conflict with another's plans. Here they will face the utter impossibility of loving neighbor as yourself, apart from the help of Christ.

Rule of Love or Rule of Desire?

A teen's responses to others will be shaped by the *rule of love:* "Do to others what you would have them do to you" (Matt. 7:12). Or his responses will be shaped by the *rule of desire:* "What causes fights and quarrels among you? Don't they come from your desires that battle within you? You want something but don't get it. You kill and covet, but you cannot have what you want. You quarrel and fight" (James 4:1–2).

The family is the context where the teenager's true heart toward relationships is consistently exposed. It provides situation after situation where what is ruling the heart gets revealed. The fight over the last drop of milk at breakfast, the shove in response to the accidental bump in the hallway, the argument over time spent in the bathroom, the discussion over borrowed clothes that weren't returned, the debate as to who gets the car, the willingness to participate in put-down humor, the demand for assistance that is coupled with an unwillingness to help others, the lack of willing and spontaneous participation in the work of the home, the willingness to participate in an escalating duel of cruel words, and a myriad of other situations must not be viewed as the groaning hassles of family life. These are the moments when God is calling us to something greater than our own comfort and ease. These are the times when God calls us to love our children with a second-great-command love, so that we are willing to take the time to do the second-great-command parenting that they so desperately need. At such moments, we need to be ruled not by the rule of personal desire, but by God's rule of love, not giving in to quick, surface solutions that give us the quiet we want, but without forming in our children the heart of Christlike love that God requires.

The Family as a Redemptive Community

Life in all its harsh realities is played out in the context of the family. Because of sin, the family is a place of unfulfilled promises, broken dreams, and disappointed expectations. The boyfriend who seemed so sensitive and attentive becomes the husband who is distant and uninvolved. The girlfriend who seemed so joyful and happy becomes the wife who is bitter and discontent. The child who seemed so sweet and responsive becomes rebellious and distant. The couple who swore that they would never repeat the failures of their parents realize they are saying and doing the very things they repudiated.

We need to face the fact that the harsh realities of the Fall are depicted in everyday family life. It is this humble admission that opens us up to one of the most wonderful functions of the Christian family. It is when we humbly face the reality of our falseness that we begin to seek and treasure the riches of the grace of the Lord Jesus Christ. As we—parents and children alike—face our need as sinners, the family becomes a truly redemptive community where the themes of grace, forgiveness, deliverance from sin, reconciliation, new life in Christ, and hope become the central themes of family life.

While writing a chapter of this book, I experienced the themes of my own sin: patterns of irritability and harsh communication toward my teenage daughter. When God reveals sin, there are only two responses for the Christian. One is to generate some system of self-justification to make wrong desires and behavior acceptable to your own conscience. The other is to admit your sin, confess it to God and man, and place yourself once again under the justifying mercy of Christ. Parents who do the former will not have a home that functions as a redemptive community. They will unwittingly teach their children to hide their sin, to explain it away, to deny its existence, or to blame others. Parents who do the latter will teach their children to rely on Christ, to confess their sin, and to believe that where sin abounds, grace abounds even more. They will teach their children to grow up to be people of hope who have seen and believe that there is no pit so deep that Jesus isn't deeper!

The key to the family functioning as a redemptive community, where the Gospel is the glue that holds the family together, is parents who so trust in Christ that they are ready and willing to confess their faults to their children. Often, even the way parents talk about their childhood is scaringly self-righteous. "Why, in my day," they say, "I never would have even considered. . . ." It is easy for parents to relate to their children like the Pharisee praying in the temple saying, "I thank God that I am not like other men . . ." (see Luke 18:9–14). However, parents who admit their sin will position themselves to model the Gospel for their children daily.

If we are not compromising God's standards by accepting a human, second-best standard, God's law will reveal sin. Scripture talks of the Word as a light, as a teacher to lead us to Christ, and as a mirror in which we see ourselves. As parents faithfully hold themselves and their children to God's high standard, children will begin to see their utter need for Christ.

I remember one night walking by my daughter's room and hearing crying. I went in and asked her what was wrong. In her tears she said, "Daddy, I can't do it, I can't do what you are asking me. It's just impossible!" I asked her to explain what she meant. She said, "You tell me that I should want to share with my brothers, but I don't. When you tell me to give them something of mine, I do, but I hate it and I am mad at you for asking me and mad at them for taking it! I don't want to share, I hate it! It's impossible to enjoy!" When she said these words, she burst into tears once again.

In her room that night, she began to experience something wonderful—the fact that there is no possibility of righteousness by the doing of the law. She began to realize that in her own strength, by the exercise of her own will, she could not obey God. In her room that night, she began to cry out for Christ. She began to see that he was her only hope. A struggle to share that wasn't covered over by some cos-

67

metic human solution became the context in which Christ the Redeemer was revealed.

As the Word is held high as the standard for the family, sin will be revealed for what it is. It is only then that the message of redemption in Christ Jesus makes any sense. As the Holy Spirit works through the faithful ministry of parents who forsake their own desire for comfort and ease, proud, self-defensive, self-excusing, self-righteous children will become seekers after grace.

Life in the Fallen World

There are things we know our children will experience in our homes. They will experience being sinned against. They are in a family populated by sinners who are not yet fully sanctified. They will hear unkind words spoken, and they will see unloving things done. They will experience the selfishness of others, and they will be the object of someone's irritation and anger. We need to greet these experiences with the message of redemption. We must teach our children that there is a Redeemer who has come, who forgives, delivers, reconciles, and restores. You model this when you do more than tell your fighting children to go to their rooms and leave one another alone. You model this as you require them to face one another, to deal with their differences, to confess sin, to ask for forgiveness, and to restore relationship. In so doing you are teaching the Gospel, you are testifying to the presence and power of the Redeemer, and you are teaching your children to be people of hope even in the midst of a fallen world.

You also know that your children will experience their own sin. Cutting, hurtful words will come flying out of their mouths. Laziness and irresponsibility will be revealed. They will respond in selfishness rather than love. They will rebel rather than submit, and they will take rather than give. Each of these experiences is an opportunity to *do re-*

demption, that is, to bring your children to the one place of hope and help, the Lord Jesus Christ.

Often we miss these opportunities because we are too busy solving the problem at hand. We expend our energies trying to keep the brothers from fighting, rather than exposing the sin behind the quar- ψ rel, leading the individuals involved to Christ, to experience his forgiveness and help as they seek him in confession and repentance. We also miss these opportunities because we see our children's sins as personal affronts. We get caught up in our own hurt and anger. Instead of words of hope and grace, we lash out with angry words of regret ("I wish for once you'd get your act together!") or words of condemnation ("You'll never change!").

We must not distance ourselves from the sins of our children as if they had a problem to which we can't relate. We need to identify with them. We, too, are sinners. Sin is a human condition. It is a problem that resides in our very nature. None of us is free of the disease. There is no sin that our children will ever commit that we are not capable of as well. As we admit that we are alike, we portray a personal excitement with the Gospel, because it is our only hope as well. We don't respond with a "How could you?" or "Why would you?" We parent with a humble awareness of our own sin. We understand the how and why of sin, because we have been there and we *would* be there apart from the glorious grace of the Lord Jesus Christ.

We do not want to communicate to our children that they would be better off if they could somehow be like us! God forbid! Rather, we need to say that it is only through Christ that we have experienced any freedom from the things with which they now struggle. We are willing to share our sin struggles with them so that the mercy of Christ would be revealed through our story (see Paul's example in 2 Cor. 1:8–11).

We know, too, that our children will face the fallenness and brokenness of the world. Paul says in Romans 8 that the whole world

69

groans waiting for redemption (v. 22). Our children will experience a world of unfulfilled promises, shattered relationships, failed institutions, corrupted government, selfish ambition, wanton violence, and broken families. They will experience the temptations, lies, and schemes of the enemy. They live in a world where there really is a Devil who seeks to devour them. They will be surprised and tricked. They will struggle with hurt, fear, disappointment, and discouragement. They will have a myriad of reasons for cynicism and hopelessness.

We will not be able to shelter them from the fallenness of their world. We cannot act as if it does not exist, because everywhere they look, they will see brokenness. Here too, we must bring the Gospel. This world is not a place of unmitigated chaos. Over all the brokenness rules the risen Christ, who reigns over all things for the sake of his people. He is bringing an end to all of the sin, sorrow, and suffering. What we face here is not comparable to the glories of eternity. There is hope! We need to find practical ways to communicate this hope to our children. There is more and better to come. There is reason to continue.

In the face of sin within and sin without, in the face of the world, the flesh, and the Devil, the family needs to function as a redemptive community, humbly admitting the reality of sin. We must also consistently and expectantly point to the amazing reality of the grace of the risen Christ, who rules over all things for the salvation of his people. Each situation where sin rears its head is an opportunity to teach grace. Each situation where the Tempter is revealed is an opportunity to point to Christ, who is greater. Each circumstance of failure is an open door for the message of forgiveness and deliverance.

There is no more consistent, effective learning community than the family. The existence and glory of God, the moral responsibility to love neighbor, and the hope of the Gospel in the face of our sin must be the constant themes that interpret, define, explain, and organize family life. As parents we must accept our position as God's primary teachers. It is a high and life-long calling. There is nothing more important that we will ever do. As we follow God's calling, we will pray for our children what Paul prayed for the Ephesian church: "That the eyes of your heart may be enlightened in order that you may know the hope to which he has called you, the riches of his glorious inheritance in the saints, and his incomparably great power for us who believe" (Eph. 1:18–19).

CHAPTER 5

PARENTS, MEET YOUR TEENAGER

DO you remember what it was like to be a teenager? Do you remember your self-consciousness, your physical self-awareness, and your general confusion? Do you remember feeling great about yourself one day and wanting to die the next? Do you remember trying to be cool, only to make a complete fool of yourself? Do you remember doing immature and irresponsible things just at the time you were trying to win your parents' respect? Effective parents of teenagers are people who are able to remember what it was like to live in the scary world of the teen years.

I remember the time I finally got my mom and dad to trust me with the car, only to run out of gas and hitchhike home, leaving the keys in the ignition! I was crushed as my mom told me in elaborate detail how dumb a thing that was.

I remember once being in a restaurant like McDonald's. Maybe this will give away my age, but I had purchased a bottle of soda. As I was walking to my table, I noticed three girls entering the restaurant whom I had met a few days before. I was excited that they were there. As I was trying to get their attention while I was sitting down, I bumped the bottle of soda and poured it into my lap. The girls looked at me and suddenly burst into laughter as I sat there with a huge brown ring of root beer in my lap! All I wanted to do was to get out of that restaurant as fast as I could, but the only entrance seemed three hundred yards away, and getting there meant walking right past the laughing trio! I will never forget that walk to the door. It must have taken me three months. I was sure everyone in the place was fixated on that brown root beer circle on the front of my khaki pants. I had suicidal thoughts in the parking lot that night. I knew that this was it, this was the big one, it was over, I would never be a normal human being! I had failed the test, and they were still laughing!

If parents fail to remember moments like this, if we fail to recognize how huge these events are to our teenagers, we will fail to take them seriously. We will minimize again and again things that are very important to our teenagers. We will miss opportunities to make these moments more than moments of human embarrassment; we will not bring the presence, power, love, and direction of the Redeemer to a crushed and confused young person. We need to get beyond saying, "What difference does it make?" to really communicating to our teenagers that we take them and their world seriously. We want them to really know that we are always there to listen, love, support, and help. We need to communicate that we will never mock the things they have taken seriously.

The problem is that teenage crises sneak up on you. I was just minding my business one morning when I turned around from the kitchen counter to find my son standing there. Before I had a chance to greet him he said, "Dad, what do you think of my ears?" *"What do I think of your ears?"* I thought. I hadn't really been thinking about his ears. I hadn't thought about his ears ever, and I know I had never discussed them with my wife! But, all of a sudden, he was very serious about his ears. He could tell that I was hesitating, so I wanted to say something quasi-intelligent! So I said, "Well, what do you think of them?"

I don't think I've been particularly opinionated about ears. I don't notice them in the mall. I've never prayed, "God, thank you for the beautiful set of ears you've given me. I don't know what I would have done if they had been like so and so's." Yet, all of a sudden, without warning, there I was in a very serious discussion about ears. My son had been looking in the mirror that morning hoping he had grown to look more like a normal human being when he saw his ears—and they didn't seem to fit his head! I tried to talk about the majesty of God's creative ability and the technology of ears, but he wasn't listening. He said, "But, Dad, they're just sort of stuck on the sides of your head. They hang out so far. What do you do with them? Mine don't fit my head; they're so embarrassing and I'm stuck with them for life!" That morning I talked longer about ears than I had before or have since.

Maybe this is why parents approach adolescence with such apprehension. We don't like the unpredictability, the spontaneity. We get nervous about how quickly things get serious, or how rapidly things can change. So we tend to buy into the survival mentality of the culture and look for another book that will help us cope with teen chaos. I saw a tee-shirt recently that said, "Of course I look tired. I have a teenager!"

We will never be able to predict what each day will bring as we raise our teenagers, but the more we understand about the age, the more we will be able to approach this time with a spirit of preparedness rather than a spirit of fear. We must reject the self-centered survivalism that sees success as making it through our children's adolescence with our sanity and our marriages intact. We must settle for nothing less than being instruments in the hands of God who is doing important things in the lives of our children.

What the Bible Says About Teenagers

We need a biblical understanding of teenagers, but there is a problem. The Bible doesn't say anything about teens! If you looked in your Bible concordance for all the verses on teenagers, you would find none. The period of life that we call adolescence is a fairly recent invention. Yet, at the same time, the Bible gives us wonderful descriptions of the tendencies of youth. Many of these are found in the book of Proverbs.

The first seven chapters of Proverbs record a wise father giving practical life advice to his son. As I have studied these chapters, I have found the sorts of things we will encounter with our teenagers. Yet none of these themes lead to the hopelessness so prevalent in our culture's view of teens. Rather, they simply and wisely begin to orient you to the kinds of struggles you will encounter as you live with your teenager. Let's look at the tendencies revealed in this section of Proverbs.

No Hunger for Wisdom or Correction

Proverbs emphasizes the value of wisdom and the importance of correction. The father of Proverbs essentially says to his son, "Whatever you get in life, get wisdom! It is more valuable than you will ever know." The importance of listening and submitting to correction is similarly emphasized. Proverbs goes so far as to say, "He who hates correction is stupid" (Prov. 12:1). These are heart-revealing emphases for teenagers (and their parents!). Most teenagers simply don't have a hunger for wisdom. In fact, most think they are much wiser than they actually are, and they mistakenly believe that their parents have little practical insight to offer. They tend to think that their parents "don't really understand" or are "pretty much out of it." Yet most teenagers sorely lack wisdom and desperately need loving, biblical, and faithfully dispensed correction.

Most teenagers don't walk into the family room and say, "You know, Dad, I was just thinking how wise you are, and what a good thing it is that God put you in my life so that I could gain wisdom too. I just thought I'd come in and talk with you for awhile and soak up some of the wisdom that you and I both know I desperately need." No, it doesn't happen that way. Teens don't tend to beg for our wisdom. Yet we cannot give in and let them set the agenda for our relationship with them.

Ask yourself, Do I respond to my teenager in ways that make wisdom appealing? Do I make the taste of correction sweet? I watch parents make correction bitter as they beat their children with demeaning words. Make wisdom attractive. Make correction something to be desired. Don't let your fear of the great "what ifs" cause you to try to produce with human control what only God can produce by his grace.

Win your children for wisdom. Be a salesman for it. You don't do this with nasty, inflammatory confrontations and ugly verbal power struggles. No wisdom is imparted in these moments. If you hit your kids with a barrage of verbal bullets, they will either run for the bunker or come out firing themselves. Here is a good rule: Deal with yourself before you deal with your teenager (Matt. 7:3–5). Sometimes I will begin a conversation with one of my children and I will notice my wife behind my son or my daughter, waving her hands back and forth at me. No, she is not flagging in ships. She is telling me that I am not ready to have the talk. I need to take time and prepare myself by considering the issues at hand biblically, discussing them with my wife, and praying for my child and for myself. By the time I have done all of this, I am in a completely different frame of mind and therefore more prepared to function as God's instrument of change.

After preparing yourself, talk with your teen in the right place at the right time. Get away into a quiet room in the house, preferably the teen's room where he is comfortable. Don't squeeze these important wisdom or corrective times into busy moments; don't do this on the fly. Don't conduct them in front of other people, or introduce them as you are running out to the car on the way to school or church. Take time, and in so doing say, "You are important and what God says is important, so I am willing to invest the time necessary to be his instrument of correction." Remember, giving wisdom is not hitting your teenager over the head with words. It is putting a lovely garland around his neck. It's giving him the world's most valuable jewels. It is gold from God's pocket to his hands. This is radically different from the way teenagers tend to think about wisdom and correction. Don't confirm their view of things and allow these times to be robbed of their value and beauty by your sin.

Teens tend to be defensive. They often will take our loving concern and parental help as an accusation of failure. In response, they will defend their thoughts and actions and will engage us in debate. We need to be very careful of the words we use. We need to be sure that we come to our children with honest questions, not accusations that come out of foregone conclusions. We need to exercise God-given self-control. We need to stay out of loud arguments that have little to do with a wise perspective on the issues at hand, but have everything to do with who is going to win or lose the debate. Proverbs says, "A gentle answer turns away wrath, but a harsh word stirs up anger" (Prov. 15:1). We must studiously avoid getting drawn into emotionally laden power struggles.

I have found it very helpful to do three things when my teenagers are being defensive. First, I clarify my actions for them. I say, "Don't misunderstand, I'm not accusing you of anything. I love you very much and because I love you, I want to do everything I can to help you as you begin to move into the adult world. Don't ever think I am against you. I am for you. And I want you to do something for me: if you ever think that I have misjudged you, if you ever think that I don't understand, or if you ever think that I have expressed sinful anger toward you, please respectfully point it out to me. I want to be used of God to help and encourage you. I don't ever want to tear you down."

Second, I help them to examine their own defensiveness. Teenagers, like all sinners, suffer from spiritual blindness. They will not see themselves as they actually are, so they need our help. I will say, "You know, there is a lot of tension in this room. Now, I haven't yelled at you, I haven't called you names, I haven't accused you of anything, but it seems like you are angry at me. Could you explain why you are so angry? I don't want this to be an uncomfortable time between us. I didn't ask to talk to you because I just felt like a good fight. I love you and want to help you in any way I can."

Third, I seek to be faithful in confessing my sins against my teenagers. Irritation, impatience, judgment of motives, name-calling, words of condemnation, raised voices, any situation where you have allowed yourself to be emotionally out of control, and any place where you have physically hit, grabbed, or pushed, all fit under the category of "provoking your children to anger" and must therefore be confessed to God and to them. Your humility and softness of heart stand as wonderful models for your teenager. Declare, with humble assurance, your confidence in the forgiveness of Christ. By so doing you let them know that they are not alone in their struggle with sin, and you demonstrate that confession produces beneficial results. Be humble enough to admit that your teenagers do push your buttons. Get to know where your buttons are. Pray before you have "the talk" that you would model the love of Christ before your teenager. If you begin to lose it, excuse yourself from the scene, pray, get yourself together, and then go back and complete the talk.

Teenagers not only tend to be defensive, they tend to be self-protective. Teenagers don't tend to live openly. They aren't usually walking around the house dying to talk with Mom and Dad. They are often masters at nonanswers. It is not unusual for them to spend an inordinate amount of time in their room. Sadly, I am afraid, many parents accept the moat that teenagers tend to build around themselves. They adjust to the lack of time and relationship with their teen who, only a few short years ago, wanted to tag along with them everywhere they went. They quit talking when their teenager quits talking. So, at the point where significant things happen, which the teenager was never meant to deal with alone, Mom and Dad are nowhere to be found.

Pursue your teenager. Daily express your love. Don't ask questions that can be answered with a yes or no. Ask questions that require description, explanation, and self-disclosure. Don't just relate to them during times of correction. Don't only catch them doing something wrong; catch them doing something right and encourage them. Pray daily with them, even if it makes them uncomfortable. Always find them in the house and say a warm "goodnight" to them before they go to bed. Because this has been our habit for years, our teens seek us out to say goodnight to us. Enter the world of your teenager and stay there. Don't ever let them view you as being outside their functional world. Teenagers will reject grenades of wisdom and correction lobbed from afar by someone who has not been on site for quite awhile.

When you ask questions about their choices and actions, teenagers tend to respond by shifting blame. They will tell you that they didn't hear your instructions or that you did not give them enough time. They might blame a sibling. Be aware that these responses can get very frustrating. (As if you didn't know!) Anticipate the fact that you will need the self-control that only the Holy Spirit can give.

One of the ways that teenagers shift blame is by accusing us of being especially hard on them and unreasonably lax on their siblings. They charge us with harshness and inconsistency. In these moments it is important to maintain your focus on the subject under discussion and not to be diverted to elaborate justifications of your parenting. Again, I try to respond at these times with humility and patience. I say, "I'm sure there are times when I miss things that I should deal with. But I think you know that I love each one of you and I seek to be what God wants me to be in each of your lives. I would be glad at another time to talk about me and the pressures of parenting. I'd love to let you know what it's like and hear what I look like from your end, but right now we need to talk about you."

Teenagers don't tend to be good listeners. Keep these conversations interesting and to the point. Don't go into lengthy descriptions of all the ways things were different "in your day." The way to deal with the short attention span of our teenagers is to make these moments of wisdom and correction interactions rather than lectures. Some of us carry invisible portable lecterns with us, which we are ready to set up in a moment. Leave them in the closet. Instead, ask stimulating questions that will cause the teen to examine his actions, his assumptions, his desires, and his choices. Help him shine the light of the Word on them. Surprise him with truth. Let wisdom sparkle before his eyes. Don't give in to soliloquies or diatribes. Engage your teenager in a stimulating conversation that doesn't flash your authority or the right you have to tell him what to do. Rather, talk to him in a way that lifts up truth and points out its beauty.

Don't get sucked in. Don't get locked out. Don't engage in interpersonal war. Faithfully bring sweet words of wisdom and loving words of correction. Hold what is valuable before your teenager and trust God to produce, in his or her heart, a love for truth.

A Tendency Toward Legalism

Proverbs doesn't give us an encyclopedia of dos and don'ts, or rights and wrongs. What Proverbs gives us is two worldviews, wisdom and foolishness. Here we find two ways of living: the way of the wise that gets its direction from the truth of God, and the way of the fool that gets its direction from human perspective and desire. God is looking for more than outward behavior. He is working so that we would be nothing less than partakers of his divine nature (2 Peter 1:4)! We cannot and we must not reduce godly living to a set of rules. Godliness is humble, thankful worship that causes us to desire what God says is valuable and to do what God says will bring him glory.

Teenagers, however, tend to be dyed-in-the-wool legalists. They tend to emphasize the letter of the law rather than the spirit. Teenagers tend to push at the fences while telling you that they are still in the yard. They tend to drive you to boundary discussions. They engage you in "how far can I go" conversations, and they tend to respond later with "but I did exactly what you told me to do."

We need to be skilled at talking about the spirit of the law with our teenagers. We need to talk about the heart issues behind the command. We need to show them the difference between an inner purity and a pharisaic performance of duty. We need to see teenage legalism as an opportunity to talk about what it means to have a heart for God and a heart for doing what is right.

My son tended to be rough in his physical play with his brother. He enjoyed his advantage of size and strength. There were many occasions when his younger brother would end up frustrated and in tears. So I went to my son and asked him not to engage in physical play with his brother. In making this request, I was actually summarizing a lot of things that were in the category of intimidation, using his size to take advantage of his younger brother. A few days later I heard his brother crying again in the family room. I said, "I thought I asked you not to do this with your brother?" His response was, "I didn't touch him." Do you see what happened? He technically kept the letter of the law, in that he did not physically touch or hurt his brother. Yet he completely disobeyed the spirit of the request by physically intimidating his brother without touching him.

As we point out this legalism to our teenagers and remind them of the true spirit of God's requirements, they will see their inability and begin to hunger for Christ. Otherwise, they will tend to be like the Pharisees who reduced the law of God to doable human standards. Christ told his followers that unless their righteousness exceeded that of the scribes and Pharisees they would not enter the kingdom of heaven! As we point our teenagers to the grandeur of the spirit of the law, they will say, "I can't do this. I can't love. I can't give. I am not a servant." They will begin to reach out for the help that only Christ can give.

The stakes here are high. Human legalism leads to human self-righteousness. Human self-righteousness denies the need for the saving, enabling grace of Christ. Human righteousness embraces the cruelest of Satan's lies, that a person can be righteous by keeping the law. If that were true, there would have been no need for the birth, life, death, and resurrection of Christ. We must help our teenagers to see their legalism, and we must not get into the endless boundary debates that legalism enjoys. We must help our children to see their rebellion of heart, and take them to Christ, who *is* their righteousness.

A Tendency to Be Unwise in Their Choice of Companions

There is a great deal of material in Proverbs about friendship and the influence that others have on you and your behavior. Teenagers often are naive and unwise in their choice of friends. Proverbs goes so far as to say that when you see certain people, you should cross the road and walk on the other side! Friendship is very important. A person is known by the company he keeps. It is impossible to be uninfluenced by one's friends. Yet teenagers typically assume that they won't be influenced and will respond to our concern with, "I can handle it."

As I was thinking about this issue, I thought of an experience from my own teenage years. As I remembered it, I was tempted to call my mother and ask for her forgiveness! Around the time that I was beginning to notice the opposite sex, I had also begun to be an avid participant in a local teen ministry. It seemed in this ministry that everyone paired off into couples. I found someone I liked and brought her home after one of the weekend meetings. I now realize as I look back that she was one of the (and I don't know what term to use here) sleaziest girls in the Christian community. I am so very glad that this is not the person I married! Looking back, I remember the surreal scene as I brought her home. My mom had the classic pained smile on her face. She was trying to be kind and polite, while at the same time wanting to rescue me from moral danger! I remember my mom asking me later that night what it was that attracted me to that particular girl. (It seemed obvious: she was pretty, fun to be around, and she liked me.) I can remember how defensive I was (although I wouldn't have admitted it at the time). I remember my mother warning me of the importance of these kind of choices. And I remember being very offended, telling her that I could handle it.

We need to approach these conversations with sensitivity and patient love. Teenagers tend to be prickly and protective when it comes to discussions of their friends. It is as if the operational rule is this: "To reject my friends is to reject me." As parents we need to be very careful about the way we have these conversations. Never resort to name-calling and character assassination. Your goal should be to get your teenager to step outside the emotion and commitment of the relationship to give it a long, honest, biblical look. They won't do this without your help. But it's also true that they won't do it if, in your own fear, you have emotionally denigrated relationships that are precious to them.

This subject must be put on the table. Teenagers need to learn the skill of wisely choosing friends. They need to understand the powerful influence of friendship upon them. It is critically important that we as parents avoid undermining our influence with our children by the unwise labeling of their friends, by unwarranted accusations, judgments of motives, and assumptions about the nature and level of influence of the friendship. We need to ask good questions that help the child to examine his thoughts, desires, motives, choices, and behaviors with respect to friendship. We want to lead our children to heart insight that will lead to much wiser decisions about friendship. We are not accomplishing anything on the heart level when we judge in fear and decide things for them. In so doing, we miss the opportunity to see lasting heart change take place in them, yet only this will lead to basic changes in their approach to friendship.

A Susceptibility to Sexual Temptation

The father in Proverbs has much to say about sexual temptation. We need to take this theme seriously, particularly in a culture that has such a distorted view of human sexuality. There is almost nowhere outside of the Christian community that a teenager will get anything close to an accurate perspective of this significant area of human life. The teenage years are a time of physical awakening. For the first time, children become desirous of relationships with the opposite sex. Lust and fantasy often become the private sins of teenagers. We cannot avoid this area or respond to it with embarrassment and ambivalence. We must put this subject on the table early with our children and keep it there as a topic for open discussion.

Many parents seem to dread having that first sex talk. They spend weeks working themselves up to it. They breathe a sigh of relief that they made it through it alive, and they never discuss the subject again. How about you? Do you know how your child is doing in this area? Do you know if he struggles with lust, fantasy, or masturbation? Do you know if he has a biblical view of relationships with the opposite sex? Do you know how many of the sexual lies of the world he has accepted? Do you understand the situations, locations, and relationships where he is experiencing temptation? Have you brainstormed with him about ways of fleeing the "lust of youth"? You cannot parent here if you have allowed the doors to be closed.

If we are going to help our teenagers with their struggle to be sexually pure, the key is to start early so that by the time the child is a teenager, parent and child alike have moved beyond any embarrassment or reticence in talking about sex. I first introduced this topic with my two oldest sons when they were eleven and nine years of age. I took them out for pizza. Little did they know what they were getting into! I asked them questions to ascertain how much they really knew. I started making explanations and drawing pictures on a napkin. My oldest son began choking on his pizza and said, "Dad, are you going to draw what I think you are?" I said, "I chose a booth where no one can see," and we began to talk. They realized that I was not embarrassed by the subject, and they soon began to open up with the questions that they had wanted to ask for awhile.

As the years have gone by, we have endeavored to keep that conversation open because new questions, new temptations, new issues, and new situations arise. Growth in understanding God's way of sexual purity is not something that can be accomplished in one conversation. Learning how to recognize and flee temptation is not a skill that is mastered after one introductory talk about sexuality. Parents need to be committed to a process that begins in the preteen years and continues, with consistency, until our children are ready to leave our homes.

Do your teenagers feel comfortable raising this topic with you? Have you given them a mixed message, on the one hand saying that sex is a wonderful gift from God, and on the other hand communicating fear, reticence, and avoidance? Have you agreed that this is a taboo topic? Do you know what your kids know and what their source of information is? Do you know where your teenager struggles with sexual temptation and how he is doing with that struggle? Is your teenager able to embrace a distinctly biblical view of sexuality? Is he able to critique the distortions of the surrounding culture? Does your teen have a heart for sexual purity or is he pushing the limits of biblical modesty and propriety? If you do not have ready answers for these questions, you have not kept the topic on the table as it needs to be.

There is an explosion of sexual awareness and sexual temptation in the teen years. Teenagers are beginning to form a sexual lifestyle that will be with them for years. It is a time when many teens fall into sexual sin that alters the course of their lives, secret patterns of sexual sin that leave them in bondage for years. We must be committed to open, positive, and consistent parenting in this area. We must be committed to pursuing our children with honest questions and patient discussions. We must put the subject of sex on the table early and leave it there to be revisited until the child leaves home.

An Absence of Eschatological Perspective

Eschatology—a focus on eternity—is not the strong point of most teenagers' functional theology. They don't tend to live with eternity in view. They don't think in terms of delayed gratification. Teenagers are shockingly present-focused. They live as if the present moment is the only moment of life. They don't think in terms of investment. They don't have a harvest mentality. Galatians 6:7 says, "God cannot be mocked. A man reaps what he sows." This is a significant spiritual principle that is seldom in the typical teenager's view.

Teenagers need to be taught to think in terms of long-term investment. This is not the typical way they think about their lives. Teenagers tend to live for whatever they want at the moment and they tend to put off their responsibilities until the very last minute. We need to teach them to examine the kinds of seeds they are now planting and the kind of harvest those seeds will bring. We must lovingly challenge their belief that this physical moment is all that matters, that present, temporal happiness is all there is. They need to understand that God is working on something bigger than this moment, that he is preparing them for something wonderful to come.

The culture around us reinforces the falsehood that life is found in present, earthly, physical treasure, and that the successful person is the one with the biggest pile. Our teenagers are told, "You are the labels that you wear. You are your body size. You are your intelligence. You are your athletic ability. You are the car you drive. You are the house you live in. You are the level of popularity that you have." They are even told that they are the toothpaste they use!

Who are the heroes of Western culture? Are they people of character who live with a harvest mentality, investing in things of eternal significance? No, they are people with good voices, expensive clothes, hot cars, big muscles, and huge bank accounts. They are people who live for the moment, people who are laying up treasure on earth. They are typically people who have no more sense of eternity than the most immature teen. In God's eyes they are, in fact, antiheroes who lead our children to believe lies and to live for what is passing away.

Our teenagers need us to be on site, teaching them to look at the long view of life, from the vantage point of eternity. Life looks radically different when viewed from that perspective! They need to see that every choice, every action is an investment, and that it is impossible to live life without planting seeds that will be the plants of life they will someday harvest.

Lack of Heart Awareness

Right in the middle of the Proverbs father's instruction of his son is this warning: "My son, pay attention to what I say; listen closely to my words. Do not let them out of your sight, keep them within your heart; for they are life to those who find them and health to a man's whole body" (Prov. 4:20–22). He is saying, "Son, listen carefully. What I have to say to you is very important. Don't blow off these words." Then he says, "Above all else, guard your heart, for it is the wellspring of life" (Prov. 4:23). In other words, "Of all that I have said, Son, focus on your heart. Know it. Protect it. Guard it. Your heart is the control center of your life, Son. What rules your heart will rule you."

As stated earlier, we must not simply parent behavior. We're not just controlling decisions and seeking to make sure that the child goes where we want him to go to do what we want him to do. God has called us to a higher agenda. We want to know the heart of our teenager, to help him see his heart as it really is, and to be used of God to help produce a heart ruled by nothing else but God and his truth.

Do you lead your teen to conversations that go deeper than solving problems of circumstance and relationship? Do you help her to see the heart behind those problems? Do you assist her in seeing the places where she has exchanged the Creator for some aspect of creation, such as peer acceptance, a certain possession, or some coveted position? Have you helped her to see the desires that rule her heart? Have you helped her confess her true treasures? Have you taken time to lovingly point out where her thinking is out of conformity to the truths of Scripture? Have you asked questions that expose the thoughts and motives of the heart? Have you shown her how her true worship is expressed in the way she responds to situations and relationships?

Whenever we talk about knowing the heart, we have to talk about the reality of spiritual blindness. All of us struggle with the lack of heart awareness, with spiritual blindness. But it seems as if teenagers particularly struggle with that because they tend to think of life in such behavioral, physical, and present terms. They don't tend to spend much time searching their hearts. They don't ask themselves challenging, revealing questions. They tend to stay focused on the external, present moment. For that reason, one of my goals with my teenagers is not only to teach them about God and his will, but to help them know themselves. I want them to become aware of the themes of their own struggle with sin, the themes of their weaknesses, and their susceptibility to temptation.

Because I want to help my teenagers to grow in self-awareness, I don't burst into their rooms announcing the rule that has been broken and the punishment that will be meted out. In times of correction we talk. I try to ask probing questions that are designed to break through the deceitfulness of sin and expose the heart. And the more my children grow in self-awareness, the more they will appreciate the things I say to them, because they will realize that they need my instruction. Part of the defensiveness so typical of teenagers comes from their utter lack of self-awareness, their utter spiritual blindness. I'm incessantly working to help my children know themselves so that this knowledge would lead them to hunger after God. I believe that every moment is self-revealing.

I use this illustration in counseling, but I think it is particularly true of teenagers. When a teenager plays the "video" of his story for you, he often is not in it. His version of his life focuses on the pressure of the situation, or on what other people did to him. As he relates his story, he does it in a way that shifts responsibility for the things he did to someone or something else!

My daughter came home from school one day waving a grade report from one of her classes. She said, "Dad, I need to talk to you about my grade in Spanish." I knew already that we were in trouble! She went on to say proudly, "I got the highest 'D' in my class!" By the time she was done talking about her grade, I thought that I should post that "D" on the refrigerator. After all, I was the proud father of a daughter who had done well under educational duress and pedagogical incompetence! She told me that all of the students, even the smart kids, got bad grades. There were only a couple "C's" in the class, and she got a high "D." Then she proceeded to tell me why. She said, "Dad, it's the new teacher. He's learning how to teach by practicing on us. Dad, it's like we're his guinea pigs." The more I listened, the prouder I got! What a disciplined daughter, to achieve despite the ineptitude of the rookie teacher!

In truth, as I listened that afternoon to her talking, I was filled with sadness because it hit me that this was not an act. I looked into her face and realized that she believed what she was saying to me. She really thought that it was not her fault. She actually did believe that the teacher was completely to blame. Somewhere between the time she received the paper and the time she arrived home, she had generated an interpretation of events that took her responsibility out of the picture. She was spiritually blind and did not see the real issues of the heart that the report revealed.

As I began to correct her, what was I going to face? She was going to be defensive. She was going to feel falsely and wrongly accused. She would probably accuse me of not understanding and think that I was unsympathetic. She would wonder why I had taken the side of the teacher against her. These are the kinds of situations we will regularly deal with as we seek to break through to the hearts of our teenagers.

As a parent, my goal is not only that my children come to know God, but that in so doing, they also come to know themselves. It's only when a person knows God that he can truly know himself, and as this happens, his hunger for God increases. This critical interplay of the spiritual life is what we want to see produced in our teenagers, a deep personal knowledge of God and an ever-growing knowledge of self.

What we need to understand here is that this is not just a "flesh and blood" struggle, with parents trying to open their teens' eyes to what they are *really* like. This is spiritual warfare. There is an enemy who is a liar, a deceiver, and a trickster. Teenagers are particularly susceptible to his lies about the self. They will believe that the problem is not with them, that they have been singled out for unfair criticism and correction. We will need to stand strong and patient, not being drawn into those debilitating verbal battles that do not open the teenager's eyes, but only make him more defensive and distant. With love and a humble dependency on Christ, we need to take every opportunity to expose critical issues of the heart (fear of man, materialism, selfishness, lust, covetousness, envy, unbelief, anger, self-righteousness, love of the world, greed, rebellion, etc.), helping our teenagers look at themselves in the perfect mirror of Scripture.

Open Doors All Around

Issues of wisdom and foolishness, legalism and true godliness, friendship, sexuality, eternity, and a personal awareness of the heart all are on the table during the teen years, providing wide open doors of opportunity. God uses discussions like these to help your teenagers come to know him, and love him, and to internalize his truth in a way that gives practical direction to their lives.

These are also the things that make this a scary time of parenting. These are issues that can cause parental panic and dread and become the occasion of parental anger. These are the issues around which parents say things they live to regret. These issues can be used of God to form a deeper bond between parent and teen, or be the thing the Enemy uses to drive a deeper wedge in the relationship.

If you respond out of anxiety, irritation, and fear, you will try to control your child all the more. Instead of seeing this as a time of preparation, you will take on a survival mentality. You will tend to see life as a minefield, and you will hope for little more than getting your teenager across it with all his limbs intact. In your desperation, you give in to raging emotions and you do foolish, unproductive things that you will later view with embarrassment and regret. You will do things like ground your child for six years or tell him that his curfew is three o'clock in the afternoon! You will promise him that you will never give him another penny as long as you live! You will grab his driver's license and tear it into pieces, or you will stomp on the CDs that have driven you crazy, sadly all the while evoking the name of the Lord and the truth of his Word. In your self-pity over the toughness of your job as a parent and the peace your child has taken away, you will resort to beating him with words and seeking to motivate him with threats. You will try to control and manipulate him into obedience, and you will initiate unproductive power struggles. All the while your relationship will disintegrate while your teenager's rebellion increases. At last, you will admit you are powerless and, as a final act of anger, you will quit parenting altogether, telling yourself that you did everything you could do.

But if instead you move toward your teenager with a confident faith in the Redeemer, whose Word is true and whose sovereign presence empowers your weak and feeble parental efforts, God will use you to communicate love, understanding, grace, hope, and life. You will ask calm but probing questions that cause your teenager to examine things that he would never examine alone. You will engage your teenager in thought-provoking debate without it ever becoming hurtfully personal and condemning. You will correct in a spirit of acceptance, forgiveness, and hope. You will smile when your child comes into the house, and she will not tense up when you enter her room. You will find her pursuing you to talk about things that many teens hide or ignore. And as your relationship deepens, you will watch her progressively taking on the character of Christ.

PART TWO   *Setting Godly Goals*

CHAPTER

GOALS, GLORY, AND GRACE

I had walked to my son's bedroom feeling a bit overwhelmed. I was physically tired that night, but I was also a tired parent. I was tired of the constant need for ministry that my children represented. I didn't want to have the same conversation with the same son that I had had ten thousand times already! I wanted to say to my wife, "You go do it. I've had it; I'm not having this conversation again!" I resented the immaturity and sin of my son that demanded so much of my attention and time.

I had spent some time in prayer before I went to his room. I felt better and thought I was prepared to have a productive conversation. Still, I was weary as I entered his room. He was tired too, and he immediately responded defensively to what I said to him. He accused me of being unloving, unkind, and lacking in understanding. He seemed to argue with every point I tried to make. This was not the way I had envisioned things going. Not only was he unresponsive, he pushed every one of my buttons.

Somewhere in the conversation I lost it. In my anger I said words to him that were as unkind as any I had ever spoken. I left the room telling him that I hoped to live long enough to see him really appreciate me. But, I told him, I wouldn't hold my breath. As

I left, he glared at me with a combination of anger and hurt.

I sat in the dark on the side of my bed, defeated and discouraged as a parent. God's call to me as a father seemed unrealistic and impossible. I struggled with the gap between what I knew and what I had done. I wondered if I would ever get it. I was torn between self-pity and conviction. I wanted my son to hurt the way that he had hurt me, yet I knew that that desire was wrong. As I sat there I realized that this job was one that I could not quit. There was no escape. Tomorrow I would wake up to the same set of demands. I cried out for God's help and forgiveness. I cried out for character and strength. I prayed for faith and perseverance. I was never more aware of my own moment-by-moment need of the Lord.

Perhaps you have already been overwhelmed by what you have read in this book. Perhaps you have been filled with regret. Perhaps the sins of your heart have been exposed. Perhaps you have been tempted to say, "Paul, I will never be able to do what you have described!" Perhaps you are thinking, *Maybe this works with your kids, Paul, but it will never work with mine!*

Before we consider God's goals for us as we parent our teenagers, we need first to reflect on who we are as God's children. It is important that we see that God's glory and grace are far greater than our sin and our struggle with parenting.

I want to show you three passages that have been friends to me in moments of discouragement and defeat. God has used these passages to radically alter the way I think about what he has called me to do in my teenagers' lives.

Awesome Power

Few things in life have the twenty-four-hour-a-day demand quality that parenting does. Few things in life have such potential for unexpected difficulty and drama. I have talked with many parents of adolescents who speak of being weary, who feel as if they do not have the strength to do what they have been called to do. It is vital in the face of this that we do not forget the strength that is ours as the children of God.

In Ephesians 3:20, Paul directs us to that power in a well-known doxology.

Now to him who is able to do immeasurably more than all we ask or imagine, according to his power that is at work within us, to him be glory in the church and in Christ Jesus throughout all generations, for ever and ever! Amen.

The God who is our Father is a God of awesome power. Through this power he is able to do things that are well beyond anything we could verbalize or grasp with our imaginations. Think of the thing in your life that seems the most impossible to accomplish. God is able to do more! Think of the thing that the Bible would say is most needed in your teenager's life, yet seems unrealistic and out of reach. God is able to do more!

It is important for us to look at our task as parents from the vantage point of the awesome power of God—the power by which he created the world, holds the universe together, raised Christ from the dead, and defeated sin. Our God is a God of glorious power far beyond what our minds can conceive. We cannot look at our parental responsibilities only from the perspective of our own weariness and weakness. We must remember that we are the children of the Almighty. He *is* Power! He *is* Strength.

But there is more that needs to be said here. Perhaps you're thinking, *Boy, Paul, would I like to get hold of some of that power!* But you don't know how to get it. In fact, many parents I have talked with have been *discouraged* by passages like Ephesians 3:20 because they seem so far from their own experience.

We need to look carefully at the words of this doxology. It says that God is "able to do immeasurably more than all we ask or imagine" (now pay attention to these words) "according to his power that is at work *within us.*" Where is his power? Is it off in the heavens somewhere, only available to those who have discovered the right spiritual mantra to call it into action? No, that is not what Paul says. Instead he says something that is glorious and radical, yet real. God's awesome power resides *within* his people and is actively *at work!* Parents, this glorious power lives within you as a child of God, and it is not dormant. God's awesome, active power resides within you, by his Spirit, so that you can do the things God has called you to do that would be otherwise impossible.

It is in our moments of weakness, when we refuse to give up, that we experience the glorious resources of power that reside within us as children of the Almighty. Paul tells us in 2 Corinthians 12:9 that God's strength is made perfect in our weakness. Often we miss the experience of his power because we tend to quit when we have hit the wall. It is when we are beyond the resources of our own strength and wisdom that we tend to succumb to the emotions of the moment, saying and doing things we will live to regret. But because of Christ's work for us, we can do something different; we can parent with courage and hope. It is important to recognize the strength we have been given as the children of God.

The Gift of Glory

In John 17, Christ is facing the cross, resurrection, and his ascension to heaven. In the final moments before his capture, he goes to his Father in prayer for his disciples and for those who would believe through their ministry. He prays for the relationships his followers will have with one another; that his children will experience the same unity that he has with the Father and the Spirit. Imagine a family where such unity reigned! Picture that kind of relationship with your teenager! Again, it is tempting to look at passages such as this and say, "Come on, get real! You can't be serious. You don't really think this is possible, do you?"

Before we cast off this passage as utter idealism, too distant from our experience to be of any practical encouragement or help, we need to pay careful attention to its words (John 17:20–23):

> *My prayer is not for them alone. I pray also for those who will believe in me through their message, that all of them may be one, Father, just as you are in me and I am in you. May they also be in us so that the world may believe that you have sent me. I have given them the glory that you gave me, that they may be one as we are one: I in them and you in me. May they be brought to complete unity. . . .*

In his prayer Christ says that he has done something magnificent for his people. Knowing the brokenness of the world and our sinful hearts, Christ saw that there would be no way that we would ever experience on our own the love and unity that are his plan for us. On earth he had seen the bitterness, anger, jealousy, greed, deceit, and vengeance that sin produces. He knew that he must make ample provision for his people or they would never live in unity and love. Brother would never love sister, husband would never love wife, friend would never love friend, and parent would never love child without his divine intervention. And that is exactly what he provided!

Pay careful attention to the words of verse 22: "I have given them the glory that you gave me, *that they may be one* as we are one." Hear what Christ is saying. When Christ came to earth and took on flesh, the glory of almighty God was placed on him so that, through him, the glory of God would be seen by us all. Christ then says that the glory that was placed on him he has placed on his children so that *they would be one!* We need to embrace this redemptive reality. What was far beyond our grasp has been placed by Christ within our reach. He has placed the glory of almighty God on us for a specific purpose: that our relationships with one another would mirror those of the Trinity. Paul says it this way in Colossians 2:9–10: "For in Christ all the fullness of the Deity lives in bodily form, and you have been given fullness in Christ. . . ."

When you try to talk with your teenager, it is not just you and he in the room alone, hoping that somehow, some way you would be able to get along with one another. The glory of God has been given as a gift to you so that you would be able to be a humble, gentle, patient, and forbearing instrument of the love and unity God has planned for his people. His gift of glory is your hope of unity.

Notice further that Christ says, "May they be brought to complete unity." It is important to see that Christ doesn't pray, "May they bring themselves to complete unity." No, Christ is saying, "Father, if your children are ever going to live in unity and love, it is you who must bring them there." Again, in those moments in the room, it is not just we who are working. God is working to produce what only he can produce. These are his moments of grace, his moments of redemption and change.

There is probably no time in our lives when we are in more need of God's gift of glory and his moment-by-moment activity than the years when we are parenting our teenagers. In these years we are faced with our weakness, sin, and inability. It is in these years that the enemy wants to turn us from the high goals to which God has called us to settle instead for human control and situational success. We need to remember that God's gift of glory was given to bridge the gap between us and our children so that his love and unity would flourish between us.

Everything We Need

There is no passage that has been more of a comfort to me as a parent than 2 Peter 1:3–9.

> *His divine power has given us everything we need for life and godliness through our knowledge of him who called us by his own glory and goodness. Through these he has given us his very great and precious promises, so that through them you may participate in the divine nature and escape the corruption in the world caused by evil desires.*
>
> *For this very reason, make every effort to add to your faith goodness; and to goodness, knowledge; and to knowledge, self-control; and to self-control, perseverance; and to perseverance, godliness; and to godliness, brotherly kindness; and to brotherly kindness, love. For if you possess these qualities in increasing measure, they will keep you from being ineffective and unproductive in your knowledge of our Lord Jesus Christ. But if anyone does not have them, he is nearsighted and blind, and has forgotten that he has been cleansed from his past sins.*

Peter says that there are believers whose lives are ineffective and unproductive. He then explains what causes this. It is because these believers are missing the qualities that make for a productive life. Faith, goodness, knowledge, self-control, perseverance, godliness, brotherly kindness, and love are the essential qualities of a Christian's effectiveness. They are also the essential qualities of productive parenting, the qualities we need in those tough moments with our teenagers.

Peter also tells why these essential qualities are missing: because these people are nearsighted and blind, forgetting that they have been cleansed from their past sins. In short, they have forgotten their *identity*. They have forgotten who they are as the children of God. Here is Peter's argument: if you forget who you are as a child of God, you will quit pursuing the qualities that will make your life effective and productive.

The first few verses of the passage lay out the glories of our identity as God's children that Peter says we must not forget. He says that God has given us *everything we need* for life and godliness. God has given everything we need, not only for eternal life, but also for the God-honoring life to which we have been called until he returns. Notice the tense of the verb. Peter says God *has given* us everything we need. It has already happened! This is a fundamental Gospel truth. God will not call us to do anything without providing a way for it to be done. If he calls us to cross the Red Sea, he will enable us to swim, send a boat, build a bridge, or part the waters!

Peter says, "Don't forget who you are. You are the children of God who have inherited riches beyond your ability to conceive. You have been given everything you need to do what God has called you to do. Don't give in to discouragement. Don't quit. Don't run away from your calling. Don't settle for a little bit of faith, goodness, knowledge, self-control, perseverance, brotherly kindness, and love. Get everything that is your inheritance as God's children."

We need to walk into the rooms of our teenagers saying to ourselves, "I have everything I need to do what God has called me to do." In these moments we can experience a little more of the inheritance of character that Christ has provided us through his death.

Awesome power dwelling within, the gift of glory given so that we can be agents of love and unity, and everything we need to do what God has called us to do—this is the Gospel. This is our identity as the children of God. These are the truths that can lift us out of our weariness and discouragement to parent our teenagers with faith, courage, and hope. They call us to hold onto God's high goals and to fight the hopelessness that the enemy wants to rule our hearts.

We have not been left alone. God has given us rich resources of grace. He is active in us and through us to produce what we could never produce on our own. The Gospel says that we can parent with hope. It tells us that we can grow, we can change, we can do more and better. In those moments when we are at the end of our strength, we can experience his power to love, to be self-controlled, to persevere, to do what is good, and to be kind, even in the face of our teenagers' resistance.

God knows our weakness. He is aware of our sin. And he has given us glorious gifts of grace so that we can be his tools of change in our children's lives. We cannot give in to discouragement and hopelessness. Christ gives us reason for hope; hope that we can be effective and productive as we parent our teenagers. The gifts of grace that he gives turn weak and failing sinners into effective and productive children of the almighty God. We can hold to his high goals with hope as we look at parenting through the lens of his grace and glory.

In the darkness that night after I left my son's room, my mind went to these passages. I recited them once again to myself. I confessed my disobedience and unbelief and prayed for a heart of faith. The truths of these passages renewed my hope and my courage. They helped me reach once more toward God's goals. As I went to sleep, I was anxious for the morning to come. I couldn't wait to talk with my son, to express my love and to ask for his forgiveness. I knew that there would be many more moments of challenge and struggle, but I had hope. I was able to look at them from the vantage point of God's grace and glory.

THERE'S A WAR OUT THERE

IT happened unexpectedly, as it almost always does. She said very hesitantly that she needed to talk with me about something. She said it was about school, that she was in trouble. She was obviously very concerned about what she had to say to me. Even while she was making her introduction, my heart began to race. What had she done? How serious was it? How long had it been going on? What was I about to hear? I invited her to sit down with me and talk.

With her head bowed in an attempt to avoid eye contact, she handed me a crumpled piece of paper. "I got caught in English class giving this note to Samantha," she said. "The teacher was very upset when he read it and made us go to Mrs. Long's [the principal] office right away. Mrs. Long said that I had to show you the note tonight, then she wants to see you tomorrow. Then she will decide what she is going to do with us." I hadn't yet read the note, but my mind again was racing as I held it wrinkled in my hand. This was my little baby. She had never been in trouble. She never behaved with a lack of respect for authority. I felt my idyllic world and my idealized view of my daughter being shattered.

I unwrinkled the paper and began to read its contents. It was brazenly offensive. It was disrespectful of authority. It used language that I could not believe would ever be in the mind of my sweet little girl, let alone written down to be passed to someone in a Christian school classroom! I felt myself flushed with a volatile combination of anger, grief, and embarrassment.

I was angry that she would dare to be so boldly rebellious and insensitive. We had faithfully schooled her in the truth. Was this the way she was going to thank us? How could she? At the same time I was grieved. A simple, sweet, uncomplicated world had suddenly died. It was over. She was no longer the innocent little girl climbing up on Daddy's lap begging to be told a story. She was no longer the playful little one squealing away as she tried to escape down the hallway from Daddy's tickling hands. I wanted that world now. I wanted the power to turn back the clock. I didn't want to have to parent the person who wrote that note. I wanted my little girl back.

There was, however, a third thing that I felt: embarrassment. I was well known in the Christian community. I was a pastor, seminary teacher, and counselor. I spoke at conferences about the Christian family and parenting. What would people think of me now? Some expert! Some example! I was filled with self-pity. I wondered what the administration at the school thought when they got that note. I wondered what they thought about me.

I kept reading and re-reading the note as she sat there. I could not bring myself to believe that she had actually written it. I asked her again if she really had. I guess I was hoping that she would say that she hadn't and that she was just covering for somebody else. But she *had* written it. The words had come from *her* mind and were written with *her* pen. She had written exactly what she wanted to say to her friend. There was no mistake here.

I wondered, too, if this was the "tip of the iceberg." What other things was she "into" that we did not know about? What language did she use with friends that she would not think of using at home? Who was she hanging around with in school? How bad was her crowd? Where had she gone? What else had she done that we would soon hear about, that would further shatter the image of our girl we carried in our hearts? I felt conflicted. I wanted to know it all, yet I was afraid to ask for fear of what I might hear.

I don't know how many minutes went by, but my thoughts were disturbed by her saying, "Dad, are you just going to sit there and stare at the note? Aren't you going to say something?" I said with emotion, "Right now I don't know what to say." I followed by asking her if there was anything else she needed to tell me.

It is because of this kind of situation, the unpredictability of the teen years and our own heart struggles in the face of them, that parents need a clear set of biblical goals that function as God-given guardrails to keep us on the road he wants us to travel. These situations can be greeted as moments of sovereignly given opportunity to shepherd the hearts God has exposed in our teenagers. Or they can become moments where a wedge of distance and anger is driven even more deeply between us and our teenage children.

We can't wait to decide what to do when these moments suddenly come upon us. We cannot expect that when the moment is tense and the emotions are high, we will be able to think clearly, biblically, and concretely. We can't expect to set long-term goals when we're dealing with the powerful feelings of sadness and disappointment. We have to enter these times with our children with a pre-commitment to a concrete set of goals. The failure to do so will keep us from accomplishing the good things that are possible as God enables us to turn a sinful situation into a redemptive opportunity.

I want to use this situation with my daughter as a real-life context for discussing five foundational goals for parenting teenagers. But let me first point out what our goal should *not* be.

Regulating Behavior

I am afraid that most parents of teenagers have the regulation of their teenagers' behavior as their most basic goal. They fear the big three vices of the teen years: drugs and alcohol, sex, and dropping out of school. They want to do anything they can to keep these from happening. So they look for ways to control their teenagers' behavior. They do whatever is necessary to maintain control of their choices and activities. They spend much of their time doing detective work. They are more like police than parents.

They seek to motivate by guilt ("After all we have done for you, this is how you are going to thank us?" or "What do you think the Lord feels as he looks down at what you are doing?"), by fear ("Do you know the diseases that you can get out there?" or "You do that and there is no telling how I will respond!"), or by manipulation ("If you _____, we would be much more willing to get you the car" or "We'll make a deal with you: if you _____, we will _____ for you").

As parents we need to confess to the fear that causes us to try to do God's job. In our inflicting of guilt, our instilling of fear, and our controlling by manipulation, we may well be trying to produce what only God can produce as he works to change the hearts of our teenagers. What we need to do is trust his work as we seek, in restful faith, to be instruments of change in his redemptive hands. It is a short-term victory at best to control the behavior of a teen whose heart is not submissive to God. Surely, the moment that he is out from under our system of control, he will begin to act in ways that are more consistent with the true thoughts and motives of his heart. He will no longer do what is right, because the right that he did was forced on him by the external parental control. His heart had never changed. We see this again and again as teenagers go off to college and seem to throw off everything they "learned" in their Christian homes.

Colossians 2:20–23 warns us against this behavior-control strategy:

> *Since you died with Christ to the basic principles of this world, why, as though you still belonged to it, do you submit to its rules: "Do not handle! Do not taste! Do not touch!"? These are all destined to perish with use, because they are based on human commands and teachings. Such regulations indeed have an appearance of wisdom, with their self-imposed worship, their false humility, and their harsh treatment of the body, but they lack any value in restraining sensual indulgence.*

The rules-and-regulations approach that focuses on keeping the teenager "out of trouble" will ultimately fail because it does not deal with the heart. As Paul so powerfully states, it "lacks any value for restraining sensual indulgence." What he means is that it does not deal with the source of a person's wrong behavior, the sinful desires of the heart. Peter says that the corruption in the world is caused by evil desires (2 Peter 1:4). We have to work at the level of the heart desires with our teenagers, or we will win lots of battles and ultimately lose the war. It is not enough to be detectives, jailers, and judges. We must pastor the hearts of our children with the kind of faithful, watchful care for their souls that we receive from our heavenly Father.

The parent who has a pastoral model of parenting will do more than hand down regulations and enforce punishments when the regulations are broken. Pastoring parents will befriend their teen. They will probe and examine. They will engage their child in provocative discussions. They will be unwilling to live with distance, avoidance, and nonanswers. They will not let the teenager set the agenda for the relationship. In times of trouble, they will have discussions rather than cross-examinations. They will not be there simply to prove the child wrong and to announce punishment. They will seek to expose the true thoughts and motives of their teenager's heart by asking heart-disclosing questions. ("What were you thinking and feeling at the time?" "Why *was* that so important to you?" "What were you seeking to accomplish when you did that?" "What was the most important thing to you at that moment?" "What was it that you were afraid of in that situation?" "What was it that you were trying to get?" "Why did you become so angry?" "If you could go back and do something differently, what would you change?" etc.) They will help their teenager to look at himself in the accurate mirror of the Word, which is able to expose and judge the heart. And they will do all of this in a spirit of humble, gentle, kind, forgiving, forbearing, and patient love.

In so doing they will incarnate the love of Christ, who is the Great Shepherd (Pastor) of their teenager's soul. Colossians 3:12–14 gives us a wonderful description of the attitudes that need to shape the ministry encounters we have with our teenagers.

> *Therefore, as God's chosen people, holy and dearly loved, clothe yourselves with compassion, kindness, humility, gentleness and patience. Bear with each other and forgive whatever grievances you may have against one another. Forgive as the Lord forgave you. And over all these virtues put on love, which binds them all together in perfect unity.*

Parents who approach their teenagers with these attitudes of heart will demonstrate the presence of the One who is truly ever-present and boundless in redemptive love. He, the great Changer of Hearts, is then able to use them as instruments in his restorative hands. How different this is from the anxious anger, fearful control, and desperate manipulation that many parents exercise in an attempt to get their teenagers to do what is right! James says that this anger "does not bring about the righteous life that God desires" (James 1:20).

Attempts to control, although appearing to be right, actually get in the way of what the Lord is seeking to do in your teen's life. Ezekiel states God's agenda very clearly, to "recapture the hearts of the people of Israel, who have all deserted me for their idols" (Ezek. 14:5). God says, "This is what I am working on, to recapture the hearts of my people so that they serve me and me alone." Can we have a lesser goal as we parent our teenagers? We must work to see the underlying idols of the heart that have shaped their behavior. They will be exposed as the Spirit works through us to shine the light of Scripture on the teen's life.

All that we do with our teenagers, from the casual encounters to the crisis moments, must be shaped by a basic commitment to heart change. This parental pastoring of the heart can be summarized with five fundamental goals that offer practical guidance in all that we do with our teenagers. These goals will form the discussion of this and the next four chapters.

GOAL 1 *Focusing on the Spiritual Struggle*

Teenagers' lives tend to be dominated by concerns about the world that can be seen, touched, and tasted. They fret tearfully about how they look. They long to be accepted by peers. They hold their "stuff" possessively. They talk in dramatic terms about what looks beautiful or tastes appealing to them. They are crushed when someone mocks an outfit. They anguish over perceived rejection. Teenagers tend to be intensely materialistic, that is, focused on the physical world.

Often the more significant unseen world of the spiritual seems unreal to them. Teens tend to believe two deadly lies. The first is that the physical is more real than the spiritual. It is not surprising that present, physical, personal happiness seems more important than eternal blessing. Second, they tend to believe in the permanence of the physical world. It doesn't seem to be passing away to them. It seems always to be there and it seems to be "where it's at."

How different this is from the biblical perspective! Asaph, in Psalm 73, says the prosperity of the wicked is like a dream. What a powerful analysis! A dream seems real, yet it is not. It passes away the moment the body wakes. The earthly goods that a person acquires are passing away even as they are being collected. The physical world is destined to perish.

In 2 Corinthians 4:16–18, Paul says it this way:

> *Therefore we do not lose heart. Though outwardly we are wasting away, yet inwardly we are being renewed day by day. For our light and momentary troubles are achieving for us an eternal weight of glory that far outweighs them all. So we fix our eyes not on what is seen, but on what is unseen. For what is seen is temporary, but what is unseen is eternal.*

Paul is preoccupied with the unseen. He is focused on the spiritual. He is not invested in the physical and material world. Why? Very simply because it is passing away. Christ said, "What good will it be for a man if he gains the whole world, yet forfeits his soul?" (Matt. 16:26). John warns us in his first letter not to "love the world or anything in the world" (1 John 2:15). The theme is everywhere in Scripture. The wise person lives for what cannot be seen. The fool lives to build another barn to store away what is perishing and useless in the world to come. The wise person longs for spiritual blessing, the fool craves physical reward. The wise person looks to eternity, the fool lives for the moment.

Not only do teenagers tend to live with a physical focus, missing or minimizing the significance of the spiritual world, but they also tend to live with a peace-time mentality. In times of peace, people give themselves to luxury, leisure, and pleasure. They focus on wants and desires. However, in times of war, people live with another focus. The factory that produced lavish stereo systems is converted to produce electronic equipment for battle. The assembly line that produced luxury cars begins to produce tanks. Young men go to military training instead of going off to school. War commands the focus not only of the professional soldiers, but the whole society as well.

Here's the point. Scripture says that *life is war!* As I have said many times to my children, "There is a war out there. It is being fought on the turf of your heart. It is fought for the control of your soul. Each situation you face today is a skirmish in the war. Be careful, be aware of the battle. Don't forget that there is a scheming enemy out there who is out to deceive, divide, and destroy. Go out knowing that to win you must fight. You must not relax, you must not forget." We cannot say this enough to our teenagers (or ourselves).

Wise, mature, godly people live aware of the spiritual; they see it in every situation of life. They never view life *"under* the sun" (see Ecclesiastes). They see the spiritual implications in everything they do, in every situation they are in. This is what we must aim to produce in our teenagers. To do this *we* must be spiritually minded ourselves. We must live aware of the war.

There are two things that keep us from teaching our children to face and fight in the spiritual struggle. First, there is a tendency on our part to be more worried about the world of the seen than about the world of the unseen, especially when it comes to our teenagers. We are more upset that they lost the job and about how that is going to affect their collegiate future than we are about the inner spiritual issues that God is revealing in that moment.

We are more concerned about the poor grades on the report card than we are about what those grades reveal about the spiritual condition of our child. We get angry that the room is a chaotic litter of dirty clothes, and we do not see the heart behind the mess. We are upset that the car is dented and make much more of the physical damage than we do the spiritual damage that may be taking place at the same time in the teen's life. We tell her that her outfit looks ridiculous, or complain that he drank the last of the milk, and that his music drives us crazy, all the while missing what is really of eternal importance.

Because of this, we do not take advantage of daily opportunities to remind our teenagers of the spiritual struggle present in every situation in this fallen world. If we are going to produce teenagers who engage in the spiritual struggle, we need to start by asking ourselves what is really important to us. Are we, by the things that concern us and the way we solve problems, actually demonstrating the opposite of what we say we believe? Are our own lives consistent with what we say that we would like to produce in our teenagers?

The second thing that gets in our way as we try to open our teenagers' eyes to the spiritual struggle is a cultural misunderstanding. Our Christian culture has tended to misunderstand spiritual warfare. We have tended to think of it as the more bizarre end of spiritual things. By most Christian thinking, if spiritual warfare became a movie, the movie would have to be produced by Stephen Spielberg with the screenplay written by Steven King! Spiritual warfare makes us think of demon possession, horrific demonstrations of satanic control, and dramatic exorcisms. But Scripture presents spiritual warfare not as the violent, bizarre end of the Christian life, but as what the Christian life *is!*

When Paul introduces the subject of spiritual warfare at the end of his letter to the Ephesians (6:10–18), he is not changing the subject to talk about the dark side of spirituality. He is doing something very different. He is summarizing everything he has said up to that point. Where does spiritual warfare take place? In the body of Christ, in the marriage relationship, in the parent-child relationship, between slave and master, and in every location in the culture around us. Our teenagers need to learn how to fight the war and use the battle equipment the Lord has provided. Paul's description needs to shape the way we think about this everyday, every-situation war.

> *Finally, be strong in the Lord and in his mighty power. Put on the full armor of God so that you can take your stand against the devil's schemes. For our struggle is not against flesh and blood, but against the rulers, against the authorities, against the powers of this dark world and against the spiritual forces of evil in the heavenly realms. Therefore put on the full armor of God, so that when the day of evil comes, you may be able to stand your ground, and after you have done everything, to stand. Stand firm then, with the belt of truth buckled around your waist, with the breastplate of righteousness in place, and with your feet fitted with the readiness that comes from the gospel of peace. In addition to all this, take up the shield of faith, with which you can extinguish all the flaming arrows of the evil one. Take the helmet of salvation and the sword of the Spirit, which is the word of God. And pray in the Spirit on all occasions with all kinds of prayers and requests. With this in mind, be alert and always keep on praying for all the saints.*

If our teenagers are going to stand strong in the spiritual war, they need to know that there *is* a spiritual world where war is taking place. They need to know who the enemy is (and who the enemy is not). They need to know the weapons of this war and how to use them, and they need to know what victory looks like in everyday life.

This is vital because spiritual warfare not only takes place *where* we live, *it is what we are living*. That is why Paul summarizes his letter to the Ephesians this way. He does not want us to think about all of these situations and relationships horizontally. He wants us to realize that there are dramatic vertical struggles taking place in them all. So he tells us to be aware of the Devil's schemes, to stand fast in the Lord's power, to put on the whole armor of God, and to pray. There is a war going on out there. It is not an *aspect* of the Christian life, it *is* the Christian life. Sadly, because they have bought into the cultural misunderstanding, most Christian parents have not constantly reminded their teenagers of the battle or prepared them for the daily victories that can be experienced by the children of God.

Our goal is to raise children who live very aware of the spiritual world. We want to be used of God to produce young adults who understand the spiritual implications of everything they do. Our goal is to produce children who exist in the world of the seen, but who live for what cannot be seen, touched, or tasted.

Qualities of a Spiritual Warrior

What will the teenager look like who understands and participates in the spiritual struggle? Let me list several qualities that will be part of his life:

1. He will have a heartfelt, internalized fear of God. This is the foundation of a spiritual life. It is the fear of God that is the beginning of a truly wise life (Prov. 1:7). The fool has no fear of God in his heart, so he lives for what the moment can deliver and for what his eyes can see. What is this fear of God? It is the nonnegotiable motivator of the spiritual person. God, his presence, his will, and his glory are the reason the spiritual person does what he does. He has a single motivation in his life—to live life so as to please his Lord. He does not live for his own pleasure or the pleasure of others. He does not live for

what he can possess. He does what he does because God is and has spoken. This is the sole guidance system for his existence. He does what he does not because someone is watching, or out of fear of the consequences, but ultimately because of a deep, worshipful love and reverence for God. The thought of knowingly and purposefully disobeying him is unthinkable.

This is the only thing that will keep our teenagers pure in times of temptation when we are far away and the pressure is on them to step outside of God's boundaries.

2. Second to the fear of God, but directly related to it is submission to authority. One of the sad things that I hear parents say is, "Come on, Paul, you have to expect teenagers to rebel. It's just part of growing up." I don't think that we should ever come to casually expect or accept rebellion from anyone. It is always wrong and always dangerous!

If a person fears God, he will be submissive to the authorities that God has placed in his life. A person who disregards, argues against, or seeks to skirt the authorities in his life is not taking advantage of God's help in fighting the spiritual battle. God placed authority in our lives to restrain sin. A person who is aware of his sinfulness and who wants to live a godly life will not chafe against authority. He will appreciate it and submit to it. This is the spirit we want to see in our teenagers.

Something is wrong when a teenager views authority as negative and punitive. Our goal is to teach our teenagers to admit their need of God-ordained authority and the importance of willing submission to it. We want them to grow to see the authority figures in their lives as instruments of help, guidance, protection, and restraint, lovingly given by a God who knows their hearts and the nature of their struggle in this fallen world. Ultimately we want them to say, "Authority— I need it, I want it, I am thankful that God has put it in my life."

This goal may seem unrealistic for two reasons. First, many of us have become so used to accepting negative responses from our teenagers that we are surprised when they respond with acceptance, respect, and willing obedience. Rather than expecting respect and being grieved in the face of rebellion, we have succumbed to the cultural belief that rebellion is an acceptable norm for the teen years.

Second, to many of us this goal sounds way too "pie in the sky," because we did not fight and win those essential authority struggles while our children were young. We spent too much time indulging their demands and giving in to their misbehavior. We would explain away their rebellion, saying that they were "teething," that they were "overtired," or that they were just trying to "get attention." Now that our children are teenagers, they don't have a heart of appreciation for our authority. They see no need to submit to it. They don't understand why we are not excusing their rebellion as we once did, and why we are now standing in their way. As teenagers they are now all too willing to take us on when we try to exercise parental authority. We, as parents, need to understand that rebellion against parental authority is never okay, at any age. Rejection of parental authority is a rejection of God's authority. And the rejection of God's authority is, in fact, claiming his authority as my own. It is an attempt to *be* God. Whether your teenager realizes it or not, the stakes could not be higher!

3. The next quality evident in a person who is engaged in spiritual warfare is liberally discussed in Proverbs. It is separation from the wicked. Let me put it in positive terms. The teenager who fears God is going to want to be with other teenagers who fear God. It is true that a person is known by the company he keeps! If a teenager is serious in his desire to participate in the spiritual struggle, if he is seriously seeking to live a life pleasing to the Lord, and if he is living in a willing submission to the authorities in his life, then he is going to want to spend his time with people who share his values. Rebellious

teenagers will not be attractive to him. Teens who have no spiritual things will not draw him. Rather, wherever he is, he will instinctively seek out those who have a heart for God. He will feel strangely out of place with kids who have no interest in the things that God says are most important.

4. It is impossible to participate in the spiritual struggle if you do not have the ability to think through your faith and apply it to the situations of life. What a teenager needs, if he is going to live a God-honoring life, is a thorough knowledge of Scripture that allows him to apply its commands, principles, and perspectives to the many different situations that arise in everyday life. He needs to be more than a person who has acquired biblical knowledge; he needs to be a person who is able to approach life with biblical wisdom.

I am convinced that many teenagers are unprepared for the spiritual struggle because they have never been taught to think biblically. They have been in Sunday school, so they know all the familiar Bible stories and they have memorized all of the favorite Bible passages, but these are not much more than isolated, unconnected biblical factoids to them. They haven't been woven into a consistent, distinctively biblical view of life. The Bible isn't a way of thinking to these teenagers. It is a book of moralistic stories, a book of dos and don'ts. The result is that, although they have lots of biblical knowledge, they have little biblical wisdom. They do not have a functional, useful, biblical view of life that would keep them from living foolishly.

We must disciple our children to think biblically, to interpret all the facts of life from a biblical perspective. We must teach them to always ask how the Bible can help them to understand whatever they are considering.

They must learn to look at themselves, life, relationships, possessions, morality, leisure, government, learning, knowledge, marriage, family, the past, the future, love, hate, character, maturity, right and wrong, good and evil, success and failure, and everything else they will encounter in life from the vantage point of Scripture. The goal is that this consistently biblical view of life will enable them to recognize what is wise to think and do in every situation. We will not accomplish this by barking orders at them. This takes time, patience, and love. It also assumes that we have taken time to think through the issues ourselves. We cannot mentor our children into something we ourselves do not have.

5. The final piece of this goal of focusing on the spiritual struggle is biblical self-awareness. Maybe it is obvious, but teenagers don't tend to be very self-aware. They are very aware of how *others* respond to them. They focus in on how they look and how they feel, but they tend to lack the essence of biblical self-awareness—an awareness of the heart. This is powerfully demonstrated when a parent points out a wrong attitude in the teenager. Most often, teenagers will respond with hurt, feeling that they have been falsely accused or wrongly singled out.

We want to be used of God to produce teens who can regularly examine themselves in the perfect mirror of the Word of God and who can humbly accept what is revealed there. A teenager who has an accurate view of himself will not only respond well to the help of his parents, he will seek it out. He will be aware of his spiritual weaknesses and will welcome the resources that God has placed in his life. He will not excuse, defend, argue, or shift blame when his wrong is pointed out. He will "not think of himself more highly than he ought to think" (Rom. 12:3). It may sound unbelievable, but it is true.

Many teenagers do not take protective measures against sin ("fleeing youthful lusts") because they believe that they are much stronger and more mature than they actually are. They really do believe that they can play with fire without getting burnt. Even when they do get burnt by their choices and behavior, their inaccurate view of self leads them to conclude that what happened was really the fault of others or the fault of the circumstances. How important it is for us to take every opportunity God gives us to hold the mirror of the Word in front of our teenagers so that they can begin to see themselves as they actually are! So often in the moments when their hearts are being revealed, our own anger and frustration cause us to beat them with words and mete out harsh punishments. We forget to function as God's instruments, and then our anger only leaves our children more defensive, more closed, and more self-deceived.

What does it mean to be biblically self-aware? It means that the teenager will live with an accurate, practical knowledge of personal themes of weakness, temptation, and sin. Each of us sins, yet we do not all sin in the same ways. There tend to be themes to our struggles with sin. The spiritually aware teenager knows where he is susceptible to temptation, and that knowledge helps him to take protective measures against it.

One Sunday as we were traveling to church I inadvertently drove into a rather large pothole. After the car quit bouncing, my wife said that she was confused. I asked her why. She said she didn't understand why Sunday after Sunday I drove into the same pothole! It was in the same place each week. The road had another lane. Why didn't I anticipate and avoid the pothole?

Teenagers will often drive into the same spiritual pothole again and again because of their blindness to the themes of their hearts. One of the most helpful things we can do for them spiritually is help them to look down the road of life, anticipating where temptation will hit them and teach them how to avoid it. As we do this, they will grow in self-awareness and in appreciation for the mercy and grace of the Lord who helps them in their time of need. They will also begin to see their parents not as judges and jailers, but as God-given resources to assist them in fighting life's most significant battles.

In times of struggle and failure, we need to do more than pronounce judgment on what's wrong and enforce punishment. We need to talk, discuss, question, evaluate, engage, and interact with our teenagers, hoping that God will use these moments of opportunity to open their eyes a little more to who they really are and to their constant need for Christ.

That night when I held that awful note written by my daughter, it was important to keep this first goal in mind. Here was a wonderful, God-ordained opportunity to talk with her about the nature of the spiritual struggle. However, that is usually the kind of moment when parents tell teens how crushed they are, how ashamed they are of them, how they would never have thought of doing such a thing when they were young, how they can't believe that this is what the teens do after all they have done for them! Too often parents announce a punishment and leave the room, missing a golden opportunity to do the work of the Lord.

My daughter's note was about more than bad language and disrespect. It pictured the spiritual war that was raging in her life. By God's grace the war had broken out into the open, yet she didn't see it. She was much more focused on the fact that at school and home she was "in trouble," and she wondered what she was "going to get" as a consequence for her behavior. She needed her parents to take her to a deeper level of concern and understanding regarding the situation. What motivated her to write such a note? It was the result of what kind of desires? How did the whole situation reveal what was important to her? What did the note reveal about her relationships with peers and her response to authority? What could she learn from this situation about her own personal susceptibility to temptation?

In thinking through these questions with her, my wife and I were helping her to understand and participate in the spiritual struggle. And this discussion gave us an opportunity to talk to her about the themes of the fear of God, submission to authority, separation from the wicked, the ability to think through and apply the faith, and biblical self-awareness. It provided an opportunity for us to help our daughter to know herself more accurately, to know God more personally, and to be much wiser in understanding the schemes of the enemy. In the midst of real failure, she took one more step in becoming an active participant in the spiritual struggle. She would have never taken these steps without our help.

CONVICTIONS AND WISDOM

MY wife and I were going away to a weekend conference. Our son asked if he could stay with a family from our church who had children his age. We agreed, dropped him off, and went on our way. It seemed as if it would be a nondescript, uneventful weekend. Little did we know that God had something else planned for our son. This was going to be a weekend of temptation, of choice, of decision, and of the costly exercise of faith.

Before our son had arrived at our friends' house, the kids in the family had gone to the video store to rent a couple of movies. Movie-watching was going to be the big event for Friday night. It just so happened that the parents of the family had to be away that evening, and after they left, the videos came out. It wasn't long before our son realized that the videos contained material he should not be watching.

What would he do now? He could watch the videos; probably neither we nor his friends' parents would know. He could protest and see if he could convince the others not to watch the movies. He thought of going somewhere else, but he really didn't have anywhere to go.

He decided to try to convince the others not to watch the videos. They thought he was "being stupid" and put the first video in. As a young teenager, not knowing what else to do, he spent the evening in the kitchen, eating more chips and drinking more soda than he ever had in his life. He had made a choice. He had exercised conviction. He had taken the heat for his faith.

When the parents of the house came home and found him in the kitchen, they asked him why he wasn't with the others. When he explained, they had two reactions. First, they were upset at their own children for the video choices they had made and for their insensitivity to their guest. Second, they were amazed at our son for the choice he had made to live out what he thought was right.

I am afraid that many of us are so busy making decisions for our children in order to keep them safe that we do not teach them to develop their own set of internalized biblical convictions. It is one thing for a teenager to do what is right under a watchful eye or under the threat of punishment. It is quite another thing to see the independent, unpressured, heartfelt exercise of personal conviction. As we are preparing our teenage children to go out into this darkened, fallen world and live a godly life, it is mandatory that we make the development of internalized convictions one of our primary goals.

GOAL 2   *Developing a Heart of Conviction and Wisdom*

Along with developing convictions, developing wisdom—the second half of this goal—is also necessary if our teenagers are to live God-pleasing lives. Let me illustrate with another story.

The call came to me at work in the middle of the day. It was my son calling from his part-time job. He had been asked to do something that was dangerous and not part of his job description. It was not a moral issue, there was no clear right or wrong, but a decision needed to be made. He called me and asked if he could fax me his job description so that we could discuss what he should do. We talked about the people involved. Who were the people in authority over him, and why were they making the request? We talked about the way he should deal with those over him. In a way, he wanted me to make the decision for him, but I would not, because I thought this situation was sent by God to develop him. There were many wisdom issues involved here. My son was open, seeking, and thinking well. After discussing the situation, I told him I would pray for him. I was confident that he had what he needed to make a wise decision.

What happened? He got fired! I couldn't believe it. He had done all the right things, yet he had lost his job. I was tempted to question God. Couldn't he encourage him just this once? But even in the firing there was an opportunity to talk about life in a broken world, the blessing of doing things God's way, and what it means to entrust yourself to God's sovereign care. Then, in a couple months he was hired back. The regional manager had been very angry over the way the situation was handled and instructed those under him to offer our son the job back.

Notice that this situation was very different from the Friday night video incident, but no less important. The first situation had to do with what I will call clear-boundary issues. These are issues to which God has plainly spoken, where there is an obvious right and wrong. What is needed is the exercise of personal, biblical, internalized conviction. The second situation had to do with what I will call wisdom issues. These are issues where there is no direct "thus says the Lord," but to which Scripture speaks with a myriad of balancing biblical principles so that we may live wisely in this fallen world. What is needed here is readily applicable biblical wisdom.

When your teenager encounters clear-boundary issues, he does not need to pray for wisdom. For example, in a department store he does not need to pray that God would give him the wisdom to know whether he should steal or not! What your teenager needs there is a heart that is submissive to God's will as revealed in his Word. He needs a heart more controlled by love for the Creator than for the created thing.

But when a teen encounters wisdom issues, he will never solve them by treating them as if they were simple boundary issues. If he tries to do this, he will begin to lose confidence in Scripture, thinking that it does not speak clearly to the issues of his life. And then, in his lack of confidence in Scripture, he will move toward one of two extremes: legalism, that is, making everything a rigid boundary issue; or foolishness, concluding that anything that is not an obvious boundary issue is unimportant and not addressed in Scripture.

I fear that many of us do an inadequate job of preparing our children to deal with wisdom issues. For some of us, this is because we live with a secular-spiritual dichotomy in our own lives. Many of us think of our lives in a two-worlds way. There is the world of the spiritual that includes our devotional, church, and formal worship life. It also tends to include those issues to which God has given us clear commands. Attention to these things makes up our definition of what is spiritual.

The other world in this two-worlds way of thinking is the secular world. It is the world outside of God's clear commands in Scripture and one's devotional-worship-church life. In a two-worlds way of thinking, Scripture has little if anything to say about life in this second world. Unfortunately, this world tends to be vastly larger than the spiritual world. It tends to be the world where I live every day and expend most of my productive effort. How can we teach our teenagers to exercise biblical wisdom there if we are not accustomed to doing it ourselves? How can we teach wisdom when we have failed to realize that *all* of life is spiritual and that Scripture speaks in some way to *every* situation of the human experience?

There is another reason why parents fail to prepare their children well for the wisdom decisions they will face as they leave home. It is, sadly, that many parents simply do not have a fluid, functional, situationally applicable knowledge of Scripture themselves. Many of us have little more than a Sunday school knowledge of the Bible. We know the popular stories, we have some grasp of the major doctrines, and we know phrases from the most-quoted passages, but we have not meditated upon or mastered the Word. We don't know how to use its wisdom to guide us in matters of everyday living, and our own lack of knowledge keeps us from discipling our children to live in a biblically wise way.

As a parent, you cannot give what you don't have yourself. We can only teach our children to be practically obedient to the Word, exercising decisive biblical conviction, if we are doing the same. We can only teach our children to wisely apply the principles of the Word to the issues of life if that is what *we* are seeking to do. Obedient students of the Word tend to produce the same kind of children.

Understanding Clear-Boundary Issues

Let me define further what I mean when I talk about clear-boundary issues versus wisdom issues. Clear-boundary issues are situations that involve the plain commands of Scripture. The call to speak the truth, to honor father and mother, to not steal or commit adultery or fornication are all examples. To live God's way in these situations, a teenager needs two primary things. First, he needs to know the commands of Scripture. A teenager cannot stay inside God's boundaries if he doesn't know what they are. Second, he needs personal conviction, that is, a heart committed to doing God's will regardless of the consequences.

I am persuaded that it is very important to define the concept of convictions for our teenagers. Too often, what we call convictions are actually preferences. Real convictions are based on revealed truth (that is, Scripture). Preferences are based on personal desire. Convictions are constant; preferences change with desire. Convictions demand faith; preferences rely on the emotions of the moment. Our teenagers need to understand the difference between a conviction and a preference.

Here are six characteristics of biblical conviction:

1. *A biblical conviction is always based on a study of, submission to, and application of Scripture.* It is knowledge of the will of God combined with a heart to obey that is carried to the situations of everyday life.

2. *A biblical conviction is always predetermined.* You do not arrive at biblical convictions on the spur of the moment or in the heat of the circumstances. Biblical convictions are predetermined first by God. He has made the decision for us; our job is simple—to obey. Second, they are predetermined by us. Long before we enter the situation, we have decided that we will live according to the clear commands of the Word. We bring this heart commitment, made long beforehand, to each new situation.

3. *A biblical conviction will not change with the circumstances.* It is not responsive to outside pressure. We see this powerfully demonstrated by Christ, the apostles, and the martyrs of old. Conviction is based on an inner commitment, not on the external pressures of people or the presence of situational consequences.

4. *Biblical convictions are inflexible.* True convictions have a nonnegotiable quality to them. They will not be offered up, dealt away, or compromised in order to get or achieve something else.

5. *True biblical conviction is bold.* There is a foundational confidence to it because it is based on the clear word of the Lord as revealed in Scripture. In conviction I realize that the God who made the world and who controls this moment has spoken; therefore, there is no safer place to be than to be actively doing his will! True conviction is not timid and doubting. It results in courageous acts of faith.

6. *True biblical conviction is always lived out.* Conviction that is not lived, that does not rule my everyday life, is not really conviction. If my heart knows, understands, acknowledges, and has submitted to what is right, it will definitely show in the decisions I make daily.

We want to be used of God to develop this kind of heart in our teenagers. Think, once again, about the incident with my daughter and the note she wrote in her school classroom. What she lacked were personal, internalized, biblical convictions. A person who does not have biblical convictions does not have an internal restraint system. This person will do right when under a watchful eye, or when under external pressure. However, when these external motivators are removed, this person will behave very differently. Her problem was not knowledge. It wasn't even an acknowledgment that God's standard was right. What was lacking was a personal *commitment* to obey God no matter what the cost. Lovingly, God revealed this gap dramatically, so that she would have a turning of heart.

Understanding Wisdom Issues

As important as biblical conviction is, and as important as it is to pay attention to the boundary issues, a believer spends most of his time grappling with wisdom issues. Because a true believer has long ago decided that he would live in submission to the lordship of Christ, he willingly lives within the boundaries. He does not live testing them. He lives a basically obedient life, but a life in which there are myriad situations where he needs wisdom, that is, he needs to apply the principles, perspectives, and themes of Scripture so that his practical everyday decisions express God's will for his life. In these situations he needs wisdom because there is no clear "thus says the Lord." At the same time he knows that Scripture speaks to every circumstance of life. We want to be used of God to develop teenagers who can go out into the world and live wisely.

Let's look back at my son and the job situation and see the many, many principles of Scripture that apply and that define what living wisely looks like in such a circumstance.

1. *There is the principle of authority.* The authorities in his life (parents, bosses, governmental officials) are clearly presented in Scripture as ordained and appointed by God. They are presented in Scripture as God's servants for my son's good. Whenever he appeals to or disagrees with these authorities, he must do so in a spirit of honor, thankfulness, and submission.

2. *There is the principle of grace.* Proverbs says that "a gentle answer turns away wrath, but a harsh word stirs up anger" (15:2). In this time of disagreement and controversy, the way he spoke was very important.

3. *There is the principle of truth,* even truth spoken in love. It is important that my son would avoid the temptation to trim or embellish the truth. At the same time, it is vital that he would not use the truth vengefully as a weapon. He must speak truth as he would want it spoken to him.

4. *There is the principle of the "higher agenda."* As a believer, he is called to work in such a way as to "make the Gospel attractive." Even at work we are to function as ambassadors of the Lord and living spokespersons for his truth.

5. *There is the principle of wise counsel.* The Scripture warns me against impulsive, independent decision-making. We are told that God will give wisdom to those who ask, without showing favoritism. And we are told that in the multitude of counsel there is wisdom. It was important for our son not to respond in haste, but to take the time to receive the wisdom God has promised.

6. *There is the principle of faithfulness or integrity.* It was important for our son to examine his job description because he had to accept the obligation to do the work he had promised to do in exchange for

his wages. Scripture calls us to be careful of the promises we make and to be faithful to what we have promised.

7. *There is the principle of the sovereignty of God.* It was tempting for our son to look at the circumstance as "rotten, bad luck" that somehow had befallen him. He needed to see that this event was under the careful control of God who rules over everything for his sake. He did not need to panic or to gain control somehow. He was free to act wisely and entrust the outcome to his heavenly Father, who judges all things justly.

8. *There is the principle of values.* In situations like this, we express what is really important to us. For our son, it was tempting to live for things that can be seen. When you are in school, a job is very important. Scripture enjoins us not to live for earthly treasure, or for what can be seen, touched, tasted, and quantified. Rather, we are called to live for things that have eternal value. Even in this job situation, our son was being called to live for God's glory, to live to keep his own heart pure, and to seek God's kingdom and his righteousness. Where the rubber meets the road, this means doing what is right, trusting God to provide.

9. *There is the principle of the heart.* Scripture, as we have earlier noted, teaches us that we "behave out of the heart." What we do expresses the thoughts and desires of our hearts. It was important for our son to be aware of his heart in this situation. To what temptations would he be particularly susceptible? Would he be tempted to give in to the fear of man? Would he be tempted to anger? Would he struggle with doubting God? Would he give in to discouragement? Would he succumb to the pressure of his peers or the pressure to make a hasty decision? It is very important in this kind of situation for the teenager to operate with heart awareness so that he can protect himself from the temptations to which he knows he is particularly weak.

10. *There is the principle of God's glory.* Our son was called to live

for something grander than his own good, comfort, success, affluence, and ease. The most important thing he must do is to respond in a way that pleases God. This is more important than solving the situation, pleasing the boss, pleasing himself, or retaining the job. He will never do what is right at the practical, everyday life level unless he has the glory of God as his ultimate goal. Whenever we disobey God, it is because our own glory and good are more important to us than the glory of God.

These ten principles bring focus to the job situation our son encountered. Each helps him to know more clearly what he should do, why he should do it, and how and when it should be done. There are many, many more principles that apply to this situation, each giving light to the heart and a lamp for the feet.

The truths of Scripture are like a great symphony orchestra. You do not really understand or experience a symphony by hearing the separate notes of one violin, oboe, or drum. You do not experience its rich beauty by hearing a duet between the trumpet and the bass viol. It is only as you hear all the instruments played together that you really understand the majesty and beauty of the symphony. In an orchestra, each instrument is made more beautiful by the other. Each complements and balances the other. Similarly, Scripture gives us a symphony of truth. Not just one note but many contribute to the rich, harmonious tones of truth.

As parents, we need to have a symphonic mentality as we train our children for godly living. We cannot hammer away at one note. We must introduce them to the whole symphony of biblical wisdom so that they can make biblically sound decisions. To do that we must know the symphony ourselves, and we must be committed to take the time to talk to our children daily about the principles that apply to their life situations. We need to get away from the quick and easy "do this, don't do that" that we dispense on the fly with little or no discussion or explanation. We need to invite our children to examine and discuss, seeing difficulty and trouble as an opportunity to help them hear a little more of God's symphony of truth and to understand how these notes make sense of life. It is of paramount importance that we do not think *for* our children, but teach *them* how to think about life, employing the symphony of perspectives God has given us in his Word.

Strategies for Developing a Wise Heart

If we are going to raise children of conviction and wisdom, we need a strategy for doing so. Let me list some things that you can do to help develop a sensitive conscience and a wise heart.

1. *See the difficult, troublesome, problem situations as God-given opportunities to develop a biblical mind in your teenager.* This is the theme of this book: problems are there because God, who loves us and who is in control, is accomplishing his wonderful purposes in them.

Several years ago, a brokenhearted parent told me that she had found pornography in her son's bedroom. She was crushed and her husband was angry. As she described it, they had been getting ready to "go after" their son when they decided to call me first. I was thankful they did. They needed perspective. Yes, I shared their sadness, but I saw something else very wonderful going on. I saw the rescuing hand of God. Their son could have gotten away with it and moved just a little closer to that world of enslaving, secret, sexual sin, but God, in his glory and goodness, had another plan. I said to this mother, "Don't you see that God's work of rescuing your son from this temptation has already begun? Thank him for his awesome love, and be a part of what he is doing. Don't go in with guns blazing. Tell your son how much he is loved by God and that today that love is being demonstrated in the way God ordained that the pornography would be found. Then help him to understand the thoughts and motives of his heart that led him into this sin."

If you look at these situations as irritants that ruin your plans for your morning, afternoon, or evening; if you respond to them impulsively with impatience, irritation, and verbal put-downs; if you fail to reflect a biblical mind ("I couldn't care less what you do when you're out of here, but I tell you one thing, you do this again and you're on the street!"), your teenager will grow up to do the same. Instead, stop, thank God for your high calling as a parent, and have a patient and heart-engaging conversation with your son or daughter.

2. *Resist making the decision for your teenager.* Remember, we need to have a goal more fundamental than keeping our teenagers safe by regulating their behavior. Take the time to teach your teenagers how to make a wise decision. Teach them the biblical content that applies to each situation and teach them the biblical process of decision-making. Our goal should be to put more and more decisions into our children's hands as they mature. To do this, you will have to deal with your own fear, your own desire to control, and your own reluctance to place your life and the life of your teenager in the capable hands of God.

You will also need to be patient and persevering in the face of resistance. Ephesians 4:2 provides the model for us. It says, "Be completely humble and gentle; be patient, bearing with one another in love." Bearing in love means patience in the face of provocation. Teenagers will say wild things. They will give weak excuses and offer illogical arguments. They will make extreme statements ("No one has ever . . . ," "You and Mom always, always . . . ," "This happens to me every time . . ."). They will accuse you of not understanding. They will compare you to the parents of their friends. They will do all of this because teenagers don't tend to hunger for wisdom. They don't tend to think that they need help. They tend to see your loving intervention and instruction as unwelcome interference. It is your job to win them for the way of the Lord. You are called to be an instrument of wisdom in your teenager's life. To do so, you must be gentle, humble, patient, and persevering.

3. *Draw out the heart of your teenager* (Prov. 20:5). Ask open-ended questions that help him to communicate what he really thinks and what he really wants. As you do this, don't scold the teenager for his honesty. You don't need to harshly lecture someone who is open, communicative, and teachable. Ask your teenager what he wants to do and why he wants to do it. Ask him what is important in the situation and why. Ask him what he fears the most when he thinks about what could possibly happen. Ask him to describe what would really make him happy in the situation. Ask him what he thinks God thinks about the circumstance.

The goal is to get your teenager looking at himself. You will need to ask good questions that he cannot answer without examining his own heart. Resist making pronouncements about what your teen did, why he did it, and what he is going to get as a result. Resist doing all the thinking and talking as you examine a situation. Resist turning a discussion of choices and decisions into another lecture, where you preach at him with pointed fingers, red face, and loud voice while he sits silently, waiting for you to leave. If we consistently handle things this way, it is not long before our teenagers determine to avoid these "talks" at any cost and feel a sense of dread when we approach their rooms. Sometimes we have unwittingly driven our teenagers into the very silence that we say we hate.

4. *Be persistent.* Don't settle for grunts, groans, no eye contact, silences, and yeses or noes that are given without explanation. Be positive, friendly, and encouraging, but be persistent. Few teenagers will draw you out. Often teenagers have many questions and much to say, but they will say nothing unless given the opportunity to talk with

someone who really does appear to care. Seek out your teenagers and patiently engage them in conversation. Don't take personal offense at their resistance, but remind them of your love and commitment. Make sure that they understand that the conversation you are having is not about catching them in the wrong and dispensing punishment, but about helping them to identify and do what is right.

5. *Help your teenager to determine whether he is dealing with a clear-boundary issue or a wisdom issue.* Discuss the difference between the two. If you are dealing with a clear-boundary issue, discuss the nature of true, personal, biblical conviction with him. Make sure that this conversation is not held in the abstract, but in the context of the particular circumstances in which he finds himself. If together you determine that you are dealing with a wisdom issue, then brainstorm with your teenager about the passages, principles, and perspectives that may apply. Share examples in your own life of how you seek to exercise biblical wisdom as you make decisions.

6. *Don't try to tell your teenager in one conversation everything you have learned.* As you talk, be sensitive to how you are being received. Is your teenager a willing and active participant? Or is he trying his best to end the conversation and get out of the room? Have you talked so long that his attention has waned? Remember, you live with your children and you will have another opportunity to get at issues again. Be wise, with a few well-thought-out and strategically positioned words. Remember, your goal is not to demonstrate the breadth of your own wisdom, but to teach your child to think and live wisely. This present opportunity will not be your last. Take advantage of the moment, but realize that you will have many more.

CHAPTER

LIFE IN THE REAL WORLD

YOU see it in the style of sneakers. You hear it in the sounds of music. You encounter it when your teenager speaks to you in a brand of English that you barely understand. You see it in the way teenagers relate to one another and to you. It beams into your home through television, radio, and the Internet, through the VCR and the stereo, through newspapers and magazines. It tells us what to think, desire, and do. It shapes relationships and defines what is important.

It is inescapable and very powerful, often unnoticed but everywhere visible, always new yet ancient in its influence, often recognized by its power to shape our actions, but more significant in its ability to shape our thoughts. It is something we create, yet daily it shapes us. It is human culture. Where there are people, there is culture. Where there are fallen people, there is fallen culture. This is life in the real world.

One of the most important skills for teenagers to develop is cultural awareness. By this I don't mean an appreciation of classical music or the opera, but an understanding of the way the spiritual struggle is played out in the culture in which we live. To do this, we need a practical understanding of the nature of the believer's struggle with culture.

The Smiths and the Joneses:
Two Typical Responses to Culture

It's a Saturday evening church supper and the Smith and Jones families find themselves together in the food line. Both families are hoping that they do not have to sit together for supper, but alas, they end up sharing the last available table. There aren't any real problems between these families—it's just that they do not understand each other at all!

Let's look around the table. The Smith children are dressed very conservatively and their conversation is about a book they are reading together as a family. Their children have little interaction with non-Christians because of the negative influence. No modern music is played in their home, and the Smiths do not go to the movies. They do own a television, but the children only watch educational programming.

Mr. and Mrs. Smith operate within a very small circle of life. Mr. Smith works with two other Christian men, and Mrs. Smith's contacts with other women occur mostly within a tiny support group of Christian friends. On the surface, the Smith children look unlike and act very differently from their peers. The Smiths' model for relating to the outside world is "Come out from among them and be separate."

It doesn't take long to see that the Joneses have had a very different response to their culture. Their children are dressed much differently from the Smith kids. For one thing, there are a lot more jewelry and earrings on the Jones children—and that includes the boys! The Jones daughter is wearing her Walkman headset around her neck, although she doesn't put it on during supper. The Jones children participate in many public-school activities. They all have stereos in their rooms and watch lots of television. The oldest son plays in a Christian alternative rock band. On the surface, the Jones children look and act like their non-Christian peers. The Joneses' model for relating to the world outside is, "Be in the world, but not of the world."

Rejection and Assimilation

The Smiths illustrate a rejection-isolation response to culture. The basic philosophy is this: *Evil is in the thing, so avoid the thing.* This strategy usually includes a list of cultural activities to be avoided (movies, music, dancing, etc.). Being separate is interpreted as meaning that the Christian family must avoid participation in the secular world wherever possible. On the surface this response may not seem so bad, yet it carries inherent dangers and deficiencies.

First, there is in this response a subtle denial of the doctrine of creation, which declares that all that God made was good (Gen. 1:31; Ps. 139:14). This is not to say that God created hard-core rock music. He did, however, create the melodic and rhythmic structures that it employs. Evil is not some organic presence within certain things, but is the result of the way things are used to express the thoughts and gratify the desires of sinful man. We need to be biblically precise in the way we think about these issues. For example, modern music is not in itself evil, as if evil were a substance present within in it. Modern music becomes problematic because it is a powerful medium for the worldview of individuals who are living in rebellion against God. Because this is true, it is important to teach our children to resist the way it panders to their sinful hearts without letting them think they win the battle with sin simply by avoiding certain things.

Second, this response tends to miss the core issue of the human struggle with evil. The core of our struggle is not with evil outside us, but with evil within. There *is* a war being fought: it is the war within, fought on the turf of the heart. Peter says that God has given his children everything they need to escape "the corruption in the world caused by evil desires" (2 Peter 1:4). As parents, we need to teach our children that we do not solve the struggle with evil by avoiding certain things, although there are times when fleeing certain situations, locations, and relationships is a principal means of avoiding the bondage of sin. Nevertheless, Paul says that such restrictions "have no value for restraining sensual indulgence" (see Col. 2:16–23). Avoiding external temptations alone does not restrain sin because it does not deal with the sin already in the heart. We want to teach our children that avoidance is not a cure, though it can be used of God to limit the damage of sin in our lives.

Third, the isolation response tends to promote a dangerous self-righteousness. Righteousness gets equated with keeping "the list." People who keep it are considered righteous and mature and people who don't are considered carnal and immature. Christ pounded away at this view of righteousness when he attacked the spiritual pride of the Pharisees (see Matt. 5:20; Matt. 23; Luke 18:9–14; Isa. 29:13). It is possible to keep this list rigidly while still having a heart that is far from God and totally reliant on self. It is clear that there must be a better way to teach our teenagers to respond to culture than modern, conservative-evangelical isolationism.

The Joneses would say that they have found a better way—assimilation. The philosophy of assimilation is this: *Things are neutral, so there is no harm in participating in the thing.* This approach, too, has defects.

Scripture teaches us that nothing is ever neutral. In this world things always carry some kind of moral freight. Christ said it very plainly: "He who is not with me is against me" (Matt. 12:30). For example, you could argue that language is in itself neutral. Individual letters, individual words, and the sounds that they make are neutral, but we never, ever encounter them that way. Language is always used to convey some kind of meaning. When employed, language is no longer neutral.

So there are certain things we must acknowledge as we think about the institutions, relationships, media, and products of the culture around us:

> All things that God created are good.

> All things that we encounter have been put together, or are used, in a way that carries meaning.

> Everything can be used for good or evil.

> Everything in culture expresses the perspectives of the creator and/or user.

> We never find things in the culture around us in a neutral context or setting.

Just as the rejection-isolation response to culture has its weaknesses, so does the assimilation response common in the evangelical church. Our children need a third way to respond to the culture around them, one that is the result of good biblical thinking. They need to understand what culture is and the nature of its power and influence, and form a biblical plan for living within it.

What Is Culture?

In the beginning, God created people with the capacity to interact with their world, and he gave them the responsibility to do so in a way that imaged him. God never intended for people to have a passive relationship to the world he made. He meant for them to "dress" the world around them. He made people in his image with creative abilities that no other creatures were given and he commanded them to use them (see Gen. 1:26–31; 2:15–20). So, since the creation, people have always had their hands on the world. It has never been left alone. We never encounter it in its original state. People are always instinctively interacting with the world. They are always organizing and re-organizing, interpreting and re-interpreting, creating and re-creating, and building and rebuilding. The presence of culture is constant and always changing.

God placed people in the primary environment of the world he created, but we never get to live in that environment alone. We are always living within the secondary environment as well—humanly created culture. Thus, the struggle with culture is an inescapable one.

How then do we define culture? People made in the image of God interact with the world God made, and culture is what results. Where there are people, there is culture. If a family isolates itself from the surrounding culture, they will not have escaped the cultural struggle, because as people made in God's image, they will form a family culture. And if an individual seeks to isolate himself from both the surrounding culture and the family, he still will not have escaped the cultural struggle, because he will create an individual culture. There is no way to escape dealing with the relationships, customs, institutions, structures, media, products, and beliefs that make up culture. We always live all of our lives in this secondary environment.

Something more needs to be said here: the Fall is the reason for this cultural struggle. Before the Fall, Adam and Eve interacted with the world God had made. They expressed their God-like creativity, but there was no problem because all that they did and said, all that they dressed and created, and all their customs and ways of relating were based on the words of God. Tragically, another voice, the Serpent's, came on the scene to give another interpretation to what God had made and said. In following this voice, Adam and Eve created the cultural struggle. Since the Fall, people build culture on the basis of many varied and competing authorities. Gone are the simple days of Genesis 1 and 2. Now the cultural canvas is stained with sin and until eternity, human culture will never again perfectly reflect the will of

God. This is why responding to culture is so important. It is one of our primary moral struggles. Teenagers need to grow up understanding this and being prepared for it.

The struggle with culture is inescapable and it is always moral. People always interact with the world in a spirit of submission to God and his Word or in rebellion and dependence on their own minds. The cultural struggle is always about right and wrong, true and false, good and bad, belief and unbelief, and human desire or God's will. Isolation is impossible. Assimilation is really capitulation. As was stated before, we need a better way.

The Need for Protection

You can see the influence in the way we dress. Very few of us are wearing Nehru jackets with wide bell-bottom pants (not that I am complaining!). In fact, few of us are wearing the same style of clothing we wore ten years ago or maybe even five. Skirt lengths go up and down and tie widths go from narrow to wide and back again. Why? Who tells us it is time to change? Why do the clothes we once thought attractive look weird and even embarrassing now? Have you ever looked at a family photo album and said, "I can't believe I wore that!"? Fashion is a pointed example of the influence of culture. It not only shapes what we do, but the way we think and the way we see.

The example I have used with my teenagers to capture the insidious influence of the surrounding culture on them (and us) is air. Like the air we constantly breathe, culture is the spiritual air that our hearts constantly absorb. Many of the pollutants in the physical air are unseen. The same is true with culture. I think that we as parents have made a great error in our tendency to emphasize the obvious (sex, drugs, violence, abortion, etc.) while neglecting the more deceptive, unseen pollutants in the cultural air around us. The result is that although our children may not participate in the "biggies," they

Figure 1. Themes (Idols) of Modern Culture

THEME	DEFINITION
RELATIVISM	• No absolute standard for life. • Each person determines what is right for him. • Right changing with the situation.
INDIVIDUALISM	• No higher goal than my happiness and pleasure. • No higher purpose than meeting my own needs, wants, rights, and desires.
EMOTIONALISM	• Feelings the most influential, most important indicator of what is right and best. • Feelings as personal guidance system.
PRESENTISM	• Focus on the present—living for the moment. • Focus on present personal happiness. • No sense of delayed gratification, investment.
MATERIALISM	• No recognition of the spiritual world. • Goal of life is experiencing physical pleasure and possessing material goods. • Focus on what is seen.
AUTONOMY	• No sense of innate, natural responsibility to a higher authority than self. • No functional recognition of the existence of God and call to live to his glory.
VICTIMISM	• No sense of personal responsibility for actions. • Belief that I am what my experience has made me. • My defects are the result of others and situations outside of my control.

FRUIT IN TEEN	BIBLICAL ALTERNATIVE
• No consistency of lifestyle or conviction. • No internal restraint. • Susceptibility to influence of others. • Dislike of rules.	TRUTH: Willing submission and obedience to the commands and principles of Scripture.
• Selfishness, self-centeredness, "rights" focus. • Lack of commitment to others. • Laziness, irresponsibility. • Grumbling, complaining.	TWO GREAT COMMANDS: Life shaped by practical commitment to love God and to love neighbor.
• Teen moved by what feels right—good feelings focus. • Seldom acts against feelings. • Sensitive to approval or disapproval of others.	BIBLICAL FAITH: Commitment to test everything by the truths of Scripture.
• A "got to have it now" mentality. • No focus on long-term investment. • No sense of consequences. • Impulsive decisions.	ETERNITY: A personal commitment to do everything that I do with an eye toward the reality of eternity.
• No independent pursuit of the things of the Lord. • No focus on character and attitude. • Focus on clothing, beauty, friends, and things.	SPIRITUALITY: A life that is shaped by a seriousness about issues of the heart and relationship with God.
• Tendency toward rebellion to authority. • No real Godward focus in life. • Authority and correction seen as negative.	CREATUREHOOD: Life guided by a recognition of the Creator and living to his glory.
• Regular patterns of blameshifting. • Excusing, rationalizing bad behavior—defensiveness. • Lack of confession. • Lack of sense of need for personal change.	SIN: Humble recognition of struggle with sin within and temptation without. Thankfulness for the forgiving grace of Christ.

end up serving the idols of the surrounding culture. (See Figure 1 for examples of these idol themes, their impact on our teenagers, and the biblical alternative.) Surely, these idols are more to be feared because they creep up on us unseen, appearing harmless and attractive (see Col. 2:1–8, especially v. 8). They also powerfully play to the desires of the sinful nature, that is, they feed the very thing that God, by his Spirit, is seeking to destroy.

Another error we have tended to make as parents is to blame the vehicle rather than focus on the idol themes these vehicles promote. A variety of vehicles—government, music, movies, magazines, education, television, and the idle talk of people on the streets—all transmit and promote the philosophy of the culture. None of these vehicles are in themselves bad or dangerous. The danger is in the way they are used to promote the things they promote. And even in a fallen world, they will be used for both good and evil. The point is not to slay the messenger. We must be aware of the power of the media to transmit a culture's ideas, but it is the ideas that are dangerous and must be the focus of our attention. For example, many Christian parents will not let their teenage children go to R-rated movies, but will permit them to watch hours of TV situation comedies, which transmit into our homes the perspectives, relationships, and values of the surrounding culture.

This is where the pollution metaphor helps us. When there are poisons in the physical air, people wear protective equipment that filters them out. In the same way our teenagers need spiritual filters against the unseen poisons in the cultural air. Our children need the protection of a biblical world and life view, and as parents we want to begin giving them one from the very earliest moments of their lives. We also want eyes of faith to see that every situation, relationship, and problem in their lives is an opportunity to rethink and carefully apply a biblical view of life to concrete situations.

Talking to Your Teenager About Culture

In light of this, don't be hesitant to talk, talk, talk to your teenagers. This cannot be a time when our relationship grows distant. They need our parenting as much as ever before, so we must seek them out. Let me suggest some strategies for these talk times.

➤ *Don't wait around for your teenager to talk to you.* Seek them out in a way that is warm, friendly, and affirming. Teenagers who are on the defensive won't talk freely and won't listen well.

➤ *Don't settle for nonanswers.* Follow up the yeses and noes. Ask questions that your teenager cannot answer with a yes or no, but that require him to disclose what he is thinking, feeling, and doing.

➤ *Be positive.* Don't be like a detective hunting for what is wrong. The purpose of these talks is not to "catch" the teenager, but to help him to understand, desire, and do what is right. So much of the talking that goes on between teenagers and their parents is negative and discouraging to the teenager.

➤ *Lovingly seek to expose the faults in your teenager's thinking without making him feel ignorant or stupid.* Teach him, in an affirming way, to see where he has breathed in the pollutants of his culture.

➤ *Become a partner in struggle with your teenager by sharing your own struggle* to live a godly life in an ungodly culture. Admit to the places where you have been influenced. Ask your teenager to pray for you as you promise to pray for him in his struggle.

➤ *Always point your teenager to Christ,* who daily gives us mercy and grace in our moments of need and who patiently continues to work in us until his work is complete.

➤ *Always keep in mind that you cannot protect your children from culture.* The only effective strategy is to prepare them to deal with culture in a biblical fashion. This will take years of loving commitment on your part.

➤ *Finally, model the character of Christ.* Don't be drawn into negative verbal power struggles. Greet anger, negativity, and accusation with soft-spoken strength. Don't beat your teenager with words, but win him with Christlike love.

What Is the Influence of Culture?

Have you ever cringed at the outfit your teenager was wearing? Have you ever complained about the fast, frenetic pace of your life? Has it ever seemed like your teenager was speaking in some unknown dialect? Does someone in your home work a forty-hour, five-day week? Have you ever contemplated retirement at sixty-five? Have you ever questioned the sanity of having an eighteen-year-old make costly and crucial career decisions as he faces college? Have you ever succumbed to buying the latest piece of exercise equipment, only to have it gather dust in some room of your home? Does your teenager own a Walkman? Is sixteen a magic year in your home because it is the year a teenager can get a license to drive? All of these things depict the distinctive influence of modern culture on the way each of our families thinks about life.

If we understand the ways that we are influenced by our culture, we can teach our teenagers to live wisely, alertly, and redemptively. *Wisely* refers to the ability to apply the principles of Scripture to practical decision-making in the context of their culture. *Alertly* means living aware of the "hollow and deceptive" philosophy of the surrounding culture and not giving in to the temptation to serve its idols. *Redemptively* means not being satisfied with isolation or living protectively, but following the command of Christ to be "salt and light" in a corrupt and darkened world.

Let me urge you not to look at your teenager and settle for survival. Thank God when they are sexually inactive and drug-free, but set your aim higher. God's will is that they would "participate in the divine nature and escape the corruption in the world caused by evil desires" (2 Peter 1:4), and that they would "shine like stars in the universe . . . in a crooked and depraved generation" (Phil. 2:15).

The influence of the surrounding culture is much more pervasive than the obviously offensive images found on television and in movies, magazines, and music. Yet we all are tempted to make these the focal points of our debates and skirmishes with our teenagers. Sometimes we even respond negatively to cultural things our teenagers bring home (music, fashion) not because they are morally corrupt, but because they are different from the culture of our own youth. We say, "You're not gonna play that racket around here!" (which expresses the exact sentiment our parents had toward *our* music). But is it morally wrong for my son or daughter to enjoy music that I find unlistenable? At other times we say, "There's no way that you're gonna wear that!" (which expresses the bewilderment our parents felt at the clothing *we* thought looked good). But is it *morally* wrong for my son to wear pants that are so big that he can take three steps before his pant legs move?

When we respond to issues of taste in the same way that we respond to moral issues, we cheapen the whole cultural discussion and weaken the positive influence that we can have with our teenagers. We need to accept that in many ways they will be different from us. The issue is not whether they are participating in things that are enjoyable to us, but whether they are participating in things that are pleasing to God! That requires an awareness of the subtle and pervasive influences of the culture in which they live.

The powerful influence of culture can be summarized in four areas. These areas, when taken together, summarize all of life. The surrounding culture will influence every area of your life in some way. This is why we must live vigilantly and teach our teenagers to do the same.

1. *Culture will set the pace of life.* Have you ever complained about how busy you are or how fast-paced your life is? How much time for quiet meditation or personal reflection do you have? How many moments of family activity do you have when all the members of the family are present? Do you have at least one meal a day when all of you eat together? Once a week? Once a month? Do you wonder how you and your children can participate in all the expected activities of church, school, Little League, and music lessons? Have you ever wondered who told you to live this way? Have you ever wanted to stop the world and get off? The pace of life in our culture is directly related to what the culture thinks is important. It is the direct result of a culture that has acquiring and achieving as two of its highest values.

The culture influences not only the daily schedule of our lives but the order of events in our lives as well. There is an unspoken but mandatory order to life in Western culture. The order moves toward the big dream, retirement, and the ultimate in personal success— early retirement. The order is high school, college, marriage, house, career, promotion, bigger house, retirement. Certainly, there are variations, but there is a remarkable similarity to the order of events in the lives of most people.

Who gave us this order? What are its strengths and weaknesses? How does it get in the way of God's revealed plan for us? Where does it tend to enslave us more than serve us? Where do we see ourselves and our teenagers following it blindly?

One of the things I enjoy doing is eavesdropping on the conversations around me in the supermarket checkout line. I find these conversations informative and enlightening even if I do get a sore neck from trying to listen without being conspicuous! I overheard two older men a few months ago. One said, "Hey, Joe, I haven't seen you for a while." "I retired last year," Joe responded. "Must be nice," the friend replied. Joe said, "I don't know why I did it. It seemed like the thing to do, but I hate it—it's driving me crazy! I've already begun looking for a job." "Man, Joe, you're raining on my parade," the friend said as he walked away. Such is the influence of culture. It dictates the conventional passages of life, and we often follow them without even knowing why we have made the decisions we have.

2. *Culture will set the agenda for life.* An agenda is a plan. It is what we are doing and why. An agenda always expresses priorities and values. A life plan is formed by determining what is of value and designing a plan to acquire it. The agenda for a person's life in any culture will express what is important to that culture. If you had to list the priorities of our culture, what would they be? How different are they from your own priorities? How different are they from biblical priorities?

Our culture is always expressing its perspective on what is important, what is of value, and what is "true." For example, when your teenager can watch a week of television sitcoms, dramas, newscasts, talk shows, and topical magazine shows and never hear God mentioned or the Bible included in the debate, the culture is powerfully telling him what is important and what is not. Imagine the influence of television on a teenager who watches it three hours a night, twenty-one hours a week. That equals nearly 7700 hours over his teen years. During these hours of cultural bombardment, he is usually relaxed and not thinking critically. He is breathing in the cultural air with little thought of protection. It would be the height of naiveté to think that he will remain uninfluenced. The view of life given to him will influence his life view and his life plan if he uncritically breathes in the culture and accepts its priorities.

How many Christian families are so committed to the teaching, relationships, fellowship, and ministry of their local church that they would refuse a promotion or a job offer because it would take them away from the body of Christ to which they are committed? Most Christian families would jump at the job and hope that they would be able to find a "good church" where they go. One of the weaknesses of the Western church is that it is so transient, it is hard for relationships to develop and gifts to be recognized so that God's people can do what he has called them to do. Is it wrong to move? No, but we must make this decision from the vantage point of biblical values and not blindly follow the surrounding culture. We won't teach our teenagers to live with their eyes open if we are not doing the same.

3. *Culture will define and shape our relationships.* Such things as our view of authority and government, our view of men and women and their roles, our view of children and their place in society, our view of the relationship between men and women, our view of sexuality, our view of the family and its role in and importance to the culture, and our view of the elderly are examples of the ways in which culture will shape our relationships.

An example of the powerful influence of culture on our relationships is the radical redefinition of the family that has occurred recently. Family was once a term that was only used to describe a husband (male) and wife (female) who were married (to each other), and their children. It now has an endless and often disturbing variety of meanings. It is tempting to think that this radical redefinition of family will never influence us, but we need not look much further than the vast number of divorces and single parent families in the church to humbly remind ourselves that we *are* being influenced.

For teenagers, the influence of culture is no less powerful. There is a pressure in our culture for boys and girls to pair off ("I'm going out with . . ."). There is a strongly physical emphasis to these relationships, which is evident in the reason a person is considered attractive ("He's so buff" or "She's such a babe") and in the emphasis on sexual expression. (The song says, "I just hunger for your touch.") "Sexy" tends to get a higher billing than "mature." And in a physically focused culture, to say someone has a nice personality (which means they are kind, polite, generous, patient, etc.) is the kiss of death.

Another evidence of culture's influence on relationships is the macho, in-your-face, can-you-top-this way that teenage boys tend to relate to one another. This trash-talking, rule-bending, "I'll do it my way" bravado is fed to our young boys in an endless stream of sporting events and commercials featuring arrogant heroes who respect no one and promote the philosophy that if you wear the right shoes, have enough muscles, believe in yourself, and make sure no one stands in your way, you can be or do anything you want. Above all, you must never appear timid or display or acknowledge weakness. This challenge-meets-challenge style of male relationship has not only trickled down to the Little Leagues of our culture but it has set the tone for relationships in the streets and hallways of life. Its materialism, independence, self-centered arrogance, and professed power could not be more appealing to the sin nature. Watch your teenager relate to peers, siblings, you, and others in authority. Do you see the influence of the surrounding culture on their style of relationship?

Our task is to make sure that the styles and rules of relationship that we promote to our children, by word or by example, meet the biblical standards of relationship (see Eph. 4; Rom. 12; Col. 2:12–14; and Matt. 5–7, the Sermon on the Mount.)

4. *Culture will powerfully influence our spiritual life.* Culture will always exert its influence on a person's religious or spiritual life. There is no middle ground here. Either a person's spiritual life is shaping

the way he thinks about and responds to his culture, or a person's religious or spiritual life becomes inculturated.

Again, begin by becoming aware of where our culture stands on these things. First, religion has virtually been barred from the cultural debate. Those representing religious institutions are rarely welcomed into the discussion of significant cultural issues. Second, religion is often presented in a subtly negative light by the popular media. Third, psychology has taken its place as the dominant "religion" of our culture. It defines who people are. It defines the meaning and purpose of our existence. It defines what is normal and what is not. It defines why people do the things they do and how change can take place. It is an understatement to say that these things have influenced the church and our personal spiritual lives.

Our teenagers need to understand that they do not live in a vacuum. They live in a culture that will exercise its influence on every area of their lives. It is important that they not only learn to protect themselves from the culture's pollutants, but also learn how to influence their culture with the truth of Jesus Christ. As we seek to prepare them, we need to be humbly honest about the places where our own lifestyles have been more shaped by cultural norms than by biblical principles. We cannot disciple our teenagers into a consistently biblical lifestyle without being willing to evaluate the places where our own lives are inconsistent.

Responding to Culture: A Plan for Our Teenagers

Do you remember the Smiths and the Joneses? Each family has chosen a radically different strategy for dealing with culture. The Smiths are convinced that *isolation* is the right strategy. They fail to realize that it is impossible to escape the struggle with culture, because where there are people, there is culture. They fail to realize that culture starts with the heart. The institutions, media, relationships, and products of a culture are the fruit of what that society craves and serves. The cultural struggle is really a struggle with the evil desires of the heart and although separation is at times the right choice, a child will not be safe just because a family avoids the physical locations, situations, relationships, and institutions of the surrounding culture. Further, the Smiths have not prepared their children to obey Christ's call to be salt and light in a corrupt and darkened world.

The Jones family looks at the Smiths and are convinced that they have found a better way to respond to culture. *Assimilation* seems so sensible to them. They see most things in their culture as being neutral and see no harm in allowing their children to be active participants. This mistaken view of neutrality leads them into an involvement with their culture that lacks analysis or evaluation. Like the Smiths, the Joneses have failed to teach their children to function as salt and light.

Parents need a third way to guide their children that does not give in to the weaknesses of isolation or assimilation. I call this third way redemptive interaction.

GOAL 3 *Teaching a Teenager to Understand and Interact Redemptively with His Culture*

The purpose of this goal is to raise teenagers who are fully able to interact with their culture without becoming enslaved to its idols. And the aim of the interaction is not personal pleasure and satisfaction, but redeeming their culture for Christ. Matthew 5:13–16 gives us the biblical basis for this strategy.

You are the salt of the earth. But if the salt loses its saltiness, how can it be made salty again? It is no longer good for anything, except to be thrown out and trampled by men. You are the light of the world. A city on a hill cannot be hidden. Neither do people light a lamp and put it under a bowl. Instead they put it on its stand, and it gives light to everyone in the house. In the same way, let your light shine before men, that they may see your good deeds and praise your Father in heaven.

In their assimilation, the Jones family has lost their saltiness, and in their isolation, the Smith family has hidden their light. We want to teach our children to do neither, but rather to move out, to be involved, protected by truth and ready to redeem. The redemptive interaction strategy has two fundamental objectives. First, we want our teenagers to thoroughly know and understand God's truth as a protection against becoming inculturated. Second, we want to teach them what it means in practical, everyday life to live truth in a way that points to their heavenly Father.

These two objectives give us the inward, outward, and upward face of Christian living in a fallen world. The inward face is a personal commitment to truth that will protect our teenagers from the subtle falsehoods and deceptive idols of the surrounding culture. The outward face is living in such a way that even when they are not verbally interacting with the culture, they witness to the reality of Jesus Christ by the way they live. And the upward face is that all of this is done in order that people would give God the Father the glory that is his due. We do not want to be afraid to set high goals, and we don't want to let the agenda be set by the reticence of our teenagers. These objectives will not be accomplished in one setting, but are achievable as the Holy Spirit empowers your faithful, day-by-day commitment to use the opportunities God gives you to prepare your teenagers to be people of God.

Let me suggest five strategies for preparing your teenagers to interact redemptively with their culture.

1. *Prepare*. The first step is to instill in our teenagers a biblical view of life. Many Christian families have years of unfocused family devotions. What their children receive during these times is not totally without merit, but it could be so much better if parents had the instilling of a biblical worldview as their goal. Without it, children end up familiar with all the popular Christian stories and with random doctrinal knowledge, but none of it is assembled into a usable system of truth that reflects God's way of thinking about life. The aim of all family Bible instruction must be that our children would be "thoroughly equipped for every good work" (2 Tim. 3:17). Everything we learn from Scripture should be attached to a biblical system of thinking. This can be done by asking several questions each time:

➤ What does this passage teach us about God, his character, and his plan?

➤ What do we learn about ourselves, our nature, our struggle, and the purpose of our lives?

➤ What does this passage teach us about right and wrong, good and bad, and true and false?

➤ What instruction is here about relationships, about love, authority, etc.?

➤ What does this passage teach us about life, its meaning and purpose?

➤ What does this passage teach us about the inner man, the heart and how it functions?

➤ What have we learned from this passage that would guide the way we live and make decisions?

➤ How does this passage help us understand and critique our culture?

As we teach our children to ask and answer these questions, we will be showing them how to use the things they read in the Bible to think about their own practical life situations. Knowing the truth will help our teenagers learn to be "in the world, but not of the world" (see Christ's prayer, John 17:15–18).

2. _Test._ In this step we teach our teenagers to critique, evaluate, interpret, and analyze the surrounding culture from a biblical perspective. This is why they must first be well-grounded in their knowledge of biblical truth.

Here is where many Christian parents make a decision that seems right on the surface, but I believe is all wrong if they hope to prepare their teenagers to be a redemptive influence in the cultural struggle. Like the Smiths, many Christian parents try their best to keep the surrounding culture out of their homes (cassette tapes, CDs, and videos). In so doing, they lose a wonderful, focused opportunity to teach their children how to use a biblical view of life to understand and critique their culture.

It is important not always to say no to your child's requests, but to invite your teenager to bring the item home, to sit with him as you listen and watch, to engage him in a discussion of the content, and then to share with him your evaluation. Help your teenager to understand what attracts him to the item (the artist, the message, the music, the visuals, the action, the pressure of peers, etc.). Then, the easiest way to critique the item is to apply to it the same set of questions that you have been using to study the Bible in your family devotional times.

It is a big temptation for parents to overreact to issues of taste that really aren't the focus of your critique. For example, resist getting into an argument about how this is not really music, or at least not like the music of your youth. Don't initiate debates over clothing, hair, and jewelry. You want to get to the heart of the matter, that is, what is the view of life (see above questions) promoted by this item? All of the externals are expressions of the heart of the artist, director, or producer. You want to spend your time looking at that.

Whenever you seize the opportunity to go to movies and concerts with your teenagers, listen to music with them in the home, or rent and watch videos together, you are making the most of a huge opportunity to raise teenagers who can learn to think with biblical and cultural clarity. Television provides great opportunities as well. The seemingly harmless sitcom will subtly promote the idols of the surrounding culture. You'll want to expose these underlying themes to your children. Our goal is to sensitize them to be alert and watchful. We want them to be insightful and wise, so we look for opportunities that will produce these results. We are interested in doing more than protecting them; we want them to influence the culture redemptively and in so doing bring glory to God.

3. _Identify._ Here we teach our children to recognize common ground. The struggles of life in this fallen world are the universal experience of all people. The cries of the angry rock performer are our cries as well. The difference comes in the way we would interpret and respond to those struggles. In modern rock music, we hear the cries of anger, fear, disappointment, and loneliness. We hear disillusionment and distrust. We hear of the quest for real love, the breaking of trust, the failure of friendship, family, and government. We hear of lust and greed, selfishness and hypocrisy. We share common ground even with the performer who offends us the most, who represents the very things from which we want to protect our children. Our families have failed, our promises have been broken, we have acted out of greed, we have seen government and church fail. Our beliefs have been challenged and our hopes dashed. We and the world have been broken by sin, and all of us have felt the pain. In fact, this is one of the reasons this material is attractive to our children. Whether we are comfortable with admitting it or not, these performers, writers, and

directors give voice to the cries of our own children, who have also experienced the harsh realities of life in the fallen world.

This is important. Many Christians buy into the lie that they have nothing in common with their culture. Yet if we look at our own sin and our own experience of being sinned against, we will humbly recognize common experience and common grief. It is the recognition of this common ground that moves us toward ministry to the culture. And to this common ground we are called to bring the message of the Gospel.

So we want to raise teenagers who have learned to identify with their culture—not agreeing with its interpretations and responses, but identifying with its struggle and humbly acknowledging why these responses seem logical to someone who does not know Christ and his Word. ("The world is broken, so get angry!" "The world is broken, so party, party, party!" "Take care of yourself and get all you can get.") Identifying means recognizing common ground. As we teach our teenagers to acknowledge humbly their own struggle to live in this fallen world, they will build platforms of ministry to their culture.

4. *Decide.* We want to teach our teenagers how to know when they can be redemptive participants in their culture and when they must separate from it. Scripture teaches us to do both, yet it also pictures how God's people have struggled with this participation-separation issue (see 1 Cor. 8, 10; 2 Cor. 6:14–18; Rom. 14).

As a Christian parent you have many ways to help your child work through these issues. Don't settle for just saying a bald no. Don't resort to saying, "Because I told you so!" Don't get into loud arguments over Friday night's proposed activities. Calmly help your teenagers learn how to think through these decisions. Require them to be part of the discussion and thinking process. Many parents not only protect their teenagers from the world, but block them out of the decision-making process as well. In so doing, they leave them unprepared for the myriad of decisions they will have to make as adults. These moments are opportunities to prepare your teenagers to respond with biblical wisdom to the many choices they will face.

5. *Redeem.* Here we teach our teenagers to take back turf that has been lost to the world by witnessing to the good news of Jesus Christ. Our voice in the culture is ordained by God not just to be negative, not just to be always speaking *against* something. The goal is to declare positively what God had in mind when he designed things in the beginning, to be part of rebuilding the culture his way, and to proclaim that this rebuilding can only be done by people who are living in proper relationship with God through Christ Jesus.

The church of Jesus Christ, the Christian family, was never meant to exist as an isolated ghetto in the middle of a darkened and broken culture. We are called by Christ to be participants in the world as his agents of redemption.

So we need to prepare our teenagers. We need to train them in truth and to teach them evaluative and analytical skills. We need to model how to think and interpret life biblically. We need to engage them in the decision-making process. We need to teach them to recognize common ground and to speak to the cries of the culture in language it understands. We need to teach them how to recognize the idols that underlie what the culture produces. We need to teach them to participate in the cultural debate, to be people of influence, and to be rebuilders. And we need to teach them to do all of this without giving way to self-righteous isolationism or the personal compromise of assimilation.

It is exciting that we can do this without fear. God has given us his Word, he has filled us with his Spirit, and he has surrounded us with the resources of the body of Christ. He will give us daily opportunities to engage our children in fruitful, wisdom-building conversations about the nature and struggles of the world and the nature of their own struggles of heart. Thankfully, we are not alone. He is with us, giving us everything we need to produce teenagers who approach the world with more than a list of dos and don'ts.

With hope we can hold onto our goal of raising teenagers who can think biblically, understand their culture, and deal with anything it produces from a biblical perspective. These teenagers will become adults who know when to separate and when to participate. They will know when to tear down and how to rebuild. They will be people of influence. They will be salt and light.

A HEART FOR GOD

BEFORE they came into the world we had dreams for them. Before we were married we talked about having children, how many we wanted, how we would raise them, and what we wanted for them. I can remember the excitement I felt when I knew there was a child growing within my wife. I remember resting my hand on her stomach because the only connection I could make with my child was when I could feel his movement with my hand.

I remember driving to work and wondering about him. Who would he or she be? What would this little one look like? Would he be physically normal? Would he be a scholar, a preacher, an athlete, or a mechanic? Would she have a good career, go to the mission field, find a decent man—what would her journey be? I remember the moment our first son was born and holding him in my hand—the thunderous collision of absolute joy and powerful fear that took place within me. He was here, healthy, alive, and warm! We had a son! Yet, in these moments I was confronted with the length, the importance, the awesomeness of the task. I was his father! No one else would be in the position of his mother and me. God had chosen us to be his primary agents of love, care, instruction, and training.

In those early years of his life, we dreamed dreams, we discussed, we bought books, and we prayed. With him, we loved, we rocked, we fed, we instructed, we played, we disciplined, and we prayed. For years we have worked hard and long. We have had thousands of after-school what-happened-today conversations. There have been thousands of moments of instruction. There have been thousands of times of comfort and encouragement. There have been a stream of Christmases and vacations that have come and gone.

There were myriad firsts and lasts. There have been many, many late night conversations between us after he had gone to bed. We have prayed for him and with him. We have instructed him daily in the Word and taken him to places where others would do the same. Yet in all of this, we have fallen short of the kind of parents that we hoped we would be. There have been irritated looks, unkind words, weary silences. We have done many things, but none of them perfectly. In all of this we have been confronted with our weaknesses and the ever-present resources of God's strength.

We have said innumerable noes and yeses. We have bought clothes, skateboards, books, and furniture. We have enrolled him in schools and taken him out of others. We have sat again and again with him in his room and had conversations about things that really matter. We have met and welcomed friends into our home. We have greeted girlfriends and heard the stories of tough bosses. We have been through science projects and SATs.

We have worked and worked and worked. We have prayed and prayed, many nights going into his room as he was sleeping, putting a hand on him, and once again committing him to the Lord. And we have done all of these things again with each of our children.

What is it that we were doing? Was it simply walking through the passages of family life? What was our goal? What was our focus? What did we want to produce?

Our Highest Goal

All of us want things for our children. We want a good education, a suitable and satisfying job, a loving marriage, healthy children of their own, a good home, and a life that isn't torn by tragedy. But what is the central wish that gives focus to all the labors and dreams? If we could wish one thing for our children, what would it be? Deeper than houses, cars, jobs, and mates, more fundamental than location and situation, what kind of person are we working so hard to produce? Deeper than where they are and what they will do, what do we want them to *be?*

David captures what should be the paramount focus of all of our parenting efforts as he describes his own desires.

> *One thing I ask of the LORD,*
> *this is what I seek:*
> *that I may dwell in the house of the LORD*
> *all the days of my life,*
> *to gaze upon the beauty of the LORD*
> *and to seek him in his temple. (Ps. 27:4)*

> *How lovely is your dwelling place,*
> *O LORD Almighty!*
> *My soul yearns, even faints,*
> *for the courts of the LORD;*
> *my heart and my flesh cry out*
> *for the living God.*
> *Even the sparrow has found a home,*
> *and the swallow a nest for herself,*
> *where she may have her young—*
> *a place near your altar,*
> *O LORD Almighty, my King and my God.*
> *Blessed are those who dwell in your house;*

they are ever praising you. . . .
Better is one day in your courts
than a thousand elsewhere;
I would rather be a doorkeeper in the house of my God
than dwell in the tents of the wicked. (Ps. 84:1–4, 10)

What David expresses in colorful Old Testament language is a *heart for God*. Above all else, this is the goal of our parenting efforts. This is *the* quality we want to see in our teenagers as they prepare to leave home. This quality will give a God-focus to all their other character qualities and to their lives as well. We cannot let ourselves elevate any other quality over this one. We cannot be too busy to invest in seeing this developed. We cannot follow the cultural norms that elevate education and career far above everything else; the Bible would say that someone who has lived only to be successful in these things has been a fool. This goal of a heart for God reflects the purpose for our creation as human beings. The Westminster Shorter Catechism says it well, that the chief end of man is to "glorify God and enjoy him forever."

Perhaps for many of us, this goal seems unrealistically high. We have become used to feeling good because our teenager is willing to go to church without putting up a fight, or is quasi-respectful around the house. Yet this is God's goal for each one of us; can we settle for anything less for our children? Maybe this goal seems unrealistic for our teenagers because we haven't had it for ourselves. We lack the faith to seek it for them because we haven't seen it as a possibility for ourselves.

GOAL 4   *Developing a Heart for God in Your Teenager*

It is a sad reality that many children leaving Christian homes do not have a heart for God. They may profess to be Christians, and they are surely not philosophical atheists, but they are worldly in the way they approach life. There is little evidence in their day-by-day living of a hunger for God. These children do not consciously deny God, but other things have replaced his functional rulership in their lives. Love of God has been replaced by love of other things. Even though they are not overtly rebellious, at the heart level there is a greater love for the "world" than there is for the "Father" (1 John 2:15). They have worshiped and served created things rather than the Creator (Rom. 1:25).

What Has Gone Wrong?

Why is this situation so common? If the Lord is the central focus of our lives, why is this value not passed on to our children? This question haunts many heartbroken Christian parents, but I believe it is a question all of us should ask. Each of us should search our hearts and examine our family life as we do so. Let me suggest some possible answers to the question.

1. The first answer is *familiarity*. The old saying goes, "Familiarity breeds contempt." As fallen human beings, we tend to take for granted the things that have been a regular part of our lives. In the physical realm we don't live with a sense of appreciation for the lavish food, clothing, housing, and health we enjoy in Western culture. We are incredibly rich by the standards of the rest of the world, yet we do not live with a sense of privilege. In fact, we often grumble and complain because we do not think we have enough! One of our teenagers will open the door of a fully stocked refrigerator and moan that there is nothing to eat! It is only since traveling in Third World countries that I have gotten back my sense of privilege and a resultant thankfulness.

This dynamic is surely present in the spiritual realm as well. Somehow we need to break through the ordinariness that characterizes Christianity for our teenagers. We need to help them appreciate what a gracious privilege it is to be born into a family of faith. We need to help them see that the "normality" of their Christian home is anything but normal in this world. Rather, it is the act of a sovereign and loving God, who has literally harnessed the forces of nature and the course of human history so that we would come to know him and his truth. Further, our teenagers need to see that he continues to be present, daily working in us so that we do not wander away and so that we would live with his glory as our highest goal. We need to faithfully point to his existence and power and evidences of his hand at work. We cannot let ourselves or our teenagers forget the single most glorious fact of our existence: that God really does exist, that he is glorious in power and goodness, and that he has made us to be his children! There will never be anything more important or wonderful than this.

We have failed our children if we don't do everything we can to have them leave our homes with a sense of awe over God and the glories of his grace. We cannot relax if our teenagers do not appreciate knowing God, being loved by him, and being chosen to live for his glory. We need to recognize humbly that one reason we have not passed this on to them is because we may have lost it ourselves. Many of us have become "nearsighted and blind, [having] forgotten that [we have] been cleansed from [our] past sins" (2 Peter 1:9). Our teenagers will not understand that redemption is a gift and a privilege if we do appreciate it ourselves.

Many of us need to hear these words not only with a humble, convicted heart, but with one that finds comfort in the forgiveness Christ has purchased. Our Redeemer not only convicts, he forgives. He not only forgives, he delivers. He not only delivers, he restores. This is all offered to you as a Christian parent. Christ's work for us means that we do not have to live paralyzed by regret. We confess our sins; he forgives and delivers. As we step forward in faith, he does more than we could ask or imagine by the power of his Spirit that is within us. The Gospel allows us to look back in rest and look forward in hope.

2. The second answer has to do with *lifestyle*. Deuteronomy 6 envisions a parenting lifestyle where we are *with* our children. ("Talk about them when you sit at home and when you walk along the road, when you lie down and when you get up" [v. 7].) In the old agrarian culture, the family was together all the time. Parents mentored their children in practical skills, in views of life, and in issues of faith. The family home and property were the focus of the family's lives and activities. In cottage industry or family farming, when there was a need or crisis in the family, the work would give way to the personal pressing need. Members of the family were physically present with one another much of the time. Parents in that culture could talk with their children literally from the time they awoke to the time they fell into bed.

It is important to recognize how radically different today's typical family lifestyle is from the home life that was the norm when Deuteronomy was written. With the industrial revolution and the rise of modern education, the family home and property are no longer the focal point for the lives of family members. In fact, family members rarely spend time together. Our homes tend to be like motels where we all arrive at night to sleep, only to go our separate ways the next morning. Go to a mall and notice how few families you see together. Look around at the worship service at your church and notice how few families even sit together. The point is not that we should demand that our teenagers be with us every waking hour, or that we should wish that we were parenting 150 years ago. Rather, we must simply recognize that the word that captures modern family lifestyle is not togetherness, but separation.

The significant degree to which most modern families live separate lives surely does affect our ability to communicate redemptive awe to our children. From the age of five or six on, most of our children will spend most of their waking hours outside the home. As they mature and begin developing friendships, participating in outside activities, and seeking employment, the time spent outside the home (and apart from the mentoring influence of their parents) will only increase. In our culture it is almost considered weird for a teenager to spend time with his parents. When you see families together, it usually involves younger children. And in our culture, at eighteen (hardly the age when most children reach full maturity!) most teens leave home for some distant college, never to live with Mom and Dad again.

Permit me to say again that I am not suggesting that all of us should home school our children and forbid them to get jobs, participate in outside activities, or go away to college. We simply need to recognize how the lifestyle of separation affects our ability to nurture our teenagers as God has called us to. If we are going to prepare our children for adulthood, we will need to be focused and disciplined. We will need to manufacture opportunities to talk in relaxed ways about significant things with our teenagers. We will need to evaluate the choices we make for our families and the degree of busyness we permit as the norm. You simply cannot mentor, pastor, disciple, or develop children whom you are seldom around.

For some of us this will mean turning off the television. For others it will mean sharing much more of our personal lives and hearts with our children. For some of us this will mean simplifying our lifestyles, and for some it will mean making a greater effort to talk daily with each child, going to our teenager's room, showing interest in his life, and sharing ours. For some of us this will mean less travel and less focus on career development. For some of us this will mean confessing our own selfishness, as we have lived closed and isolated lives with the ever-available excuse of a busy schedule. For all of us it means asking whether we have passed down to our teenagers a love for God and a commitment to live to his glory. If this has not happened, it means asking if busyness and separation are part of the reason why.

3. The third answer to the question of why we have not passed an appreciation for God down to our children is hard to face, but it must be considered. It is *hypocrisy*. Children whose parents have vocalized a strong commitment to their faith but have not lived consistently with it will tend to despise that faith. Living consistently with the faith does not mean living perfectly, but living in a way that reveals that God and his Word are the most important things to you. Such a parent can even honor God in his failure, with his humility in confession and his determination to change (repent).

Parents who talk about sin but live self-righteously ("In my day . . ." "I get up and go to work every day, you don't see me complaining!") are functionally denying the Gospel. Parents who talk about the sacrificial love of Christ but live selfishly ("Who took my newspaper?" "Turn off that infernal racket, it is driving me crazy!") are functionally denying the Gospel. Parents who talk about the grace of Christ, but are verbally condemning as they discipline their children ("You'll never make anything of yourself." "What are you trying to do, see how many stupid things you can do in one day?") functionally deny the Gospel.

Parents who talk of the forgiveness of Christ, but who live with an angry, unforgiving spirit toward their children ("Get out of my sight! Right now I can't stand to look at your face." "The next time you want something from me, remember how you treated me today!") functionally deny the Gospel. Parents who talk of seeking God's kingdom, but get swept up into Western culture's materialism (living for better clothes, a better and bigger house, car, and vacations) functionally deny the Gospel. God's call is that we would live lives that are worthy of the Gospel that we have received (Eph. 4:1). If we don't do this as parents, our teenagers will tend to dismiss or even despise the very Gospel we say is of paramount importance. They will tend to reject the God we have so poorly represented, and they, too, will end up serving the idols of the surrounding culture (see Judg. 2:6–15).

Search Your Heart

How do you react to what I am saying? Are you defensive? Ashamed? Discouraged? Don't be! That is functionally denying the Gospel too. If you see your sins and failures, you don't have to justify yourself to me, your child, or God. You don't have to live with the heavy burden of regret or be tempted to give up. The Gospel not only gives you hope for your children, it also gives you hope for yourself. Christ lovingly invites you to repent and let him do a new work in your life.

As parents, we need to be willing to search our hearts and examine our lives. We need to be willing to confess and repent of ways that our lives have contradicted our words about the most important thing in our lives. And we need to confess our sins, not with bitter feelings of defeat and failure, but with the joyful recognition that there is forgiveness and deliverance in Christ! He who forgives will also empower us to live in a new way!

If you look at yourself and say, "Yes, the life that I have lived before my teenager is in many ways a contradiction of the Gospel," don't give in to thinking that there is no hope. Go to your teenager and confess. Say, "You know, son (or daughter), the way I have lived and responded to you has often been a contradiction of how I have taught you to live and how God has responded to me. I know that this has often discouraged you and made you angry. I know that I have been self-righteous, unloving, condemning, and unforgiving, and I am here to ask for your forgiveness. I have come to realize that as your parent, I have not represented God very well. I ask that you would pray for me, and I would welcome you to come to me whenever you think I have responded to you in a hypocritical or unloving manner. I have committed myself before God to live in a way that makes him and his Word attractive to you and your brothers and sisters. Please pray for me."

I am convinced that these are healing words that God can use to fundamentally alter your teenager's appreciation for God. It is never too late to confess and repent! Don't give in to defeatism. Recognize that God is able to restore what the locusts have eaten (Joel 2:25). He is the God of restoration, the Creator who is able to tear down and re-create! Humbly be part of his work of rescue and restoration.

Signs of a Heart for God

What does a heart for God look like in a teenager's everyday life? The central characteristic of a heart for God is its deep, sincere hunger to know and honor God. This needs to be contrasted with a pharisaical performance of Christianity's external duties, or living for its temporal benefits. God communicated his rejection of the heartless "obedience" of the Israelites using the strongest of terms. He said,

> "The multitude of your sacrifices—
>   what are they to me?" says the LORD.
> "I have more than enough of burnt offerings,
>   of rams and the fat of fattened animals;
> I have no pleasure
>   in the blood of bulls and lambs and goats.
> When you come to appear before me,
>   who has asked this of you,
>   this trampling of my courts?
> Stop bringing meaningless offerings!

Your incense is detestable to me.
New Moons, Sabbaths and convocations—
    I cannot bear your evil assemblies.
Your New Moon festivals and your appointed feasts
    my soul hates.
They have become a burden to me;
    I am weary of bearing them.
When you spread out your hands in prayer,
    I will hide my eyes from you;
even if you offer many prayers,
    I will not listen.
Your hands are full of blood;
    wash and make yourselves clean.
Take your evil deeds
    out of my sight!
Stop doing wrong,
    learn to do right!
Seek justice,
    encourage the oppressed.
Defend the cause of the fatherless,
    plead the case of the widow." (Isa. 1:11–17)

The LORD says:
"These people come near to me with their mouth
    and honor me with their lips,
        but their hearts are far from me.
Their worship of me
    is made up only of rules taught by men." (Isa. 29:13)

Christ had the same kind of response to the heartless, self-righteous duty of the Pharisees.

Woe to you, teachers of the law and Pharisees, you hypocrites! You clean the outside of the cup and dish, but inside they are full of greed and self-indulgence. Blind Pharisee! First clean the inside of the cup and dish, and then the outside also will be clean. Woe to you, teachers of the law and Pharisees, you hypocrites! You are like whitewashed tombs, which look beautiful on the outside but on the inside are full of dead men's bones and everything unclean. In the same way, on the outside you appear to people as righteous but on the inside you are full of hypocrisy and wickedness. (Matt. 23:25–28)

For I tell you that unless your righteousness surpasses that of the Pharisees and the teachers of the law, you will certainly not enter the kingdom of heaven. (Matt. 5:20)

The warnings of these passages can help us look honestly at ourselves and at our teenagers. Godliness is defined as something more than keeping a list of behaviors (the received list of dos and don'ts that every Christian community has, which typically combines biblical injunctions and prohibitions with many man-made standards of conduct). True godliness flows out of the heart and produces a harvest of good fruit in a person's life. This is what we seek for our teenagers.

What you *will* see in a teenager who has a heart for God is a catalog of behaviors, attitudes, relationships, and activities that reflect a *personal pursuit of God*. This is not the begrudging performance of duty. It is not motivated by threats, guilt, ultimatums, and parental manipulation. All such parental interventions are attempts to produce what only God can produce. They will not produce a lasting harvest of godliness, only fruit that decays as soon as the pressure is removed (as, for example, when the teenager goes away to college and drops all the Christian pursuits he was pressured into at home).

Notice the terms I have used. We want God to use us to develop in our teenagers a *personal* pursuit of God, a seriousness about relationship with him that is internally motivated. This teenager will be a spiritual self-starter. He will not need to be coerced or manipulated. He will involve himself in spiritual things because he genuinely wants to, because they are important to him.

Notice further that what we are describing is a personal *pursuit* of God. Pursuit has to do with running after something. This teenager is a seeker. He is hungry. He is looking for situations, locations, and relationships that will help him to do what is most important to him—to know God. He will find time. He will go out of his way. He will be decisive and intentional in his faith. He will be open and teachable. He will not be looking for excuses for missing a service or a Bible study. He will read, study, meditate, and memorize. He will independently, of his own volition, run after God.

Third, what we are seeking to mentor is a personal pursuit of *God*. This is not the same as hanging around the body of Christ because the "cool" relationships are there. It is not about placating parents by participating in the "stuff" going on at church. Rather, this is a teenager who has come to know and love God, and who wants to know him better. There is in his heart a real desire for fellowship with God, a real desire that his life would be pleasing to him. This is a young person who really does love God, and his lifestyle reveals that love.

As I stated earlier, this personal pursuit of God will reveal itself in behaviors, activities, and relationships in the teenager's life. If your teenager does have a heart for God, these are the things you will see.

Signs of a Pursuit of God

1. *There will be an independent life of personal worship and devotion.* This teenager will spend personal time with the Lord. He will

want to read the Bible and spend time in prayer. No, he probably won't be getting up at 5:00 A.M. to read and pray for two hours, but there will be a developing life of personal devotion.

I remember going into my teenage son's room not long ago to look for the cordless phone and noticing a well-used New Testament next to his bed. He had been daily reading his way through it. He had not been dramatic or vocal about his devotional life, but there was a hunger for God that made him find time in his often chaotic schedule to study Scripture.

2. *There will be a desire for corporate worship and instruction.* A teenager who is glad to go to church services, who does not need to be threatened into being there, will be there for two primary reasons. First, because he enjoys worship. For him worship expresses his heartfelt love and thanksgiving for God and his work. For him worship expresses the basis of his hope. And he will find enjoyment in being with people who share his desire to praise God. He will be there because he finds that corporate worship helps him focus on the most important thing in his life, the existence of God and his glory. He may not be able to verbalize all of these things, but he will be there because he *wants* to be there.

It was a Sunday after I had returned from a lengthy overseas trip. We were heading, as a family, into what looked like a very busy time. I had decided that we would hibernate for the weekend, including Sunday. We would have a quiet time of family worship together and then go out for Sunday lunch. My oldest son came and told me that he wanted to go to our church's morning worship service. He asked if I would be offended if he took the train to the service and then joined us for lunch. Would I be offended? I was delighted! (His desire for worship also caused me to re-examine the choice I had made.) I wanted to do nothing that would dampen his desire to participate in the corporate gatherings of the church.

This points to another positive sign in a teen's desire to participate in the gatherings of the body of Christ: he has *a hungry and teachable spirit.* Teens often don't recognize their need of instruction. They can get defensive when you seek to advise or teach them. They often think that they know much more than they actually know. They assume that they are much more prepared for life than they are in reality.

It is a sign of God's grace at work when a teenager seeks out instruction. It is a sign of spiritual hunger when a teenager has a teachable spirit. Teenagers who have a heart for God will not avoid times of teaching and preaching; they will look for them. And they will not be in the back row of the church, slouched down in their seats, looking as if they will barely be able to endure the boredom. No, somehow, some way they will demonstrate a hunger to learn more about God, his will, and his way. They will appreciate the teachers that God has raised up in the body of Christ, and they will want to be where biblical instruction is being offered.

3. *A teenager who has a heart for God will also pursue fellowship with the body of Christ.* He will want to spend time with others of like mind. He will look for peers who share his faith and his desire to be involved in the Christian community. This is the teenager who arrives at college and immediately begins checking out the Christian student fellowships available on campus. This is the teenager who will find the fellow Christians in his high school. When he is out and about, he will be excited about meeting fellow Christians. He will also value the help, prayers, encouragement, experience, insight, and wisdom of the older members of the body of Christ.

I remember one teenager who sat in my office, slumped down in the chair in that "okay, do something that will impress me" posture. He obviously didn't want to be there. I was doing my best to get inside of his defenses and in the middle of my efforts he said, "I gotta get out of here. This is driving me crazy! It's not enough that she [his mother] has brought God into every discussion that we have ever had! Now she forces me to come here so you can close the door and do more of the same. Just tell me what you want me to do and I will do it, so I can get out of here!" Sad words, spoken by an angry young man who had no time for the things of the Lord. Sadly, too, his reaction pictured the wrong way that the Word had been used in his home. (We will be discussing this later.)

4. *The teenager who has a heart for God will be relaxed and open to discussions about spiritual things.* We should not expect or accept our teenagers' being closed and defensive, unwilling to listen to the Word of God. We are seeking to produce young adults who love the Lord and his Word, who understand that it speaks in some way to every situation of life, and who are hungry to be guided and corrected by it. Not only do we not want to produce teenagers who are spiritually defensive; we want to produce teens who are humble and open, who know that they need God's help, and who seek it.

Evaluate your teenager. How does she respond when the Bible or the Lord's will is mentioned in a conversation? Does he talk about the truths of the Word in any way? Do they ever talk about praying or seeking biblical direction for a decision? Do they seek out your help with a morning conversation, with a brief call in the middle of the day to see what you think about an issue, with one of those deep, late night discussions where they are baring their hearts, or with a request that you would pray for them about something coming up? Are they increasingly devoted consumers of the things of the Lord, hungry, needy, seeking? Are they relaxed and at home with God's truth and with people who hold it dear?

My daughter was in a tough situation with a very competitive and often catty group of friends. There was a real temptation to give in to anger, bitterness, gossip, and returning evil for evil. One night at the supper table she shared some of the things that were going on with this group of friends. Then she said, "I've thought about this a lot and I know what is right to do." Maybe this doesn't seem like a remarkable statement to you, but it was very encouraging to me. She was saying that she hadn't gone with the flow of the group, that she had stepped back to take a look, and that she had sought to determine what was right to think, to say, and to do.

5. *Teenagers who have a heart for God will approach decision-making from a biblical perspective.* They will have a heart for what is right. What encouraged us is that our daughter wanted to do what was right, and she had taken time to consider God's will. We cannot be content with raising teens whose decisions are impulsive, emotion-driven, and self-centered. We must hold a higher standard before them. We want to be used of God to develop a constant Godward reference to everything they do, to raise young people who really do live for God's glory. We want them to really believe that the most important question in any situation is, "What does God want me to think, desire, say, and do?" And we want them to see the Bible as their most important tool in making the critical and practical decisions of life.

Our highest goal must be that our teenagers would have a heart for God. This is the root that will produce all the other fruits of godliness in their lives. So we look for the evidence of a personal devotional life, for a desire for corporate worship and instruction, for friendship and fellowship with the body of Christ, for a relaxed openness to the things of the Lord, and for decision-making from a biblical perspective. We do not look for these in a legalistic way, but as natural signs of a heart that really does love God, that really does desire to know him and to live in a way that brings him glory. And we do not want to give in to thinking that this is impossible for our teenagers. The Gospel is for teenagers and the Holy Spirit can work godliness in the heart of a teenager as well as anyone else! If we believe these things, we will try to function as God's instruments of godliness in their lives.

Strategies for Encouraging a Heart for God

If a heart for God is our ultimate goal for our teens, then we need to ask what practical things we can do to encourage it in them. As in anything else, if we are going to be successful, we need to know where we are going and how to get there. Let me suggest several things you can do to encourage a hunger for God in your teenagers. Keep in mind that all of these things will apply to younger children as well, but are particularly important during the teen years.

1. *Make family worship a priority and make it engaging.* To engage your teenager first of all means to hold his attention. It means to draw him in and get him involved. It also means to attract him and win him over to God's will and way. In order to do this, our times of family worship need to be enjoyable, relevant, challenging, and interactive. Family worship needn't be a boring drudgery for our children; it can be an enjoyable family time that is Scripture-centered. Let me mention some things we have done to engage our teenagers.

We have tried to keep them interested and challenged by using good Christian books as the basis of our instruction and discussion. I have found that much of the Christian devotional literature aimed at teens is much too fluffy and often over-psychologized. (For example, much of this literature deals with self-esteem, a category that you do not see heavily developed in Scripture.) Our family has looked for good, practical, fun-to-read books that are aimed at adults and read them to our children. Good examples are the writings of Steve Brown and Max Lucado.

I read ahead in the book and "dumb down" the vocabulary to the level of the youngest child participating in the devotions. The purpose is to make the book understandable to the youngest child and yet conceptually challenging to the oldest. I have recommended Steve Brown and Max Lucado because they are excellent storytellers and they constantly build bridges from the truths of God to every-day life.

As you are challenging your teenagers in family worship, make these times conversational. Draw the teens out to see if they under-stand, to see if they have doubts or confusion, and to see if they can connect the things being discussed to what is happening in their own lives.

We have found that spending time in Proverbs and the Gospels is very helpful in keeping our teens engaged. You could not find a more readily practical portion of Scripture than the Proverbs! It is literally impossible to read a chapter of it that does not speak directly to things that each of us encounters. The Proverbs often spark good discussions.

The Gospels also bristle with real life. God has come in the flesh, and he is walking among people, engaging them in a consideration of the truths of the kingdom of God. Christ, the master questioner, the master storyteller, the master illustrator, can hold the attention of your teenagers as you help them understand the important issues he discussed.

We have found it important not to enter the family worship time with rigid expectations and a rigid plan. We want an atmosphere of freedom, where our teenagers feel free to ask questions, verbalize doubts, express confusion, debate applications, and try to draw in-ferences and applications, all without the fear of being silenced, re-buked, or ridiculed. We want the truth to connect, to convict, and to capture our teenagers, so we are in no hurry. We want to give them time to understand and the Spirit time to work. This time is for them. We have no expectations about the amount of material we cover and our goal is not to get our teenagers to agree with us. The goal is to stimulate in them a hunger for God, so we want to be re-laxed, patient, and creative.

2. *Look for opportunities to point your teenager to God.* Don't let

them live in functional atheism, a practical view of life in which God is absent. Look for natural ways of pointing to the presence, power, and provision of the Lord. We know he is there, we know he is always active, and we know that whatever he does is good. There should be many opportunities to point him out to our teenagers. We have to protect our teens from distant, passive-God theology. Many teenagers believe in a God who simply doesn't make any difference, so their faith and their lives exist on two completely different levels.

Point out direct answers to prayer. Talk about situations in which he has given strength and wisdom. Help your teenager to recognize instances of the Lord's protection and provision. Note the places where Scripture prepared your teenager for something that he was facing. Discuss those situations where Scripture gave guidance and direction in a time of decision. Point out the "good gifts" that God lovingly supplies. Don't let your teenager live in a functional world where God does not exist.

3. *Be positive and Christ centered in your use of Scripture.* There are many teens who develop a negative attitude toward Scripture because of the way it has been used by their parents. Don't use Scripture as a club to inflict guilt, to put your teenager down, or to condemn. Don't embarrass your teenagers with Scripture. Don't beat them with the Bible. Remember that the truth must always be spoken in love. The purpose of the Word in your teenager's life is not to beat them down and discourage them, but to prepare them to be "adequate and equipped for every good work" (2 Tim. 3:17).

Your use of Scripture with your teenager should be drenched with hope because Scripture always moves from human failure and sin toward forgiveness and deliverance in Christ. Don't use the Bible in a way that causes your teenager to run and hide from God. Use it in a way that encourages him to run to Jesus for the help that only he can give.

4. Be willing to use yourself as an example of the forgiving, enabling, and delivering grace of Christ. Our story as parents is the story of God's work; it is very important that we do not take the credit. Refrain from having those all-too-typical "In my day . . ." or "When I was your age . . ." conversations. We should not see ourselves as pictures on which our children are to gaze, but rather as windows through which our children can see the glory of Christ. We powerfully point to Christ when we humbly admit to our teenagers that we were and are people in need of the Lord's help.

5. Be willing to ask for forgiveness, accountability, and prayer. Even your parental failure can be used by God to soften the heart of your teenager! What hope there is in the Gospel! Don't let those moments of selfishness, irritation, harsh words, impatience, and anger just fade away. Go to your teenager and confess your faults. Ask him to pray for you, and invite him to come to you any time he has been hurt by the things you have said and done. Be a picture of humility, dependence on Christ, and hope.

I saw my son's progress report from school at the end of the day. I looked at his grades and immediately was angry. Although the grades were not terrible, I knew that he could do better. Lashing out at him, I told him how hard we worked to get him through school (guilt). I told him I sometimes wondered if he would ever get his act together (condemnation). And I told him that when I was his age, I was very serious about school (self-righteousness). He sat across from me with his head down. He said nothing. And when I was done, he went down to his room.

Immediately, I was convicted for the way I had behaved. I prayed and asked the Lord to forgive me. Later that night, I asked my son once again to sit down with me. I told him that I had come to realize that he was not the only sinner in the house! He smiled. I asked for his forgiveness. I confessed my need for God's help and for his prayer. I told him that I was his father, but I also wanted to be a faithful friend. I told him that I wanted to leave him with hope even in moments of correction. He thanked me for talking with him, and he went to bed. The next afternoon, when he came home from school, he grabbed my arm and said, "I want to be your friend, too." Precious words. They represented a softening of his heart, and they represented God's working redemptively through my failure. Remember, it is not your weakness that will get in the way of God's working through you, but your delusions of strength. His strength is made perfect in our weakness! Point to his strength by being willing to admit your weakness.

6. *Be a model of prayer without ceasing.* Make prayer a regular and important part of family life. Pray with your teenager constantly. If they tell you they are facing a tough test, don't promise to pray for them; do it right then and there. If they share with you that they are struggling with a relationship, don't simply tell them how to handle it; pray with them. When you are starting out on a family trip or vacation, gather as a family and pray. When your teenager is struggling to get along with his siblings, don't give in to constant yelling; sit down and pray with him. Ask your teenager where he struggles with doubts, fears, anger, discouragement, and other temptations, and pray with him. Go back later and tell him you have continued to pray and ask him how things are going. Pray, pray, pray, pray. In family life, there are a thousand natural opportunities to pray with and for your teenager.

7. *Be an example of hunger for God.* Let your teenager see your commitment to personal and family Bible study, to be under the regular teaching of God's Word, and to be in robust fellowship and ministry with the body of Christ. Ask yourself, "Do I hunger after God and does my teenager see it?" Are you a model of the thing you are seeking to instill in your teenager?

My father was very faithful in gathering us for daily family devotions. He was not a teacher, but he would read a passage to us and then we would all pray. I remember one period of time when my older brother Tedd was working first shift at a factory. He had to be there between 6:00 and 6:30 A.M. Dad got the rest of us up at 5:00 A.M. so that we could read and pray together. Then the family would go back to bed as Tedd went off to work. I don't remember much of what we read, but I remember how the unaltering commitment to family worship impressed me. I remember thinking that it must be very important because nothing got in the way of our family time of reading and prayer!

My parents did the same with Sunday worship. It was a nonnegotiable part of our family schedule. The only thing we ever did on Sunday morning was attend our church's service of worship. Even when we were on vacation, my parents would find a place for us to worship on Sunday morning. They demonstrated a commitment that pictured the importance of these spiritual priorities. We need to do the same.

God has chosen us to be his children! He has opened our eyes to his truth. He has forgiven us, adopted us as his children, and empowered us by his Spirit. In the face of our disobedience and unbelief, he has responded with patient, loving correction. We have experienced his amazing grace. If we accomplish nothing else, we want our children to know him, to value his love, to wonder at his grace, and to live for his glory. We want them to experience his redeeming love and to surrender their hearts to him. So we will make public worship and teaching, personal Bible study, fellowship, family worship, and ministry top priorities. We will endeavor to be parents who daily live out what it means to "seek first his kingdom," making the pursuit of Christ our priority. In so doing, we allow God to work through us to instill a hunger for him in the hearts of our teenagers.

C H A P T E R

LEAVING HOME

SHE stood on the porch watching him squeeze another box of "stuff" into the car. She tried her best to blink back her tears and see a well-prepared young man, but every time she looked, her mind was filled with the little boy wearing dirty jeans, sporting a milk mustache, and asking for just one more "chocklit" cookie. She wondered how he would do. He was going to be a thousand miles away at a major university. They had been there together and all the necessary arrangements had been made, but this time he was going alone. He wanted it that way, so she agreed to follow him later. Yes, she wondered how he would do, but she knew *she* wasn't ready for this.

She wanted to do it all over again. She wanted to do it better. She wanted to grab her son and ask for forgiveness for all those times she should have been there, but wasn't. She wanted to express regret for all the times she had responded in irritation at another request for help. She wanted to take back all the words spoken in anger. She wished for another chance at the science project that was such a disaster and caused such conflict between them. She wanted to go back to all the Little League games that seemed so unimportant and this time be there for all of them.

She wished she had been more faithful in talking about the things of the Lord. She wished she had lectured him less and prayed with him more. She wanted to go back and be more welcoming with his friends. She wished she had gone to his room more, just to ask him about his day, simply to find another excuse to express her love. There was an unspoken fear in her that he would "blow up" in college like so many other children from Christian families. She stood there and prayed, not noticing that the packing process was done and he was standing, with her husband, on the porch with her.

Her racing thoughts and silent prayers were interrupted by his voice. "Mom, I'm all packed and I gotta go. I can't tell you how thankful I am for all you and Dad have done. Don't worry about me, you guys have done a good job. I know what's right and wrong. I'll be okay." With the last words they embraced. Tears streamed down her face. She didn't see it, but he cried too. Dad said, "Let's pray before you go." And with that prayer and one final hug, he hopped off the porch and into the car.

She stood on the porch in the arms of her husband long after the car was gone. She wasn't quite sure why she stood there and what she was looking at. It just seemed like a way to hold onto her son a little longer. Then her husband broke into her tearful thoughts and said, "Dear, this is what we have been working for all those years. He is a good kid and he is ready. He knows the Lord. He'll be okay. Besides, he'll be back for Christmas in just a few months."

As they walked into the house he said, "I know we're going to miss him, but we really ought to be happy. We can see the fruit of all of our efforts. It's been worth it. We have a lot to be thankful for." She didn't respond. It was hard for her not to imagine herself in the car with her son, giving him just a few more last-minute words of advice. And it was hard for her mind not to run to a myriad of "what ifs." She knew her husband was right. The goal of parenting is to work yourself out of a job. The goal of parenting is to send young adults out into the world who are prepared to live as God's children and as salt and light in a corrupt and broken world. She was aware that her son wasn't her possession, that he belonged to God, and that she and his father were but instruments in God's hands. She knew that this was a good moment, a graduation, an emancipation, but it was hard to be happy and hard not to want him back for just a little more parenting. Yet she knew that this phase of her work in her son's life was over and that she must entrust him into the hands of a better Father.

GOAL 5 *Preparing Teenagers for Leaving Home*

Thousands and thousands of parents have lived this scene, all knowing that it was coming, yet all a bit unprepared for the day when it actually takes place. This is the final goal that needs to be in place. As parents, we need to see emancipation from the home as an important and godly goal. It is what God has called us to do, to prepare our children to be meaningful contributors to the work of the kingdom of God. So we spend years preparing, and then we send them out. No, they do not belong to us; they never did. They have always belonged to the God who appointed us to be his agents of growth, maturity, and preparation. We don't want them to be dependent and clinging. We want them to be able to stand strong and contribute much. We want to be able to say a happy "Go free!," knowing that they have everything they need to do what God has called them to do. This is the goal of all of those years of parental labor.

Leaving the Home Too Soon

It doesn't take much of a look around to see that many teens in our culture and in our churches are leaving home too soon and too little prepared. Their leaving isn't the warm family scene that I described. These are children who, from the age of thirteen, fourteen, or fifteen, begin to tell themselves that they are going to get away from home as soon as possible. They live for the age of eighteen, when they have graduated from high school and can effect their own liberation. When these children leave, they don't say a warm thanks. They leave either with angry words or with no words at all because the relationship with their parents was broken long before.

As I have counseled many teenagers and their parents, it has become very clear to me that few teenagers leave because of the *rules*. No, they leave because of the *relationship*. They leave because the relationship with their parents has gotten so bad, so angry, so confrontational, so adversarial that they cannot stand to live under the same roof with them. Sadly, this happens frequently in the homes of believers. This is not to say that these teenagers are not rebellious. They usually are, but it is relational breakdown that ultimately drives them out, unprepared to live godly and productive lives in a fallen world.

What happens is that parents, in their desire to get their teenager to do what is right, allow their own anger, bitterness, and unforgiving spirit to corrupt and distort the whole process. Before long they are almost unable to have a conversation with their son or daughter that is not dyed with their anger. Their words increasingly become disparaging, judgmental, and condemning. They allow themselves to get sucked into battles of words, using the weapon of the other person's failure, to win the war for power. In so doing they forget their own experience of the parenting love of Christ. It was while they were yet sinners that he died for them. It is his goodness that leads them to repentance. It is his grace that overpowers the depth and breadth of their sin. His grace never compromises what is right, it never says sin is okay, but it brings powerfully persevering love to the one who could never earn it by his righteousness.

Parents who follow Christ's example do not correct without the

Gospel of grace as part of the message. They do not admonish without pointing to the reality of the love of Christ. They see every instance of trouble, failure, and sin as another opportunity to teach their teenager to cast himself on Christ. They never call wrong right, but they always deal with wrong in a way that depicts the glorious realities of the Gospel. And they never try to do with the power of their words or the gravity of their discipline what only Christ can do as he enters into a teenager's heart by his grace. The preeminent theme of their home will not be their disappointment and their anger at their teenager's failure. The preeminent theme will be Christ. He will dominate the times of failure as Forgiver and Deliverer, and he will dominate the times of obedience as the Guide and Strength. In each experience he will be sought and he will be given glory. Teenagers who live in homes like this will be regularly surprised at the love of their parents and the grace of Christ who has chosen them to live in a family where the redeeming love of Christ reigns supreme.

Four Verbs for Parents

Let me suggest four verbs that can set the agenda for parents who want to model Christ with their teenagers.

The first verb is *accept*. We must greet the sin of our teenagers with the accepting grace of Christ. Not acceptance that compromises God's high standard or his call for confession and repentance, but acceptance that leads to change. This acceptance holds God's standard high, but in the context of the hope found in the cross of Christ. Our job as parents is not to condemn, judge, reject, or break relationship. Our job is to function as God's instruments of change, and the most powerful tool we have is our relationship with our teenagers. We want to conduct this relationship in such a way that his work will thrive in the midst of it.

The next verb is *incarnate*. As Christ was called to reveal God in the flesh, we are called to reveal Christ. As parents, we are called to incarnate the love of Christ in all of our interactions with our teenagers. We reveal his love, patience, gentleness, kindness, and forgiveness as we respond with the same toward our children (see Col. 3:12–14). This must be one of our highest goals—that Christ, his character, and his Gospel work would be depicted in the way we relate to our teenagers.

The third verb is *identify*. Hebrews 2:10 says that Christ is not "ashamed to call us brothers" because he suffered the same things that we suffer. He is able to identify fully with the harsh realities and temptations of life in this fallen world. He went through the process that we are now enduring. If Christ can identify with us, how much more should we be able to identify with our teenagers! Often parents of teens communicate that they are not at all like their teenagers and, in fact, have real difficulty relating to them and their struggles. However, we *are* the same. There is no struggle that our teenager might have that we haven't had or aren't still having. There are times when we want to shuck our responsibility and forget the things that we don't like to do. There are times when we are willful, wanting our own way. There are times when we are defensive and unapproachable. There are times when we think we know more than we do.

We share a fallen nature with our teenagers, and we share progressive growth unto holiness with them. We must not act as if we are people of a different sort or stand self-righteously above them. We must stand alongside them as the older brother and sister and point them to the only place of hope—Christ. We must communicate that there is no answer we give them that we ourselves don't need.

The final verb is *enter*. As Christ entered our world and spent thirty-three years getting to know our experiences, we must take the time to enter the world of our teenager (see Heb. 4:14ff.). That means spending as much time asking good questions and listening as it does speaking. In fact, our speaking to our teenagers would be much more loving and insightful if we took the time to get to know the people, the pressures, the responsibilities, the opportunities, and the temptations they face every day. One of the tragic things that happens to parents and teens is that they quit talking meaningfully, honestly, and personally. All of the correction, instruction, discussion, debate, and discipline is done on the platform of ignorance.

Take time to enter the world of your teenager. Know what he faces every day, know how he is emotionally and spiritually gripped by those experiences, know where he is being tempted and where he is succumbing. Understand what the worlds of home, school, work, and leisure look like to him. Let him know that his world and the way he experiences it are important to you. Find ways to let him know that you are on board, that you understand, and that you care. When he says that you don't understand, tell him that you love him and that you want to understand. Ask him to explain what needs to be explained so that you *will* understand. Ask him not to be frustrated when he thinks that you don't understand, but to give you help so that you would.

Teenagers whose parents have accepted them with the grace of Christ, who have incarnated the love of Christ, who have identified like Christ, and have entered their teenager's world following Christ's example will not have teenagers who are trying to get out of the home as soon as they can. Rather, they will be drawn by the powerful love and grace that has been their daily experience. They will tend to treasure the one human relationship in which they have been consistently loved when they deserved it least. This will give their parents the freedom and the time to prepare them just a little more for their important entry into the world where they will stand with God on their own.

What Does Maturity Look Like?

Before we define maturity, it is important to note that the Bible presents maturity as a lifelong goal. God is still at work bringing *us* as parents to maturity in Christ. Your teenagers will not leave your home as finished products. So what are we looking for here? As our children are preparing to leave home, we want to see the *seeds* of maturity in their lives. If the seeds are there, we know that they will continue to grow long after they have moved beyond our parental care. Don't be discouraged as we examine these goals. Our job is not to complete the final harvest, but to plant seeds of maturity in our children. God will water them and make them grow.

Many parents have asked me how they would know when their children were ready to leave home. It is a good question, one that needs to be asked throughout a child's life so that readiness becomes a goal we are working toward. To be a functional goal, readiness needs to be defined practically. You cannot produce something you do not understand.

What we are really asking is what biblical maturity looks like. Paul gives us a wonderful summary in Colossians 1:9–14:

> *For this reason, since the day we heard about you, we have not stopped praying for you and asking God to fill you with the knowledge of his will through all spiritual wisdom and understanding. And we pray this in order that you may live a life worthy of the LORD and may please him in every way: bearing fruit in every good work, growing in the knowledge of God, being strengthened with all power according to his glorious might so that you may have great endurance and patience, and joyfully giving thanks to the Father, who has qualified you to share in the inheritance of the saints in the kingdom of light. For he has*

rescued us from the dominion of darkness and brought us into the kingdom of the Son he loves, in whom we have redemption, the forgiveness of sins.

Six characteristics form Paul's prayer for maturity for the Colossian church. These make a wonderful functional definition for us as we seek to evaluate our teenagers and their not-too-distant emancipation from our homes. Remember that these are lifelong goals. As we consider them, think beginnings, not final ends.

1. *Sensitivity to God's revealed will.* It is hard to think of something more important for our teenagers than a wisdom that gives them a knowledge of God's will in the varied situations of life. Teenagers tend to live with a bubble around their heads—all they seem to experience is what they think and what they want. How important it is that they get a vision for something bigger than their own happiness—that is, living to God's glory, coupled with a desire to know how the principles of Scripture apply to everyday life!

2. *Functional godliness.* Paul prays that they would "live a life worthy of the Lord and please him in every way, bearing fruit in every good work." What a goal for our teenagers (and us)! Not that they would agree to go to church with us, not that they would be drug- and sex-free, not that they would get a job and do fairly well in school. These goals are not high enough for Paul, and they should not be for us! We need to believe that God, by his Spirit, can produce in our teenagers a desire to please the Lord in *everything* they do. We cannot settle for anything less.

3. *Progressive spiritual growth.* We want to see our teenagers daily growing in the knowledge of the Lord. We want to show them that every situation in life is an opportunity to know God and his Word better. We need to ask, "Are they teachable, are they seekers, are they humble, are they learning their spiritual lessons?" If they are, we will

see the fruit of growth in their lives. We will see strength replacing weakness, we will see wisdom replacing foolishness, we will see the courage of faith replacing doubt and fear, we will see thankfulness replacing selfishness and discontent, and we will see the fear of the Lord replacing slavery to the opinions and acceptance of peers.

4. *Perseverance.* What an important sign of maturity and what an important goal for parenting teens! We want to raise teenagers who have acknowledged their weakness, but have come to see that God's strength is made perfect in their weaknesses. As they rely on his strength and as God empowers them, they don't give up, run away, or quit in the face of trouble. They endure with patience things that would have once caused them to throw in the towel. They no longer succumb to the pressure of peers, but stand strong, unwilling to compromise their convictions. They don't quit when their responsibilities get tough, and they don't blame others for their failures. They stay in a hard conversation with you even when they are tempted to shut down in anger, self-pity, or defensiveness. They are learning what it means to "be strong in the Lord and the power of his might."

5. *An appreciation of God's grace.* How many teenagers seem to have little or no awareness of the great privilege of being born into a family of faith? How many teenagers take for granted the heritage that has been passed down to them? How many fail to recognize the value of godly examples that have been around them as they have grown up? Many teens not only fail to recognize the grace of God in these experiences, but they often wish that they were raised in families where they had more "freedom."

Paul says, in effect, "Do you realize what God has done? He has qualified you for his inheritance! You are part of his family! You are the inheritors of the riches of his grace!" Paul didn't want the Colossian Christians to miss the most phenomenal fact of their lives. We must work so that our teenagers don't miss it either. Maturity means not taking for granted what deserves to be highly prized.

6. *Kingdom awareness.* Paul ends his description of maturity with a very important principle. Christ does not free us from the kingdom of darkness so that we can live unto ourselves, as our own king. He brings us from the kingdom of darkness into *his* kingdom. We go from being slaves to sin to being slaves to Christ! Our lives never belonged to us, but to him. His will is our duty. His glory is to be our goal. His purposes become our life agenda. We live through him and for him. In everything we do, there is a higher agenda—his kingdom and his righteousness.

How important it is for teenagers who tend to be self-focused, nearsighted, impulsive, and emotion-driven to have a wider focus, a higher agenda! Imagine how different the life of the average teenager would be if he lived with an awareness of God and his kingdom work. Imagine how the life of your teenager would change if he wanted to be part of what God is doing on earth more than he wanted to fulfill his own desires and dreams! (Imagine how our own lives would change!) We need to hold God's kingdom before our children so that they would grow up to see themselves as kingdom citizens, kingdom workers, kingdom builders. Our goal is that this focus would shape each area of their lives—friendship, work, school, homes, leisure, thoughts, and possessions.

Do these standards seem unattainable? They *are* high, and I have plenty of growing to do in them myself. But I want to encourage you to set your standards high. Don't give in to any perspective on parenting that convinces you that the promises and goals of the Gospel are beyond your teenager's reach. Believe that God is able to do more than you could ask or think, through you and in them. Take every opportunity to encourage your teenager toward these goals. Have a biblical vision of maturity that guides all you do as you prepare your teenager for his eventual emancipation from your home.

The Daily Fruit of Maturity

"Mom," she said, "can I ask you something?" It was quite early in the morning, and everyone was rushing to get out the door. Although she didn't really have the time, Mom said, "Sure, what's on your mind?" "Well," she said hesitatingly, "you know that weekend camping trip that I asked you about? Like, there are going to be guys there. I didn't want you to think I was sneaking around behind your back, and I wanted to know what you think I should do. I really want to go, but not if it's the wrong thing to do." Mom smiled inside at the maturity that she was seeing in this brief morning conversation.

If your teenager is growing in sensitivity to God's revealed will, growing in living a godly life, if you are seeing perseverance, thankfulness, and kingdom awareness, then this growing maturity will bear fruit in the way he or she responds to everyday duties, decisions, relationships, and temptations. You need to know what the practical fruit of maturity will look like so that you can evaluate whether your sons or daughters are ready to make their break with your home. Let's look at the practical fruit of biblical maturity.

1. *Acceptance of personal responsibility.* A maturing teenager will begin to step away from the "life is supposed to be fun and enjoyable all the time—please entertain me or I'll get bored" view of life. (Remember that boredom tends to be one of the daily fears of youth.) As she matures, she will grow to accept and even find satisfaction in the God-ordained responsibilities that are hers. She will not have to be threatened, manipulated, or otherwise coerced into doing what she is called to do. She won't excuse her irresponsibility with, "Oh, I'm sorry, I forgot," "I didn't know I was supposed to . . . ," or "I guess I misunderstood what you said." She won't need to be watched or

checked up on. She will begin to develop a reputation for being trust-worthy and dependable outside your home.

There are several areas where you will see a growing acceptance of personal responsibility. Your teenager will take responsibility for maintaining a day-by-day communion with the Lord. In the early years of a child's life, Christian parents are almost totally in control of the child's exposure to the things of the Lord. At some point the child must internalize these values and take responsibility for his own relationship with God. He must have a desire for the Lord that will cause him to pursue fellowship, Bible teaching, personal worship, and ministry.

He will also take responsibility for maintaining healthy, produc-tive, and God-glorifying relationships with the people in his life. This would include parents, siblings, friends, neighbors, and other au-thority figures outside the home. Young children constantly require the intervention of adults to maintain relationships with one another. They tend not to understand how they create problems in their rela-tionships, and they tend not to know how to solve the problems they have created. You should be looking to see if your teenager is devel-oping healthy, lasting relationships that do not require the consistent intervention of others to be sustained.

You should also see the teenager growing in a responsible attitude toward work and productivity. In our pleasure-oriented, materialis-tic society, work is considered a necessary evil and an interruption, something we must do to afford the pleasures of life. Yet the culture also tends to see work as hampering our pursuit of those pleasures. Many teens in Christian homes (and maybe their parents as well) have bought into the hedonistic worldview of our culture. The result is a disdain for work and an attempt to avoid it whenever possible.

The biblical view of work is radically different. The call to mean-ingful, necessary, productive, and creative labor goes to the very heart of our identity as creatures made in the image of God. Work was a significant part of God's original mandate to Adam and Eve. It was part of the perfect life in a perfect world. The fall of man into sin didn't create work; it dramatically complicated it. The fact remains that in working we image God. We submit to the fact that we are creatures in his world. In working we find joy and meaning in living as he purposed for us to live. We become the tools by which he maintains his world and provides for his creatures.

As we are evaluating our teenagers, we look for a positive, responsible attitude toward labor, inside and outside the home. We listen to see if there is a grumbling, complaining, avoiding spirit about work. And we look for the results of a disciplined work life in our teenagers (the praise of a boss, the thankfulness of a youth leader for the teen's helpfulness, a willingness to participate in the work of the home, etc.).

2. *Applied biblical convictions.* As we have discussed earlier, the maturing teenager will erect his own moral boundaries. He will not need a lecture to do what's right with the threat of punishment as his motivation. A desire to do what is right in the sight of God will produce the fruit of carefulness in his life. You will not feel like you're living with someone who is always inching to the edge of the cliff, or someone who is constantly trying to put something over on you.

Teens who live with conviction prove that they can be trusted. They make hard choices even when their parents aren't present and would never know. They tend to hang around with others who do the same. These teens may make decisions that are different from those you would make, but they are not outside God's boundaries. After all, the goal is not that your children would agree with you in every decision, but that their lives would be a practical picture of submission to God.

Finally, teens who are living within God's boundaries don't tend to be hiders. There is no reason to hide. What they desire, decide, and do can be done in the open because it is consistent with the will of God. I've asked my teenagers this question many times: "Is there anything that you are doing out there that you would be afraid or embarrassed to do in front of me?" This question can be a practical way of getting them to think about whether they are living within God's boundaries.

3. *An approachable, teachable, seeking spirit.* Teens who are maturing and getting ready to leave home will recognize the awesome task before them. They will want all the help and preparation they can get. They won't be intolerant of conversations about what they are doing. They won't get defensive when their choices are questioned. They won't distance you with nonanswers or be impatient and argumentative when drawn into discussion. And they won't turn friendly discussions into unfriendly debates as soon as the subject touches their behavior and choices. This assumes, of course, that our attitudes and interactions are what God wants them to be as we relate to them.

If we *are* relating to our teenagers in a godly way, something is wrong if we constantly feel as if we are walking on eggshells when we are around them. Mature teens are approachable. They are able to be taught without a fight. You can go to their room to talk without feeling like an unwelcome intruder. You can lovingly challenge their thinking, choices, and actions, and they will discuss them without anger. They will not only allow you to approach them, but they will seek out your advice and wisdom.

4. *Accurate self-assessment.* Teens who are maturing will have an increasingly accurate view of themselves. They will have a sense of their strengths and weaknesses that will guide their choices in relationships and responsibilities. They will have a growing sense of where they are particularly susceptible to temptation. They will not be surprised when you lovingly point out a weakness that needs at-

tention. They won't have one of those "What are you talking about, I never do that" reactions. They will receive your help because they will have already recognized their weakness and their need for help.

I went down to my son's room one night because there was something we needed to talk about. I knocked on the door and he answered. "Do you have a moment?" I asked. "Sure," he said, "I wasn't doing anything important." "I want to talk about our relationship," I said. "I have been concerned about something for a while and I thought it was time for us to talk. It seems like you have been real defensive lately. You seem to get impatient every time we try to talk to you about your decisions. We don't look for ways to hassle you and we don't want to wreck your life. We love you and only want you to be all that God has purposed for you to be."

I waited for him to respond. "I guess you're right," he said. "I guess there are times when it's kinda hard to talk to me. I just feel like I should have a life of my own and be making my own decisions. Sometimes I feel like you guys forget how old I actually am. But I know I still need your help, and even when I don't want it, I should accept it. I'm sorry, I know I have made it tough for you lately." "I forgive you," I said. "We don't want to make your decisions for you, and we don't want to treat you like a little kid; but we do sense that there are ways that you still need us, and we are committed to giving you the help God has called us to give you. We couldn't love you and do anything less. I love you." "I love you too," he replied, and I left his room.

This is what you are looking for. Not teens who are perfect, who do everything in the right time and in the right way. No, you are looking for teens who are mature enough to realize that they are not finished products and, because of their accurate view of themselves, are able to receive the help you are there to offer.

5. *Proper perspective on things.* We have already noted that we live in an intensely materialistic culture that really does worship and

serve created things rather than the Creator. "Whoever has the most toys wins" is the way someone captured the materialism of Western culture. We tend to define success in terms of the size of a person's house and the brand and luxury level of his car. The labels that used to be sewn on the inside of clothes now appear on the outside in huge letters, announcing our good taste and affluence. It is naive to think that our teenagers can breathe the air of this materialistic culture without taking in some of its values.

As a parent, you should look for signs of an inordinate preoccupation with material things. These questions will help you recognize the signs. Do your teenagers express a "gotta have" mentality? Do they have a short contentment span, quickly moving on to the next craving? Do they tend to evaluate people by looks and clothing, only associating with people who meet their appearance standards? Do they tend to describe their future goals in materialistic, monetary terms? Do they tend to be happiest with you and their lives when they are surrounded by the "stuff" they want? Do they tend to get on the bandwagon of all the current fads of the culture? How do they spend the money you give them and the money they earn? Do they have a giving spirit, using their money to serve others and the Lord?

The maturing teenager will be thankful for the things he has, but he also will be learning that life does not consist in the abundance of his possessions. At the same time, he will be a good steward of the things God has given him, and he will be someone who can be trusted with the possessions of others. He will have a sense of the proper way to think about and use the things God has provided.

It's Just a Matter of Time

Sooner or later, every one of us who has teenagers will be like the Mom and Dad we saw on the porch. Maybe we will be begging an angry teenager not to go, or maybe we will be saying a tearful farewell to a son or daughter who is ready. We all know that our teenagers won't live with us forever. We all know that God's goal for our parenting is that we work ourselves out of a job. His plan is that we would be his instruments in producing children who are biblically mature, ready to face life in the fallen world, ready to be salt and light, ready to be contributors to his kingdom work, no longer needing the day-by-day guidance that we have given them for so many years.

Because this is where we are headed, we need a clear definition of maturity and a clear sense of what the fruit of maturity will look like in our teenager's everyday life. It is hard to reach a destination without knowing where it is!

Finally, we need to once again face the fact that we cannot give our teenagers what we do not have ourselves. Being a Christian parent does not guarantee that we are biblically mature. We, too, need to look intently into the mirror of the Word of God. Do we meet the biblical standard of maturity? Where do we need to grow? Do we model a winsome, mature godliness before our teenagers? Are we living responsible lives? Are we approachable and teachable ourselves? Do we live with moral boundaries that give shape to our decisions and actions? Do we have an accurate sense of where we are weak and where we are strong, and are we open to the help of others? Do we hold physical things in proper balance, or are we parents who work too much and owe too much because we have followed the culture's values?

We need to stand before God and ask if we hold our children to standards that we are not keeping ourselves (see Christ's words to the Pharisees in Matt. 23:1–4). Do our lives contradict our message? Is it possible that the reason our children reject us and reject God is not because of our standards, but because of our own hypocrisy? Do we humbly communicate to our teenagers that we, too, are people in process? That we need the grace of God today as much as we needed it the first day we believed? That we recognize the proneness of our hearts to wander away from the Creator, only to deify the created thing? That we need God's help to remain faithful and grow just as much as they do? Are we willing to go to them in times of failure, seeking their forgiveness and communicating a vibrant reliance on the forgiving and delivering mercy of Christ?

Do our teenagers respect the lives we lead? Do they consider being like us part of their definition of successful living? Do they say within themselves, "I live in a world where much is wrong and much is fake, but my parents are genuine. I don't always like what they say to me or what they ask me to do, but I want to be like them." Do our teenagers look at us and see truth, love, grace, faithfulness, and hope? Do they look at us and see Christ?

Successful parenting means that we admit that we, as parents, are still children in need of our Father's help. It means going to him and saying, "We cannot be what you have called us to be without the lavish resources of your grace. We have believed, but help us in our unbelief. We have obeyed, but strengthen us where we are still tempted to disobey. We have loved, but help us when we are more moved by love of self than we are by love for you. Work in us, Lord, so that you may work *through* us to capture the lives of our teenagers by your grace. We ask this that their lives and ours may be lived as hymns to your glory."

PART THREE *Practical Strategies for Parenting Teens*

THREE STRATEGIES FOR PARENTING TEENS

BILL and Jean sat in my office looking worn out and discouraged. They had looked forward to raising a family and had very much enjoyed the early years of parenting. They told of great vacations and wonderful holidays. They remembered those sweet moments of reading their children to sleep, surprising them with breakfast in bed, and bringing home, at the end of the work day, the occasional unexpected toy. But somewhere, somehow they lost sight of what they were doing and why. They were still interacting with their children, but it all seemed to lack continuity and purpose.

They had read most of the Christian parenting books and had even attended a weekend seminar, yet they saw their relationship with their teenager in particular growing more and more distant. They sensed that most of the time they corrected him out of irritation, rather than with biblical purpose. They felt as if the whole process was slipping out of their grip like sand through their fingers.

Jean spoke out, "We've had so many people tell us what to do, but we don't know how to do it. We get excited once again when we read a book or hear a speaker, but things just don't work the way they were described and they don't turn out the way we expected." Bill interjected, "I think what she is saying is that we need a sense of focus or purpose. We're here because we want to have the same sense of direction with our kids that we had when they were younger. We have one teenager and two more who are on the way. We don't want to lose them now." "Besides, we're tired," Jean said, "and I think it's because we seem to complicate problems rather than solve them. There's always some mess that we're cleaning up."

I wondered later that day how many other couples shared Bill and Jean's experience. They look back with nostalgia to the golden days of parenting. The days when your children couldn't wait till you came home from work, when they carried a book around begging for you to read to them. The days when you could satisfy them with a few moments of wrestling on the floor. How many parents secretly wish for the earlier years to return? They know that their relationship with their teenager is not what it was when he was younger, but instead of making changes in the present, they give in to grieving the loss of the past.

As parents, all of us need to bring two things into every stage of parenting: biblical goals and biblical strategies for accomplishing those goals. In the last several chapters we have laid out five fundamental goals for parenting teens. Now we must turn to strategies for realizing those goals. I want to suggest three things to do if you want to raise godly teenagers who are prepared to live as salt and light in a fallen world. These strategies will bring a sense of purpose and focus to your life with your teenager.

In all of this, there is a basic truth we need to remember: what we observe about teenagers applies to us as well. All of the biblical insights, principles, and strategies apply to our teenagers because they apply to people in general. This exposes the core truth of this book. Our teenagers are more like us than they are unlike us. They face a different set of pressures, temptations, and opportunities, but deal with them in ways that mirror us. And like us, they are not finished products.

All of the spiritual needs we will recognize in our teenagers are in some way identifiable in us. So each of these strategies must be applied with a humble willingness to identify with the teen's struggle, a humble recognition that God is still working to change us, and a humble readiness to offer our teenagers the same grace that God has given us.

Strategy #1: Project Parenting

Many parents make the mistake of parenting without any sense of "project" to guide their daily encounters with their teenagers. They try to warn, admonish, teach, and correct, but it all doesn't seem to hang together. They don't see the fruit of change in the teenager's life. The phrase "project parenting" implies being focused, being purposeful, being goal-oriented in our daily encounters with our teenagers. When we are parenting with a sense of project, we will know why we are going after what we are going after. Parenting without a sense of project is like going into the shop, collecting wood, glue, hardware, and tools, and starting to work, hoping that as you measure, saw, hammer, and glue, it will all turn into something! None of us has ever done this because it wouldn't work. We need to know what we want to build, the materials required, and the process of construction.

We need the same sense of project with our teenagers. What should we be working on with this particular child at this particular time in his life? How should we work on it? Again, project parenting means being focused, being purposeful, being goal-oriented in our day-by-day encounters with our teenagers and emphasizing certain themes. It means we will have discussed how to pursue these issues with our children. It means we will parent with *prepared spontaneity;* we will come to those unexpected, spontaneous moments of parenting with preparedness and purpose.

Project parenting means that we won't just be thinking on the fly. We will have asked ourselves where our teenager is weak, where he is susceptible to temptation, where he seems to be regularly struggling, and where we see rebellion and resistance. These things become our projects. We will not try to do everything at once; we will examine our child, pray, and consider our focus. We will realize that God, in his sovereignty, will give us daily opportunities to deal with those issues. We will have a sense of what is important at this moment in the life of the teen, and we will be looking for opportunities to deal with it.

A Biblical Model

Psalm 36:1–4 provides a wonderful model for project parenting.

> *An oracle is within my heart*
> *concerning the sinfulness of the wicked:*
> *There is no fear of God*
> *before his eyes.*
> *For in his own eyes he flatters himself*
> *too much to detect or hate his sin.*
> *The words of his mouth are wicked and deceitful;*
> *he has ceased to be wise and to do good.*
> *Even on his bed he plots evil;*
> *he commits himself to a sinful course*
> *and he does not reject what is wrong.*

In describing the "sinfulness of the wicked," David gives us a model for understanding the struggles of our teenagers and for doing the work of God in the midst of them.

David directs us to two deficiencies in the heart of the "wicked." These sinful deficiencies exist in the hearts of many, if not most, of our teenagers (and often us as well). First, he observes that there is "no fear of God before his eyes." He lacks an awareness of the existence and glory of God, and he has not submitted his life to that fact of facts. To fear God means that my life is structured by a sense of awe, worship, and obedience that flows out of recognizing him and his glory. He becomes the single most important reference point for all that I desire, think, do, and say. God is my motive and God is my goal. The fear of God is meant to be *the* central organizing force in my life.

Most teenagers do not live with the "fear of God before their eyes." Their private universe tends to be dominated by things that they are convinced they need, or by fear of man issues (desire for peer acceptance or fear of peer rejection), or by identity issues (Am I ugly? Am I a "geek"? Do people find me attractive? Will the parts of my body ever match one another?). Not only does God not dominate the scene, he is not there at all! He is not their reason and their goal. Whatever their profession of faith, God does not exist in the functional world where they live daily.

David also points to a second deficiency: that the wicked "flatters himself too much." Again, this describes many teenagers. Teens don't tend to live with an accurate view of themselves. They think that they know more than they actually know. They think that they are more mature than they really are. They tend to believe that they are spiritually stronger and wiser. They are convinced that they have outgrown their need for parenting long before they actually have. When they look at themselves, they don't use the perfect mirror of the Word of God, but the carnival mirrors of peer opinion, personal evaluation, and cultural norm. In those mirrors, you do see yourself, but what you see is distorted, so that your legs look fat and stubby or your neck looks three feet long. The typical self-analysis of the teenager is similarly distorted. He does not see himself with clarity or accuracy. He tends to "think of himself more highly than he ought to think" (Rom. 12:3).

These two deficiencies must remain in our minds as we seek to parent our teenagers. We must seek not just to correct the wrong of the moment, but to gain greater ground. We want to see our children grow in their awareness of and submission to God and in an accurate knowledge of themselves. We see each situation, each discussion, each problem, each encounter, each interchange as an opportunity to work on these fundamental deficiencies. And we need to remember that these struggles are present in our lives as well. They are true of teens because they are true of people in general.

Psalm 36 has given us direction and purpose, but we still need to be more focused, with a personal sense of project with each of our teens. How does this psalm help us to do that? Let's look at it together.

Let's begin with the *goal*. David gives us one of Scripture's best summaries of God's goal for us and our teenagers. David states it negatively, but it is nonetheless clear. He says that because the "wicked" lacks a fear of God and an accurate self-concept, he has "ceased to be wise and to do good." These qualities are the ultimate goal of all that we do as parents. We want to help our children *be wise and do good*.

Who is the wise person? It is the person who fears the Lord, whose life is organized by God's existence and his revealed will. He will bring a quality of wisdom to his everyday life that can only come from above. Who is the person who does good? Isn't it the person who has committed himself to do everything in a way that pleases the Lord and is consistent with the commands and principles of Scripture? The one who does good pays attention to God's boundaries and seeks never to step over them. The person who is wise seeks to bring that wisdom to every circumstance, to every decision, and to every relationship. He is always asking, "What decision, attitude, or action would best express the will of God for me in this particular situation?" In short, practical, functional godliness is our goal.

Parenting with a sense of project means having clear goals in mind, but we also need to help our teenagers live with a sense of the situation. God, in his sovereign plan, has placed each of them in a particular setting, a particular life context. This will be different for each of our teenagers. The teenager going to a public school is in a very different daily situation from the one in a Christian school. The teenager attending a small rural high school has a very different situation from the teen attending a huge inner-city school. Perhaps your family is not affluent, but your teen goes to a suburban school where most of the children are from fairly wealthy families. This difference will be a daily source of struggle and temptation to your teenager.

I need to know what God has placed on my teenager's plate so that I can teach him to live with his eyes open to the particular pressures, opportunities, responsibilities, and temptations he faces. What significant relationships must he deal with? Who are the voices of influence and what are they saying? What values are being promoted in his world? Where are the places of daily struggle? Who are the authority figures to whom he must relate? We need to ask these questions to gain an accurate sense of our teenager's particular situation because godliness is never general. Godliness is always specific. It is always lived out in the details of situations and relationships. To be godly means to *be wise and do good* in the particular setting where God has placed me. Our teenagers not only need focused goals, they also need an *accurate understanding of their situation.*

We now turn to the third focus of project parenting. If our teenagers are ever going to be godly (Goal #1: Be wise and do good), and if they are ever going to live out this godliness in their world (Goal #2: Know their situation), then they need to be prepared (Goal #3: Biblical personal insight). They need to enter their situation with an accurate sense of themselves and an accurate sense of the war within. If our teenagers lack this personal insight, they will tend to lack self-control. Self-control is the internal restraint system of the heart, the conscience responding to the knowledge of self and the knowledge of right that God has given us. It is the heart responding to the ministry of the Holy Spirit to make us humble and obedient.

David's words in Psalm 36 point out two important parts to personal insight. First, your teenager must detect his own sin. We have already observed that teenagers (not unlike the rest of us) are not good at this. They tend to have an inflated view of self. We need to ask, "What things about himself does my teenager miss that God wants him to see?" What weakness, failures, sins, attitudes, values, desires, idols, thoughts, or motives does he need to see that he does not see? And how can we use the normal situations in his life to help detect these problems?

The second element in personal insight is equally important. It is not enough for our teenagers to *detect* their sin; they must also come to *hate* it. One of Satan's favorite tricks is to present sin as not so bad. This has been one of his principal schemes since the Garden, and teens (again, not unlike us) are very susceptible. Even in times when they recognize wrong, they will tend to color it as less than what it really is. When they fail to keep a promise, they will tell us they forgot. When they disobey, they will tell us that they didn't understand. When they speak unkindly, they will tell us that we misunderstood them. When we speak to them about a failure, they will refer to the same failure in one of their siblings. They won't tend to see their sin as arrogant rebellion against God, as something dangerous, destructive, and leading to death. They won't tend to see it as repulsive. In fact, it will sometimes even seem attractive and appealing. And remember that all of these insights apply to us as well.

If our teens do not hate their sin, they will not run from it. Our job is to work with them in the daily circumstances of life to help them see sin as God sees it. As they do, our goal and prayer is that they would hate that sin and cast themselves on Christ saying, "What a wretched man I am! Who will rescue me from this body of death? Thanks be to God—through Jesus Christ our Lord!" (Rom. 7:24–25).

Biblical personal insight always has these two factors present: the detection of sin and the hatred of sin. When our teenagers gain this kind of personal insight, they will know where they are weak and recognize the nature of their own struggle with sin. They will be sensitive toward temptation. They will live vigilantly, and because they do, instead of falling again and again into the same sin, they will respond with self-control and, with God's help, live wisely and do good.

We want our children to live with a wartime rather than a peacetime mentality. There is a war going on—a spiritual war, fought on the turf of their hearts in the midst of their daily situation. Our children must move out into the battle prepared if they are ever going to be and do what God has called them to.

To recap, here are the three goals of project parenting. Our goals are to focus all our parenting efforts on being used of God (1) to produce teens who are wise and who do good; (2) to help them maintain an accurate knowledge of their current life situation; and (3) to prepare them to pursue godliness by helping them to detect and hate their own sin. All of this must be done in a spirit of humility, recognizing that these things must be goals for our lives as well. We must not approach project parenting as judges who have solved all of our own problems, but as those who recognize our own sin and our continuing need of Christ.

My wife and I have sought to do this by sitting down a couple times a year to take a good look at each of our children. This is the usual way we start the school year. We seek to recognize what our "projects" are with each child at this particular time. We ask ourselves, "What important struggles are present in his or her life that we need to go after?" We ask ourselves how our child currently views these areas. We want to know where he is encountering temptation in his daily situation. We seek to discern the ways in which he tends to minimize or rationalize these things. We seek to recognize the places where we can expose his struggle with sin and encourage him with the ever-present help of Christ. Finally, this gives us an opportunity to be honest about our own struggles with sin as we deal with our children's blindness, rationalization, and resistance.

The point is that we are not working on everything at once. We are not just hoping that somehow, some way our parenting will be beneficial. We are working with purpose, focus, and priorities. My wife and I have seen the benefits of project parenting in our children, and we have seen the benefit to us as well. Project parenting keeps us focused on God's priorities rather than the personal irritations and differences that cause so much conflict between parents and teenagers.

Strategy #2: Constant Conversation

For years it has been my habit to "visit" each of my four children when I come home at night. I remember the night when I went down to one of my sons' rooms to talk. I asked him how he was doing and how his day had been. He said "Okay," but he wasn't very convincing. "You don't sound okay," I said. "What's wrong?" "Nothing," he said, "Just the same old stuff." "There must be something on your mind; you look discouraged," I replied. "It's hard to explain, you know, it's just life . . . it stinks," he mumbled. "Yeah, it can be really hard sometimes," I said. "But I still don't know what we are talking about." "Do we have to talk about this now?" he said with an edge of impatience. I said, "Look, you know I love you, I come down here every day because I care. I'm not trying to hassle you. If you don't want to talk right now that's okay."

"It just seems impossible sometimes," he said. "It seems like things never turn out right. . . . It seems like you never get credit for what you do. If you do what is right, nobody notices, but there is always somebody around to catch you when you mess up. Right now I wish they would take school and my job and shove it! I'm tired of the hassle. Sometimes I feel like I'm wearing a tee shirt that says, 'I'm a jerk, please hassle me.' I wonder if it's worth it, why I put myself in such torture. I don't think I can keep doing this. . . . Something has got to change."

As parents of teenagers, it is important to realize that these conversations don't just happen. You make them happen by a daily pursuit of your child. This daily pursuit does not have to be negative, something your teenager dreads before it happens and barely tolerates as it's going on. Rather, these times can be loving and encouraging, a habit of your relationship with your teenager that both of you have grown to appreciate.

Why do our teenagers need constant (daily) conversation? Why is it dangerous for us to let days, weeks, sometimes even months go by between personal, self-disclosing conversations with them? Hebrews 3:12–13 answers this question for us and provides a model for our daily interchanges with our teenagers.

> See to it, brothers, that none of you has a sinful, unbelieving heart that turns away from the living God. But encourage one another daily, as long as it is called Today, so that none of you may be hardened by sin's deceitfulness.

This passage gives us a reason for constant conversation with our teenagers. The reason comes in the form of a warning against turning away from God. Notice that the turning away refers to a turning away of the heart. The heart always turns before the eyes, the mouth, the ears, the hands, and the feet.

223

There are many teens living in Christian homes who attend worship services, participate in family devotions, and are active in their church's youth group, but whose hearts have long since turned away from the living God. When these teenagers go off to college and fall away from the faith, something new and radical isn't taking place. It is the fruit of a turning away from God that took place in their hearts months and maybe even years before.

This passage characterizes this turning away in four ways. Each aspect helps us to understand the nature of the warning. First, we are warned against a *sinful* heart—a heart that no longer desires to please the Lord and no longer submits to Scripture. Next, the passage warns us against an *unbelieving* heart. This refers to a loss of faith, confidence, appreciation for, and trust in God and his Word. Third, the passage talks of falling away as a *turning away* from the living God. Falling away is not just breaking the moral law; it is a personal forsaking of communion and fellowship with God himself. Finally, falling away is characterized as the heart being *hardened*. This has to do with the searing of the conscience, making it insensitive to the convicting ministry of the Holy Spirit. The heart is no longer bothered by things that would have once caused much concern and guilt.

As parents we want to do everything we can to protect our teenagers from falling away. We want to protect them from rebellion, unbelief, rejection of God, and the hardening of their hearts. To do so, the writer of Hebrews says, we need *constant conversation,* that is, we need to encourage them daily. Our teenagers (like all of us) need daily contact and daily help. They need daily encouragement and daily exhortation. They need daily pleading. They need constant conversation.

Notice that the passage tells us why they need this daily ministry. It is because of *sin's deceitfulness.* Sin is deceitful and guess who it deceives first? Your teenager will easily see the sins of others around him, but will often be surprised when his are pointed out. What we are dealing with here is spiritual blindness. It is a universal problem. As long as there is sin remaining within, there will be some degree of spiritual blindness *in all of us.*

When you think of the needs of your teenager, put the issue of spiritual blindness high on the list. It is surely one of the most significant results of the Fall. Remember, physically blind people know they are blind and structure their lives accordingly. But spiritually blind people don't know they are blind; they think they see and see well. Surely this explains why our teenagers often feel hurt and falsely accused and become defensive when we point out areas of failure to them.

It is very important to understand the spiritual dynamic at work here. We are being urged to have daily contact *not* because we have caught a person in sin and we must confront him or her. This passage is not *confrontational* and *restorative* in its focus. It is *preventative.* We are urged to have daily contact because as long as there is indwelling sin in your teenager, there will be some degree of spiritual blindness. And since spiritually blind people don't tend to know it, they don't ordinarily seek help. Your teenager won't tend to seek you out because he won't think he needs it. That is why you need to commit yourself to this preventative, constant-conversation model. You want to have a home environment where there is always conversation going on, where children cannot mumble greetings, sit at the kitchen table in silence, and spend the rest of their time alone in their rooms. You have to be determined to talk to them and to get them to talk to you, preferably every day. As we do this, we need to face our own spiritual blindness. There is nothing that we have looked at here to which we are immune. In those conversations with our teenagers, God is working to open not only their eyes, but ours as well.

Spiritual blindness tends to distort our view of ourselves, of God, of others, of the past, of the present and the future, and of where and how change needs to take place. If these things are viewed with distortion or not seen at all, there is no way that the teenager will respond to the issues in his life in a biblical, God-honoring way.

The constant conversation model means being willing to pursue your teenager. It means not living with the distance that he has introduced into the relationship. It means hanging in through those uncomfortable moments when you're not really wanted and not really appreciated, and forsaking a negative relationship where you only have meaningful talks when your teenager has done something wrong.

Be committed to prevention. Don't settle for nonanswers. Ask good questions that cannot be answered without the teenager disclosing his heart (thoughts, motive, purposes, goals, desires, beliefs, values, etc.). Finally, always bring the Gospel to each of those conversations. There *is* a Redeemer. He has conquered sin and death. He is present as the Helper in all my trouble. There is hope! Goliaths do die! Change—radical heart and life change—is possible!

A parent who has his hope in the Gospel will pursue his teenagers and will not stop until they leave the home. We won't wait for them to come to us for help. We won't argue with them as to whether we are needed or not. The call of the Word is clear. With hearts filled with Gospel hope, we will question and probe, listen and consider, plead and encourage, admonish and warn, and instruct and pray. We will awake every day with a sense of mission, knowing that God has given us a high calling. We are walls of protection that God has lovingly placed around our teenagers. We are eyes that he has given that they might see. So we converse and converse and converse.

Strategy #3: Leading Your Teenager to Repentance

Secretly (and sometimes not so secretly) many parents of teenagers wish for some means of control. They wish they could wield some power over their teenagers so that they would do what they were asked to do. What many parents mourn, as their children enter the teen years, is their loss of power. So by harsh words, dramatic punishments, shame, and guilt, they try to control the thoughts and behavior of their son or daughter. What happens instead is that they find themselves in an escalating war for power and control with their teenager. The more they chase, the more the teen hides. The more they beat with words, the more the teen responds in kind. The more they punish, the more the teen works to get beyond the boundaries they have set up. The more they probe, the less the teen talks. The more they lay out what they want, the more the teen determines to do the opposite. Each side, parent and teen, is determined to break down the resolve of the other. It becomes a tense, negative, debilitating, destructive way to live, where anger grows and the only change that takes place is change for the worse.

This is surely not God's way to prepare our teenagers for a productive, God-glorifying life! Rather than seeking to get our teenagers under our control, we want to be used of God so that they would joyfully submit to his. Rather than seeing ourselves as agents of control, we need to see ourselves as ambassadors of reconciliation. Our desire should be to lead our teens to the Lord with repentant hearts. Paul says it well in 2 Corinthians 5:17–21.

Therefore, if anyone is in Christ, he is a new creation; the old has gone, the new has come! All this is from God, who reconciled us to himself through Christ and gave us the ministry of reconciliation: that God was reconciling the world to himself in Christ, not counting men's sins against them. And he has committed to us the message of reconciliation. We are therefore Christ's ambassadors, as though God were making his appeal through us. We implore you on Christ's behalf: Be reconciled to God. God

227

made him who had no sin to be sin for us, so that in him we might become the righteousness of God.

As parents, God has reconciled us to himself so that we would be his ambassadors of reconciliation. It is as though God makes his personal appeal to our teenagers through us! So we seek to lead our teenagers to the Lord with words of confession, with a commitment to repentance, and with hope in the effective work of Christ on the cross. We will not lead them to the Lord just once, but again and again and again, to receive his forgiveness and his help.

There are four steps to this process of repentance and reconciliation that make our job as God's ambassadors very clear.

1. *The first step is consideration.* As God's agents, we need to ask ourselves, "What does God want my teenager to see about himself that he is not seeing? How can I help him to see these things?" This relates to the issues we discussed regarding spiritual blindness. But many parents begin down the wrong path right here. Instead of engaging their teenagers in a conversation that leads them to consider things they would not consider alone, the parents *declare* what is wrong and what is going to happen as a result. In the whole encounter, the heart of the teen remains either passive or defensive. His eyes haven't been opened at all. The interpretations and conclusions are all made by the parent. This kind of encounter creates no turning of the teen's heart.

Contrast this with the way Nathan confronted David about his adultery and murder. Nathan did not storm into David's throne room (as parents of teens are tempted to do) and say, "You, David, are a murderer and an adulterer, and the jig is up!" Rather, Nathan told David a story to which he could relate. Its purpose was to get David to consider what he had done, to stimulate his conscience, and to open his eyes.

When I am seeking to get my teenagers to look at things about themselves, I try to focus on concrete situations, and I regularly ask these five questions:

➤ What was going on? (Tell me about the situation.)

➤ What were you thinking and feeling? (Heart response to situation.)

➤ What did you do? (Active, behavioral response to situation.)

➤ Why did you do it? (Motives, goals, desires that shaped the active response.)

➤ What was the result? (How their response affected the situation.)

These questions shift the focus from other people and the details of the situation onto my child. They have been very helpful in helping my teenagers consider what God wants them to see.

2. *The second step is confession.* I am convinced that one of the great mistakes we make when we confront our teenagers is that we tend to make their confessions for them. We burst into their rooms, telling them what they have done and why they have done it. When we do this, we are not leading our teenagers to confession; we are doing it for them. In fact, it is even worse. Since we have not attempted to open their eyes, in their spiritual blindness they think we are wrong. They feel as if they have been falsely accused, and they are angry with us rather than being grieved at their own sin. Instead of breaking down spiritual blindness, the encounter tends to promote it. And instead of the conscience of the teen being softened, it in fact becomes harder.

We need to enter the rooms of our teenagers recognizing that, in our own blindness, our evaluation of and attitude toward our teenagers may be wrong. We want to be willing to let God correct us as we seek to correct them.

The harsh, inflammatory words we are tempted to use during these times will not encourage repentance in our teenagers; they will produce the opposite. They will drive the teenager in anger away from us and God. Remember, God is seeking to make his appeal for the hearts of our teenagers through us! Are we acting in a way that advances his work or that gets in the way? Our goal must be to lead our teenagers to make statements of confession.

3. *The third step in leading our teenager to repentance is commitment.* This step must not be omitted or assumed. It involves the teenager's promise to live, act, and respond in a new way. This commitment must be to God and to the appropriate people. It must involve a turning of the heart as well as changed behavior. This is the heart of repentance—a determination to turn and go in the opposite direction. We need to discuss what this new commitment will look like in the particular relationships and situations that the teenager will face every day. We also need to help him anticipate when he will be tempted to forsake his commitment and go back to Egypt.

4. *The final step of the repentance process is change.* True repentance will always result in concrete changes in the teenager's life. Here again, we need to be specific. We need to help our teenagers think about particular situations and relationships, and how they will do old things in a new, God-glorifying way. We need to keep reminding them that in Christ they have everything they need to do what God has called them to do. He will provide a way to do all that he asks.

Our job as parents is not to crank up our control, but to lead our sons and daughters to a heartfelt submission to the control of the Lord. So we work daily to engage them in consideration, confession, commitment, and change. God has chosen to use us to make his appeal to our teenagers! As parents, we submit to his lordship by serving with an ambassadorial spirit in the kitchens, family rooms, bedrooms, and hallways of life.

In this chapter we have considered three fundamental strategies for parenting teenagers: Project parenting (focusing on what we need to work on at the moment); constant conversation (daily contact and encouragement because of spiritual blindness); and leading your child to repentance (producing consideration, confession, commitment, and change). None of these strategies can stand alone. Each complements the others. Together they give focus and direction to your daily interactions with your teenager. They give you a daily sense that you know *what* you are doing, *why* you are doing it, and *how* it needs to be done. These strategies also will be used of God to restrain your own sin as you deal with your son or daughter. They will expose in your heart the places where your anger, impatience, and frustration get in the way of the work God has called you to do.

Remember, the God who has called us is parenting *us*. He is with us in every situation and relationship. Our Father will guide, direct, protect, forgive, deliver, and love us. He will never leave us alone. When we are weary and heavy laden, he will give us rest. His strength working in us will accomplish more than anything we could ask or imagine. Our job as parents is not to deliver our children from sin, but to be agents of the only One who can. Isn't it wonderful that as we parent the children he has placed in our care, we can rest in his!

CHAPTER

13

SMALL STEPS TO BIG CHANGE

IT was the Friday night of a typical weekend seminar at a midwestern local church. I was laying out biblical goals for parenting teens. In the middle of my second talk, a man sitting halfway back in the auditorium raised his hand. "This is totally unrealistic," he said. "Nobody does this stuff with teenagers! You don't really talk this way to your kids, do you? Do you really think you can reach these goals? I don't know where your kids came from, but they're not like mine! I came here to get some help. . . . This stuff is just unrealistic!"

I could see the pastor slumping down in his seat, red-faced in embarrassment. I think he wanted to bail me out, but I understood the father's feelings and I thought it was a wonderfully honest moment. It was a great opportunity for the parents there to talk honestly about how discouraged they were with their relationships with their teens. It was true: what I had laid out to them looked like a huge and impassable mountain. They had no idea how to get from the valley where they were to the peaks where they needed to be. That's the way a lot of parents feel when they first hear this material. Maybe that's how you feel as you read this book. If so, don't lose hope.

The vocal father grabbed me the next morning. "I am so sorry that I attacked you as I did. . . . I was wrong to put you on the spot," he said. "Everything you said to us was biblical and right. The way you described what our relationship to our teenagers could be was beautiful. I was just discouraged because my relationship with my son is so far from that. We seem to be angry at one another all the time. He only talks to me when he has to and I seem only to talk to him when he is in trouble. Last night I just didn't see how to get from where we are to what you have described."

Mountains are not conquered in a single step. Relationships do not change overnight. Change is a process, not an event. God does his miraculous work of change through the small, faithful steps we take. That is what this chapter is about. We have discussed high goals for our teenagers. We have laid out three fundamental strategies for accomplishing those goals. This chapter is about the small steps that can change your relationship with your teenager, and the changes in you that God can use to change your teenager's life. These little steps will not be presented in any particular order of importance. Each is worth remembering. Emphasize and prioritize the ones that apply most to you.

Never give in to thinking it is too late. Many of you have read this book with remorse. You have wished that you had known this information sooner. You are tempted to think that the die is cast and that there is no hope for altering the dynamics of your relationship to your teenager. You are tempted to think that God has a poor sense of timing. The opposite is true. God knows when it is the exactly right moment to teach us. He is never early and never too late.

As long as your teenager is still alive and close enough for you to have a relationship, there is hope. Go to her and start fresh. Begin by asking for her forgiveness. Admit that your impatience, unforgiving spirit, selfishness, and self-righteousness have gotten in the way of the relationship God meant for you to have with her. Be specific in your confession. Next, tell her you have determined to establish a loving relationship with her, that you are committed to talking to her, and that her life is important to you, and you want to be a help wherever you can. Then begin to follow through.

I have seen relationship after relationship between parents and teenagers change dramatically because parents refused to be discouraged. They stepped out in humility and love and began to relate to their teenager in a new, more biblical way. Before long, the teenagers began to let down old walls of defensiveness and became open and communicative once again.

Stay calm. There is a God. He is in control. All that he does is good. He knows what he is doing even when we don't! As parents of teens, there are three things you can do to avoid panic, impulsive decisions, and making a tough situation worse.

First, make sure you listen well enough (and ask good enough questions) to get all the facts straight. Make sure that you have an accurate picture of what you are dealing with. Once my parents came home after an evening out to see my younger brother's head totally covered in a makeshift bandage we had fashioned from a bed sheet. He had hit his head on a radiator. My mom immediately panicked, started screaming, and was ready to call the ambulance. When my dad took off the wrapping, what he discovered was a fairly deep, but relatively small wound. My brother is still alive today! Take the time to get the facts.

Second, don't overreact emotionally. Don't give in to the impulses of anger. Don't give way to fear. Don't be overcome by discouragement. Take time to think, pray, and discuss things with your spouse before you talk with your teenager. So much relational and spiritual damage is done by parents who don't prepare themselves for those moments of trouble that are God-given opportunities to minister to your teenager.

Third, don't over-personalize your teenager's failure. Over-personalizing turns his failure into a personal offense against you. A father in my office angrily said to his son, who had failed two of his high school courses, "How could you do this to me after all that I have done for you?" He saw the failure as an act against him, not a God-given illustration of his son's struggle and need. Because of that, he was unable to minister to his son. He could not get past his own anger and hurt. It is hard to minister lovingly to your teenager when you are very angry at what he has done. Remember, "man's anger does not bring about the righteous life that God desires" (James 1:20).

Keep the conversation open. We were driving to the store and all of a sudden we were in a very important conversation. She was opening up, sharing her struggles at school in a way I had never heard before. As I dropped her off, it hit me that the most important thing I would do with that conversation would be what I did now that it was over. Many parents make the mistake of letting the open door of their teenager's self-disclosure close once again. They fail to keep the conversation open. They fail to pursue their teenager with expressions of concern, commitments to prayer, and simple questions of how it is going.

It is very helpful to get into the habit of doing regular checkups after an issue, problem, temptation, disappointment, fear, struggle, or failure has been disclosed. Is your teenager experiencing regular, ongoing temptation and is she succumbing to it? Are there new, related situations that she needs to discuss with you? What new questions or doubts have arisen? Does she feel that she has grown? I have gone back again and again to my daughter to talk about the subject she introduced that afternoon. I have learned more about her world and she has become less reserved in her communication. She knows I care, and she has come to believe that God does as well.

Demonstrate how the Bible interprets, explains, and organizes life.

Don't resort to on-the-fly, "This is what I think about it" or "Do it because I said so" responses. Your teenager needs confidence in Scripture as God's source of wisdom and understanding about life. He needs to grow in his ability to use this amazingly sufficient resource. Each situation provides an opportunity to help him realize that he is responding not simply to his experiences, but to his *interpretation* of those experiences. Each circumstance also provides an opportunity to demonstrate how the Bible makes sense out of the things your child faces each day. The goal is that he would really embrace Scripture as a "lamp to my feet and a light for my path" (Ps. 119:105).

Be willing to bare your own struggle. Many parents make the error of presenting a "just do it" view of life to their teenager. They minimize the reality and intensity of the struggle to live a pure, productive, and responsible life by failing to reveal their own struggles. They make it seem as if it is all a piece of cake to them. They subtly communicate that it works this way: you learn what is right and you just do it. Their impatience and frustration with their teenager often communicates an "I'm able to do it, why aren't you?" attitude. What comfort, instruction, wisdom, and hope can come when you share with your teenagers how you have struggled with the Goliaths in your life! (In 2 Cor. 1:3–11 Paul models this for us.)

Keep Christ and his work central. The most important relationship in your teenager's life is not his relationship with you, but his relationship with Christ. Your primary job is to lead your teenager to Christ in a spirit of worship, trust, and obedience. Be alert for opportunities to point to the forgiveness, deliverance, and power that is found in him. Make sure that all your instruction moves toward Christ.

Remember, sinners tend to be hiders. They tend to love darkness rather than light because their deeds are evil (John 3:19). They let shame and guilt drive them undercover. Christ gives your teenager a reason to come out of hiding into the light. Once your teenager begins to grasp the depth and magnitude of the grace of Christ, thoughts of hiding, denial, defensiveness, and blameshifting make no sense. The message of the grace of Jesus Christ needs to color each conversation.

Remember, too, that you have been called to incarnate Christ in your teenager's life. This means that it is not enough for you to speak of his grace; you must also be an example of it as you help your teenager deal with his own sins. Times of correction must not be times where a loud voice, pointed finger, inflammatory words, and stomping off in parental disgust are the norm. You can powerfully and pointedly discipline in an atmosphere of grace. If you fail to speak the truth in love, it will cease to be the truth as the purity of its content becomes corrupted by your frustration, impatience, and anger.

You're a sinner. Don't act surprised at your teenager's struggle with sin. You know that your teenager lives in a fallen world. You know that he is a sinner by nature. You know that Satan exists as a liar, schemer, and tempter. As a parent of a teen, you should not be shocked or surprised at the presence and power of sin in your child's life. You should expect war. You should come to your relationship with your teenager armed for war, not with him, but with the true enemy (see Eph. 6.). If you are honest about your own experience, you will recognize that the battle with sin still rages within you. (Read Paul's description of this war in Rom. 7.) You will recognize that it is dangerous for you to live with a relaxed, peace-time mentality. And you will acknowledge that this war will continue to be waged in your life and your teenager's until Christ returns.

This does not mean that we minimize sin. No, it means the opposite. When we respond with shock, we tend to minimize the reality and power of indwelling sin. This reaction tends to present sin as an aberration, as something out of the ordinary, rather than an ever-present element in every human situation, action, thought, desire, and word. The deepest issues of our teenagers' experience are not their pain and their loss of self-esteem, but their moment-by-moment struggle with rebellion and unbelief. Wise parents expect that battle, arm themselves for it, and teach their sons and daughters to use the effective weapons that only Christ can give.

Identify the "voices" in your teenager's life. Who are the people your teenager listens to and respects? Who has influence in his life? What are these people saying? When a child is young, his parents are almost the sole voices of influence in his life. But when the child goes off to school, many other voices enter his world. As we interact with our teenagers, there is always a sense in which we are in a debate with the other voices in their lives. What view of life is promoted by the friend, the rock band, the coach, the sitcom, the boss, the teacher, the magazine, the youth leader?

You will need to expose yourself to some of these voices. Listen to the CD while reading the lyrics printed on the case. Read the skateboard magazine. Sit down and watch the sitcom. Take time to get to know the coach and the teacher. Know what you are dealing with as you have those spontaneous, casual, but very critical conversations with your teenager. Determine to become familiar with the influential voices in the world inside his head. Your goal is to encourage his willingness to stand back and biblically evaluate the voices and the fruit of their influence in the way he thinks, speaks, and acts.

When you challenge the influential voices in your teenager's life, be sure you know what you are talking about. Parents often lose credibility because they are ill-informed. When you haven't done your homework, you will resort to stereotypes, generalizations, rumors, and straw man characterizations. This weakens your teenager's respect for the important things you have to contribute. She walks away thinking that you simply do not know what you are talking about. If you want to instruct your teenager effectively and help her to learn to filter the voices in her life, take time to do your research.

Plan for temptation. You live with certain temptations every day, some to which you are particularly susceptible. The same is true of your teenager. She lives in a world where temptation is a daily reality. It is not enough to point out temptation after the fact in a "this is what you should have done" conversation. All of us need to teach our sons and daughters to look ahead and identify the potholes in the road so that they do not "drive" into them once again.

We need to establish a *temptation plan* with our teenagers. First, find out where the teen is currently struggling with temptation. Then, with each temptation devise a concrete "what to do when" plan of escape, always being careful to point the teenager to the resources found in the Lord Jesus Christ. Finally, revisit and revise the plan periodically. Are the means of escape sufficient and practically workable? Is the teenager taking the way of escape that the Lord has provided? Are there new temptations that need to become part of the plan? The result will be a teenager who is becoming wise about temptation, increasingly appreciative of your practical help, and confident in the Lord's deliverance.

Make accountability your teenager's responsibility. If your teenager will admit that he is less than perfect, if he will admit that daily, in word, thought, or deed, he does things that he should not do, if he will admit that he does not yet know everything, if he will recognize that he lives in a fallen world where there are temptations to do wrong all around him, if he will admit that there are times when he is blind to his own weakness and wrong, then what he is saying is that he is a person in need of help.

A teenager who has recognized that he needs help isn't irritated when it is offered. He doesn't run away from it; rather, he seeks it out. It doesn't make any sense to recognize physical sickness and avoid the doctor, or to go to the doctor and refuse to follow his healing advice. In the same way, a teenager who has begun to recognize the war with sin will seek out help. He will want to have people in his life who love him enough to have conversations, to ask questions, to hold him accountable.

There is an important principle of personal ministry here. Accountability always works when the person being held accountable wants the help and seeks to be accountable. God's world is big. There are always places to hide. An army of people cannot successfully hold a person accountable who does not want the help. We need to acknowledge to our teenagers that we will never be successful in following them into the secret corners of their lives if they don't want us there. If they want to, they will be able to hide from us. We need to teach them that maturity means admitting the need for help and seeking it out. Mature teenagers grow in their willingness to recognize their need, spend less time running away from help, and spend more time seeking it out.

Be a good listener and a good observer. Parenting is doing home-based pastoral work. Like a pastor, parents are called to watch for the souls of those under their care. People who are successful at soul care are not just good students of Scripture; they are also good students of their "congregation." As parents, God has placed a "congregation" under our daily care, but many of us lack a *soul care* or *shepherding* model of parenting. Our model is more of a "control behavior, regulate outcomes" model. Many who are in the midst of parenting teens tend to forget the powerful things that the Bible has to say about the heart.

If you understand your parental mission as shepherding the heart or caring for the soul, you will want to know well the children God has placed in your care. You are going to want to model the Wonderful Counselor, who is able to sympathize with our weaknesses and give us mercy and grace in our time of need because He took the time to get to know us and our world (see Heb. 4:14ff.). To model Christ, we need to slow down our lives so that we have time to listen to our teenagers and observe what they do. Many spend little time with their teenagers and when they do, they are the ones doing the talking. This tends to be the case because they are around them only during moments of correction.

The words of your teenager should be important to you. What do his casual observations about life tell you about his heart? What kind of advice does he give his younger siblings? What do his peer interactions tell you about what is going on inside? What do you learn about caring for his soul from the interpretations he makes about his life? Where do you hear words of anger, disappointment, regret, fear, cynicism, and loss? Do you hear words of faith, truth, and hope? What is the content of his God-talk? What is the content of his self-talk? We need to be students of our teenagers' inner worlds.

The actions of your teenager need to be important to you. How does he respond to you? To his siblings? To his friends? How does he deal with responsibilities at home, work, or school? How does he treat possessions—his own and others? How does he respond to authority figures in his life? What does he do when he faces decisions? How does he deal with the problems he encounters? How does he respond to conflict? Do you see evidences of a heart that wants to do what is right? Do you see humility, love, and patience? Are there places where he gives and situations where he serves? Is his life self-absorbed and self-focused? Watch, remembering that our teenagers speak and act out of the heart. As we observe them, God is revealing to us the fruit of root issues in the heart.

Don't give in to "problem allergy." Many parents seem to have allergic reactions to the problems their teenagers bring into their lives. Their responses to those problems tend to be swollen and inflamed. They try to avoid knowing about their teens' problems (don't ask, don't tell), and they long for days where everything goes smoothly (no muss, no fuss). When we live this way, we are losing sight of what God is doing in our teenager's life and what he desires to do through us.

Two biblical principles should be constantly kept in focus. The first is that God is at work in every situation to accomplish what is redemptively good. From his perspective there are no out-of-control moments. He is good and he is always sovereignly working for the good (Rom. 8:28ff.). The second principle is that trial is one of the main tools God uses to mature and complete us. We cannot give in to thinking that difficulty comes because God is absent or passive. He is in the difficulty, using it as an instrument of maturity (James 1:2–8).

These two principles should radically alter the way we think about and respond to problem situations with our teenagers. We have to argue with ourselves against a disaster mentality. Those dark days are meant by God to be times of growth and repentance. These are the times when God is exposing the hearts of our sons and daughters for the purpose of rescuing them from the domain of darkness and transporting them to the kingdom of his dear Son (Col. 1:13–14). Rather than getting angry and frustrated—lashing out at our teenagers and telling them they are wrecking our lives—we need to see these tough times as huge, God-given redemptive opportunities. In everything that we say and do, we need to commit ourselves to being part of what God is doing in their lives. These are God's moments. We cannot lose sight of him and give in to responses of anger, fear, and hopelessness.

Finally, we need to be humble enough to admit that we tend to be "problem allergic" because we tend to live selfishly rather than redemptively. We want regularity, peace, comfort, and ease. We want our lives to be predictable and unencumbered. The problems that our teenagers bring home are an intrusion on our desires and plans for our lives. We tend to get angry, not because they are messing up their own lives, but because they are messing up ours. We get captivated by our own plan, and we tend to lose sight of God's. We begin to think of our children as agents for our happiness, rather than remembering that we are called to be God's agents of growth in godliness for them. So in times of trouble, we angrily fight for our dream instead of happily doing God's work. If we are ever consistently going to see problems as opportunities, we need to begin with humble confession of our selfishness to the Lord.

Always keep the heart in focus. Don't give in to a parenting lifestyle in which pronouncements and lectures are delivered with an edge of irritation. Don't settle for getting your teenager to do what you want him to do. I have watched parents embarrass their teen in front of others, manipulate their teen with things, threaten him with ultimatums, load him with guilt, and even use the Gospel in a manipulative way, in an attempt to produce the behavior they want at that moment. Our job is to draw out the purposes of our teenager's heart (Prov. 20:5). In every situation we need to ask what heart issues God is seeking to expose and how we can be his instruments in the process.

We need to enter each situation with soft answers, with penetrating questions that cannot be answered without self-disclosure, and with a willingness to take time to listen, observe, and discuss. We need to enter armed with the Gospel of grace and hope. We need to tell stories that engage the heart and stimulate the conscience. We need to be willing to bare our own struggle. We need to do everything we can to get our teenagers to step out of their defensiveness and look at themselves in the perfect mirror of the Word. We need to do all of this remembering that the words and actions we are dealing with are the fruit of thoughts and motives that have taken root in our teenager's heart. We do not want to settle for being fruit pickers when we can be root diggers. Lasting change in our teenagers always begins at the level of the heart.

Do your biblical homework first. Our job as parents is not to clone ourselves in our children, getting them to submit to our style, our desires, and our preferences. Our goal is that they would live lives submissive to the God's will as revealed in his Word. Our job is not to produce ourselves in our teenagers, but Christ. So we need to prepare ourselves biblically for our own sakes, so that our responses would not be emotion-driven, but driven by biblical purpose. What is biblically important in each situation and how can we go after those issues?

We also need to do our biblical homework for the sake of our children. We should be able to demonstrate that what we are requiring of our teenagers is biblical. We should be able to demonstrate the way each situation is interpreted (made sense of) by the commands, principles, promises, and themes of Scripture. We want to model the Word in our behavior and teach our teenagers to look at life through the lens of the Word. We want to call them to be obedient to that Word. Our hope is that our sons and daughters would grow in their appreciation for Scripture and in their love for the God revealed in Scripture. Ultimately, our prayer is that they would live as people of the Word.

I am afraid that many of us fall short of these purposes because we are in too great a rush. We give in to impulsive reactions and allow our emotions to take over. We react quickly and we want change to result quickly. We enter the scene unprepared to think and respond biblically, and we end up saying things we regret and announcing punishments we will not enforce. In the process, God's purposes and the resources of Christ get completely lost. Advance biblical preparation wards off a lot of this.

Always talk to your teenager lovingly and constructively. This seems so obvious that it doesn't seem worth mentioning. However, we need to be aware of the temptation to talk to our teenagers in a way that is less than biblical. There are several reasons we are tempted to do so. First, living with a teenager means living with the unexpected. Life is often more disordered than ordered. These years we are often hit with things we didn't see coming and for which we feel unprepared. We often give in to speaking out of our unpreparedness.

Second, in the ever-widening world of a teenager with more activities, more responsibilities, and a wider circle of relationships, our teenager doesn't tend to be around as much as he once was. When the already busy life of the family combines with the frenetic life of a teenager, there often isn't much down time left. We tend to get into trouble when we try to squeeze significant conversation into brief little moments along the way. We resort to trying to talk as the teen is running out the door, as he is gulping down his breakfast, or as we happen to be briefly in the car together. When the teenager is not receptive, we take offense, and the conversation heads in the wrong direction.

Third, the teen is aware that he is growing up, and out of this awareness comes a desire to be independent. This is not, in and of itself, a bad thing. However, it can create tension during times of discussion. The teenager will tend to see our interventions as a failure to recognize his maturity, and he will tend to respond defensively. He will start out thinking that he does not need the help that is offered. (Obviously, we need to admit humbly that teenagers are not the only ones who have this struggle.) When the teen does not receive our help with appreciation, parents tend to get hurt, frustrated, or irritated, and lash back emotionally by making some disparaging comment. The teenager responds in kind, and the conversation takes a negative turn.

One final point, maybe the most important of all. Teenagers will instinctively find and trash our idols. (Surely, this is God's doing rather than our teenager's intent.) Our sons and daughters will tend to find our "hot buttons" and regularly press them. If we have an inordinate love for things, the teenager will dent the car the first time he drives it alone. In his nervousness to explain what happened, he will inadvertently sit on—and break—the plastic cover to the new stereo, while spilling his soda on your new oriental rug! There is a great temptation to lash out and say, "Why don't you just trash every valuable thing in the house? It seems to be the one thing you're good at!" This is but one example of a very important principle we need to keep in mind. *Our communication problems with our teenager exist not simply because of our child's character, but also because of our idolatry.* When desire for things (possessions, positions, love, respect, appreciation, peace, comfort) takes the functional rulership over our hearts that the Lord alone should have, the result will inevitably be conflict in our relationships (see James 4:1–10).

When tempted to communicate with our teenagers unbiblically, we need to examine ourselves. Paul reminds us of three important things here: "Be completely humble and gentle; be patient, bearing with one another in love." "Speak the truth in love." "Do not let any unwholesome talk come out of your mouths, but only what is helpful for building others up . . ." (Eph. 4:2, 15, 29). These commands must guide our communication with our teenagers. What do they look like in practice?

This kind of communication avoids an "us versus them," adversarial stance. Rather, we will stand alongside our teenagers as those who fully understand their struggles. We will not stand above them as those who can't relate to their failure and are irritated by it. There is no place for a "know-it-all," "I have all of the answers and none of the questions" mentality. We want to stand with our teenagers as people who are still being taught by the Lord and still learning how to properly apply his truth to life.

Communicating biblically also means learning to respect perspectives and accept differences. Our teenagers are going to look at life differently than we will. Our goal isn't perfect agreement with us on all things, but their faithful submission to the Lord and his truth. Communicating biblically means taking time to listen to the content, emotions, and intentions that are communicated in everything our teenager says. It will mean learning to ask good questions instead of entering the room making accusations. It will mean learning to lead the teenager to confession, instead of making confession for him.

As we talk to our teenagers, we need to be careful to correct without belittling. We need to be patient, realizing that change may not happen in one sitting. We need to be willing to come back again and again, giving the Spirit time to work in our teenager's hearts. We need to learn how to accept and love while disapproving. We need to learn to acknowledge respectfully those things our sons and daughters think are important. We need to avoid clichés and overused stories that cheapen conversation and cause the teenager to hit the mental "kill" switch. We need to minimize the use of personal examples that tend to communicate that we went through the teen years without difficulty, or that we are presently perfectly righteous and struggle-free. And we need to try not to over-personalize or catastrophize the problems we encounter with our teens.

Since it is only by the power of Christ that we can do these things, we need to greet each day saying, "Father, we want to follow your example as we parent our teenagers, yet daily we find ourselves falling short in many ways. Today we ask that you would empower us so that we may use every situation to think, speak, and act in a way that pictures you and what you, through your Son, have done for us."

Be willing to overlook minor offenses. Everything in your teenager's life is not of equal importance. You do not want to go after all failures with the same intensity and seriousness. The hairstyle is not as important as the disrespect. The less-than-perfect table manners are not as important as the growing materialism that is eating away the teenager's heart. The room that is not immaculate is not as important as temptations to lust and sexual sin. The point is not that the hair, the manners, and the room are unimportant, but that they are minor in comparison to the other things.

Love is willing to overlook minor offenses. Wisdom lives with a sense of priority, with a biblical sense of project. We must not have "life as a final exam" relationships with our teenagers, where they are constantly evaluated and incessantly critiqued. We don't want them to feel that they can never relax and must always be on their guard. Rather, our life with our teenagers needs to be shaped by unfailing grace, boundless love, and persevering patience. In short, our life with them must be shaped by Christ. As we, by his grace, incarnate him before our children, we will be able to greet failure with grace, and they will be encouraged to live honestly and in the open.

Always deal honestly with your own attitudes. Remember, your teenager is not the only sinner in the house. God is still working to conform *us* to the image of his Son. There is still sin remaining in every parent of every teenager. Because of this, it is vital that we not only have an eye toward them, but also toward ourselves. We need to face humbly our own defensiveness, our own selfishness, our own self-righteousness, our own anger, and our own impatience. We need to regularly go to God and our teenagers and ask for forgiveness.

Your spouse can help you here. Remember that sin is deceitful: you will tend to see the speck of dust in your neighbor's eye and not even notice the log jutting out of your own. Ask for help in evaluating your attitude and actions toward your teenager, and be willing to receive it even when you have not asked for it.

There are many biblical attitudes that should be our personal goals as we parent our teenagers. First, we must always do what we do because we are committed to live to God's glory. This must be the desire that overwhelms all others. We must be people who have forsaken bitterness and the willingness to hold a grudge. We must be willing to forgive our teenagers over and over again. We must not only be lawgivers, detectives, and judges. We must hold God's high standard before our teenagers in a patient spirit of love, mercy, and grace. We must be people who speak carefully, who promise cautiously, and who are always true to our words. We must be people who can be fully trusted by our teenagers. We must always do what we have said and follow through with all of our commitments.

As we have already stated, it is vital that we bring a spirit of humility to our relationship with our teenagers. We must commit ourselves to being approachable. We must always be willing to admit, confess, and forsake our wrongs. Finally, we must continue to examine whether our relationship to our teenagers is being shaped by a heart-felt concern for their spiritual well-being or by our own selfishness and self-interest (see Phil. 2:1–12).

Expect, welcome, and respect differences. God is glorious in his creativity! Look at the human face. There are no two noses alike! You would think that sooner or later God would simply run out of designs and begin to recycle old models. Yet the variety is as endless as his ability to create. Your teenager won't be just like you. There will be ways in which he will be very different. Don't see this as some kind of personal defeat; see it as a testimony to the glory and grandeur of God. Stand back and be amazed and amused that even within your own family gene pool there is such wide variety and difference! See differences not as a cause for consternation, but as a cause for worship.

Our second son is an artist. It didn't take long for me to realize that he was totally different from me. He simply does not see the universe the way I do. I remember when he was given an assignment in second grade to write a one-paragraph composition on the Revolutionary War. This assignment was to be done with a parent. He came into the house announcing that we had homework to do together. After he had explained the assignment, I thought it would be a piece of cake.

We live in Philadelphia, so writing about the Revolutionary War would be no problem. I asked my son what topic he had chosen. He said, "Architecture during the Revolutionary War." I couldn't believe my ears. I looked at this scruffy, smiling, little boy and wondered how he had come up with that! So I asked him and he said, "Daddy, today as the teacher was reading to us about the battles, I just kept thinking, *But what did the buildings look like?*" "*What did the buildings look like?*" I thought. "*Who cares about the buildings! What about George Washington, Valley Forge, Ben Franklin, and the Declaration of Independence?*"

That little boy is now a young man in art college. I wonder at the gift that God has given him. I am so glad that he is not like me! He has opened my eyes to parts of the world I would never have seen. He has contributed to my life and to our family in ways I could never express. I worship God for creating my son as he is and for the ways we are different. Yet I am still aware of the irritation that those differences can create and the tendency that is still there to wish he were like me.

We need to be careful to distinguish between difference and sin, between alternative perspectives and rebellion against authority. We need to see the difference between an appropriate choice and disobedience. We need to wisely welcome and encourage differences while lovingly confronting sin.

Look for opportunities to put your teenager in the decision-making role. The Bible teaches us that maturity comes as the result of practice (see Heb. 5:11–14). If we want to send young adults out into the world who are prepared to make wise and godly decisions, we need to give our teenagers opportunities to hone that skill. We tend to struggle with this for the same reason that the boss of a company struggles with delegating authority. We don't want to have to clean up after someone else's failure, so we decide that we will not put them in the position where it can happen.

We need to school our teenagers in the decision-making process (thinking, deciding, acting, reaping consequences, and evaluating). To do this, we need to resist the temptation to see an ordered life as more important than developing in them the ability to make wise and mature decisions. We must resist the temptation to turn back the clock when our teenagers fail, once again taking over their decisions. Finally, we need to resist making arbitrary regulations. Our teenagers should have as wide a belt of freedom as Scripture allows so that they can learn the skills of wise living.

Humbly admit your limits. Always remember that you are not God. (This will surprise no one but you!) Unlike him, you and I have limits to our strength and wisdom. There is a limit to the change we can create. Change in the hearts and lives of our teenagers is always the result of the gracious work of God. We must not try to do, by human force, what only God can do. We will never force our teenagers to submit and obey, because submission is by definition the willing act of a heart that belongs to God. We are not the authors of change; we will never be anything more or less than instruments in the hands of the One who creates change. We should not try to do his work, but instead be people who understand what it means to pray without ceasing.

In all these things, we must remember the truths of the Word. We are not alone (Josh. 1:1–9). God is an ever-present help in times of trouble (Ps. 46). He is at work in every situation, location, and relationship to accomplish what is good (Rom. 8:28ff.). He is powerfully at work in *us* to accomplish things that are greater than anything we could ask or imagine (Eph. 3:14–20). We do not need to be afraid of our weaknesses, because his grace is sufficient and his strength is made perfect when we are weak (2 Cor. 12:7–10). We have already been given in Christ everything we need to do God's will (2 Peter 1:3–4). God has promised to give us wisdom without favoritism (James 1:5). He is gracious and just to forgive us and to cleanse us from all unrighteousness (1 John 1:9). Because of the victorious work of Christ, our labors in his name are never in vain (1 Cor. 15: 58). A day is coming when this struggle will be over and there will be no more sin or sorrow (1 Cor. 15:50–57).

What do these promises do for us? They totally change the way we think about the job of parenting our teenagers. Our goal cannot be survival. This goal is too low because it forgets the glorious things that God is doing in us and has promised to do through us. Ours is a wonderful opportunity—to be a daily part of God's glorious work of redemption. We could not have a higher calling! We need to see our parenting task as more than a duty. It is a great privilege. How could it be that God would entrust such a significant task to us? We need to embrace our calling with hope. He *is* here, he *is* at work! We have a reason to get up in the morning, reminding ourselves that our lives have eternal meaning and purpose! We have reason to step out in faith and do with courage the things God has called for us to do as we parent our teenagers.

May God fill you with the knowledge of his glory as you serve him by parenting those he has placed in your care.

Study Guide

STEP back for a moment from the daily pressures, interactions, and decisions of child rearing to reflect on our calling as parents. God has chosen us to be part of the most significant work on earth—the formation of a human soul. He has called us to prepare human beings for life in a broken and fallen world. He has commissioned us to teach young hearts how to think, desire, and choose. He has allowed us to be his voice as he unfolds the deepest mysteries of the universe to children who are still learning how to think. Most importantly, he has called us to help rescue them—not just from an evil world, but from their own sinful and foolish hearts—by leading them to Christ. There is no higher, more holy calling than this!

Much of this work takes place in the teen years. As teens assume greater responsibilities, enjoy new relationships, and experience greater independence, their hearts are exposed. This provides us with some of the deepest heartaches and greatest opportunities of our parenting years.

The question is, Are we ready to make the most of the opportunities? The answer is, Only as God enables us. As parents, most of us long for comfort and peace. We instinctively hate the tumult that teenagers bring into our lives. We don't like wondering what will come next as our lives career from crisis to crisis. Yet standing in the middle of this turmoil is Christ the Redeemer. He really *is* "an ever present help in trouble." He really *is* up to something good. In his love for our teens, he fights for their hearts by exposing them to us, so that he can use us to turn their hearts to him.

This is a drama of eternal significance, but it is easy to miss, even when it is happening right in front of us. It takes place in the mundane little moments and

255

the boring, familiar locations of our daily lives. That's why we need to open our eyes to what is happening around us. Life is not lived in the "grand" moments of existence! Most of us only make three or four big decisions in a lifetime. Most of us will never be written up in history books. Not long after our deaths, the ones we leave behind will struggle to remember us. The fact is that most of the important things we do will take place *in the midst* of the utterly mundane. *This* is the place where God does his miraculous work of reclaiming and redirecting hearts. He is the sovereign Lord of the everyday and ordinary! His glory is waiting to be revealed in every little moment. As we see this, we can share it with our teenagers.

One more thing should be said about this glorious task of parenting: we are not up to the job! We simply don't have the love, patience, wisdom, and perseverance it requires. We are parents who still need parenting ourselves. We are wisdom givers who find ourselves in the grip of our own foolishness. We are sinners calling our teenagers away from sin. We are idolaters who want to help our teenagers smash their idols. We fall woefully short of the job description!

Yet there is hope when we face our foolishness and inability. The hope is found in Christ. *He* is our wisdom! *He* is our strength! His grace reaches to the deepest level of our weakness. He died not only to give us eternal life, but also to give us everything we need to do what he calls us to do in the here and now. He *does* meet the demands of our job description and we find our capability in him. Because of him, we can approach this awesome task with courage and hope. He is here in his power and glory, and he is for us!

This truth is the foundation for *Age of Opportunity* and this study guide. (For a free Leaders Guide, visit our websites: www.ccef.org and www.prpbooks.com.) The guide is meant to help you deepen your knowledge of yourself and your teenager, and increase your practical skill at being part of what God is doing in his or her life. Take time to answer the questions that reinforce the essentials of a chapter. Prayerfully work through the personal evaluations, asking God to reveal your heart. Humbly confess. Joyfully commit to new ways of parenting. Look expectantly for a harvest of new fruit.

My sincere thanks go to Amy Knicely, who did the major work on the study guide. I have added chapter summaries and core goals. These together give you a biblical model for approaching the teen years.

May God richly bless you as you work through this guide. May he demolish strongholds in you and your teenager. May he deepen his claim on your heart and, in so doing, position you to minister to your teenager's heart. Finally, may he give you a sense of the magnificence of his grace and the stunning wisdom of his Word—and may this direct the way you walk with your teenagers through the familiar rooms of their everyday world.

Paul David Tripp
March 14, 2001

1 AGE OF OPPORTUNITY OR SEASON OF SURVIVAL?

Core principle We live in a culture of cynicism when it comes to teenagers. This cultural negativity has infiltrated the Christian family as well. This cynicism has its roots in a biological view of teenagers that sees them as little more than a collection of raging, rebel hormones, physically incapable of living responsibly.

Chapter goals Our goal is to help parents identify the ways in which the cynicism of the culture has influenced the ways they think about and respond to their teenage children. This chapter also calls parents to learn to recognize the big moments of change that are embedded in the little of moments of life that we share with them. We want to look for daily opportunities to be part of what God is doing in the life of our teenagers. Finally, this chapter is meant to help parents recognize attitudes that stand in the way of what God is seeking to do through them in their teenagers' lives.

Study Questions

1. What attitude do many parents have toward the teen years?
2. What does it mean to have a biological view of teens?
3. What parenting goal typically flows from a biological view of teens?
4. What view of God's Word is demonstrated in a biological view of teens?
5. What would be a naive view of the teen years?
6. What does the author mean when he says that the battle raging in the lives of young people is not the battle of biology but a battle for the heart?
7. Why is the battle for the heart so dramatically important?
8. What does the author mean when he says that the struggle of the teen years is not only about teen biology and teen rebellion?
9. What kinds of things might teens expose in the lives of their parents?
10. What heart issues are displayed in the father described on pages 18 and 19?
11. What is the significance of the author's statement that we live in the world of the incredibly mundane?

12. What three fundamental doors of opportunity exist for every parent of teens?
13. What desires make teenagers susceptible to the temptation to rebel?
14. List some truths that can help teens handle their widening world.
15. What truths can help parents escape a cynical view of the teenage years?

Application Questions

1. Cite an example from your experience (with others or your own life) that illustrates the way parents see the teen years as something to be dreaded.
2. Evaluate the way you respond to trials. Use the following rating scale:

    1 - Rarely
    2 - Occasionally
    3 - Regularly

With self-righteousness	1 2 3
With impatience	1 2 3
With an unforgiving spirit	1 2 3
With a lack of servant love	1 2 3
Showing weak faith	1 2 3
Craving comfort and ease	1 2 3

3. Think of the last three trials you faced. Describe the trial and then describe what Christ-like (or unChrist-like) characteristics you displayed in each.
4. List the ministry opportunities that are present in the following scenarios:
    * The last Pop Tart.
    * The cry of nothing to wear half an hour before school.
    * The report card crumpled in the pocket of jeans headed for the wash.
    * The pouting expression when the parent says "No."
    * The third fender-bender in a month.
    * Constant words of discontent.
    * "Everybody else does."
    * "I'm the only one whose parents make them . . ."
5. What biblical principles can help a teen struggling with his or her looks?

2 WHOSE IDOLS ARE IN THE WAY?

Core principle The anger, frustration, discouragement, irritation, impatience, and fear that parents feel during the teen years not only reveal that the teen is struggling, but that the parents are as well. If our hearts are controlled by something other than God, the great opportunities of the teen years will not be viewed as opportunities at all, but as a constant stream of hassles brought on by a selfish, immature person who upsets our otherwise comfortable life. Failure to deal with our idolatry will mean we will turn God-given moments of ministry into moments of anger. We will personalize what is not personal, become adversarial in our approach to our teen, and settle for quick, situational solutions that do not focus on the teenager's heart.

Chapter goals The goal of this chapter is best summarized by Proverbs 20:5, "The purposes of a man's heart are deep waters, but a man of understanding draws them out." The goal is that parents would use the mirror of the Word (Luke 6:34–36; Ezek. 14:1–5; James 4:1–10) to examine their hearts. Which of the typical parental idols listed below best describes you?

Comfort ("I just wish life were a little easier, a little more peaceful, and a little more predictable.")

Respect ("If it is the last thing I do, I am going to get her to respect me!")

Appreciation ("I have done and done for them and this is the thanks I get? It is about time that I got a little credit for all of my hard work!")

Success ("Do you know what it is like to do all this work and have him behave this way? What are people thinking about our family now?")

Control ("If I had a little more control around here, life would be much easier and he would be in far less trouble!")

The goal is that parents would understand that they must be willing to start with their own hearts if they want to be used by God to help transform the hearts of their teenagers. If we do not do this, we will be a hindrance, not a help, in what God is doing.

Study Questions

1. What is an idol?
2. Why is it a waste of time for parents to think about strategies for parenting without first examining themselves?
3. What is wrong with wanting life to be a resort?
4. Why will parents who demand comfort, ease, regularity, peace, space, quiet and harmony be ill-equipped to fight the war they are called to fight?
5. How might an idol of respect manifest itself?
6. Since children should appreciate their parents, what is wrong with parents having this as their goal?
7. What questions can parents ask themselves to avoid making appreciation their goal?

8. What is wrong with the belief that if parents do their part, their children will be model citizens?
9. Since it is so easy to lose sight of the fact that these are God's children, what should parents remind themselves of regularly?
10. List three truths from God's Word that are vital to remember if we want to avoid an idol of control.

Application Questions

1. Do you have an idol of comfort? Give specific reasons for your answer.
2. Evaluate the way you respond when your comfort is challenged. Use the following rating scale:

    1 - Rarely
    2 - Occasionally
    3 - Regularly

Fail to be effective and productive in strategic ministry moments	1 2 3
Tend to see the teen as the enemy	1 2 3
Tend to fight *with* teen rather than *for* him or her	1 2 3
Tend to do and say regrettable things	1 2 3

3. Give a recent example of a situation in which your comfort was disrupted. Record how you responded.
4. Rate yourself on how frequently you function as though you were entitled to this "right."[1] Use the following rating scale:

    1 - Rarely
    2 - Occasionally
    3 - Regularly

1. Right to have and control personal belongings	1 2 3
2. Right to privacy	1 2 3
3. Right to have and express personal opinions	1 2 3
4. Right to earn and use money	1 2 3
5. Right to plan your own schedule	1 2 3
6. Right to respect	1 2 3
7. Right to have and choose friends	1 2 3
8. Right to belong, be loved, be accepted	1 2 3
9. Right to be understood	1 2 3
10. Right to be supported	1 2 3

---

1 Adapted from *A Homework Manual for Biblical Living, Volume* 1, by Wayne A. Mack (Phillipsburg, N.J.: P&R Publishing, 1979), pp. 5-6.

11. Right to make your own decisions   1 2 3
12. Right to determine your own future   1 2 3
13. Right to have good health   1 2 3
14. Right to have pleasure   1 2 3
15. Right to have comfort   1 2 3
16. Right to have ease   1 2 3
17. Right to be considered worthwhile and important   1 2 3
18. Right to be protected and cared for   1 2 3
19. Right to be appreciated   1 2 3
20. Right to have time off   1 2 3
21. Right to have harmony   1 2 3
22. Right to have quiet   1 2 3
23. Right to have predictability and a regular schedule   1 2 3
24. Right to be treated fairly   1 2 3
25. Right to be desired   1 2 3
26. Right to have fun   1 2 3
27. Right to raise children your way   1 2 3
28. Right to security and safety   1 2 3
29. Right to fulfilled hopes and aspirations   1 2 3
30. Right to be successful   1 2 3
31. Right to have others obey you   1 2 3
32. Right to have your own way   1 2 3
33. Right to be free of difficulties and problems   1 2 3

Are we really entitled to anything?

5. Do you have an idol of respect? Give specific reasons for your answers.

6. Describe a recent situation in which you were not shown proper respect. How did you respond?

7. Describe a time when you did something for someone else and received no appreciation. What was your response?

8. How do you generally respond when you are not appreciated?

9. On the scale of 1 to 3 below, rate yourself on the following:

   1 - Rarely

   2 - Occasionally

   3 - Regularly

   Do you have an attitude of ownership and entitlement?   1 2 3
   Have you subtly become ruled by reputation?   1 2 3

Is it a struggle to love your child? Is your relationship distant
because of that struggle?   1 2 3
Are you oppressed by what others might think?   1 2 3
Have you ever doubted the principles of God's Word and
wondered why they haven't worked for you?   1 2 3

10. Do you have an idol of control? Give specific reasons for your answers.

3 WHAT IS A FAMILY? A DEFINITION

Core principle In Deuteronomy 6, God makes it very clear that he intends
the family to function as his primary learning community. God has ordained that
children would learn the most fundamental facts (truths) of human existence in
the context of the family. The family is the best place for this to happen because,
unlike a separated classroom, *life* takes place in the family. The many experiences
and relationships that make up daily family life present natural opportunities to
talk with our children about things that really matter. To understand the importance of the family's educational calling, parents need a biblical understanding of
who their children are. Parents will relate to their teenagers based on the way
they have defined them.

Chapter goals The goal is to help parents think in a distinctly biblical way
about their teenager's basic makeup as a creature of God. First, the Bible would
call us to view our teenagers as *covenantal beings*. This means that teenagers
were made for a relationship with God. They were created to be worshippers,
and if they do not worship God, they will give their hearts to God substitutes.
(See Rom. 1:25.) Second, we must see our teenagers as *social beings*. They were
made to live in loving community with others. In fact, God has given them the
moral responsibility to live with their neighbor's welfare in view. Third,
teenagers are *interpreters*. This means that as they live life, they are always
seeking to organize, interpret, and explain what is going on around them—and
inside them. Teenagers think, so they do not live life based solely on the facts
of their experiences, but also on how they have interpreted those facts.
Teenagers are always assembling a functional worldview (God, self, authority,
responsibility, right and wrong, past, future, etc.) that shapes their choices and
behavior. As parents recognize the true identity of their teenagers, the goal is
that parents would also recognize the need for the family to function as a vibrant learning community.

Study Questions

1. What is shocking and sad about the situation in Judges 2:6–15?
2. What does Deuteronomy 6 say is God's purpose for the family?
3. What are some of the opportunities parents will have to teach as they live with their children?
4. What does the author mean when he says that children are covenantal beings?
5. If children do not live in joyful submission to God, what will happen?
6. What is wrong with the self-sufficient, self-made individualism of Western culture?
7. What does the author mean by his statement that children are interpreters?
8. What do we need in order to interpret life correctly?
9. What controls our behavior? Support your answer biblically.
10. What does the author mean when he says that much of what we call Christian parenting is nothing more than "fruit stapling"?
11. If the heart does not change, what kind of fruit will result?

Application Questions

1. Describe one of the last times you took the time to learn what your child was thinking. How long ago was it? How often do you take time to do this?
2. How often do you do this spontaneously as issues arise in the course of family life?
3. Describe a situation in which you learned what your children were thinking and worked to instill in them a biblical view of life.
4. Your teen yells, "Someone stole my bookbag!" What biblical principles would help this teen arrive at a different interpretation?
5. What heart issues might influence a bright student to get poor grades?
6. What heart issues might influence a sibling to borrow things without permission?
7. What would you say to the teen who mutters that she hates her face so much she is embarrassed to leave the house?
   Passages like Psalm 139 and Ephesians 2:10 point to God's perfect knowledge of each person and his loving purposes in creating them as they are, so that they can accomplish the work that God has tailor-made for them.

8. Give an example of a way that a teen might demonstrate worship, not of God, but of some aspect of the created world.
9. What would you want to teach the child who takes the last chocolate donut? What would you want to teach the children who did not get the last chocolate donut?

4 WHAT IS A FAMILY? A JOB DESCRIPTION

Core principle To follow God's design for the family, parents must do two things. First, they must approach parenting with an educator's mentality. It is not enough to tell your teenager what to do or to correct and discipline him when he has done wrong. Rather, we are to constantly look for teaching opportunities to help our teenager look at life from God's perspective. Second, parents need to know their subject matter. What are the foundational things that every teenager needs to know about life? This foundational body of thought can be organized into three areas:

The family as a theological community. Theology in its purest form is the study of God. All of life is connected to him. God (his existence, his character, and his plan) is the ultimate fact of human existence, and it is impossible to understand life if this fact is omitted. Since the "whole world is filled with his glory," family life presents daily opportunities to talk about him.

The family as a sociological community. Here we recognize the Second Great Command by looking for opportunities to teach our teenagers God's way of love. There is no better place to teach a teenager how to love his neighbor as himself, because in the family he is required to live with people with whom he did not choose to live.

The family as a redemptive community. Here the focus is on the gravity of our condition as sinners and the glories of God's provision of grace in Christ Jesus. As we teach the teenager to admit his sin, we point him to a God of love who has not offered him a *system* of redemption, but instead has given his Son as Redeemer. In Jesus we find the only true place of hope as we admit that we are fallen people living in a fallen world.

Chapter goals Our first goal is to encourage parents to structure their family life to promote this teaching function. We cannot hope to teach our children such important truths in forty-five second intervals between activities. Our second goal is to help parents to master these biblical themes themselves. A parent cannot give his teenager something that he does not have himself. Our final goal is that parents would grow in their ability to recognize the God-given teaching moments that are sprinkled throughout every day.

Study Questions

1. Why do we often present Bible passages out of context to our children, in the hope that it will somehow motivate them to do what is right?
2. What is theology?
3. What does this statement mean? "It is God's plan that the family function as a theological community."
4. All of life becomes meaningless unless it is rooted in what?
5. Why is there no divine 911 telephone line?
6. What do teens (and adults) tend to mistakenly believe is most important?
7. When teens express their desires as needs and demand that we fulfill them, how should we respond?
8. Many teens would say that all they want out of life is to be happy. What is wrong with this?
9. Why is it important that teens see their lives embedded in the story of God?
10. What does the author mean when he states that we live life in the utterly mundane?
11. Once one has biblically clarified one's responsibilities, what is the only proper response?
12. What is the teen's job in situations that are outside of his or her control?
13. What is wrong with the thinking of the girl who told her mom, "If it's the last thing I do, I am going to teach my brother to stay out of my room"?
14. When the parents tried to eliminate their children's arguments over the CD player by devising a weekly schedule for its use, what teaching opportunity did they miss?
15. Why is the family an ideal environment to uncover issues of the heart?
16. How does facing the harsh realities of the Fall revealed in family life pave the way for something wonderful?
17. How can the family function as a redemptive community?
18. What is the key to the family functioning a redemptive community?
19. Why is it helpful to recognize the utter impossibility of fulfilling the law?
20. Why do we often miss opportunities to "do redemption"?

21. What are you communicating when you ask a sinning child, "How could you?" or "Why would you?"

Application Questions

1. When Joey is mocked because of his "bobo" sneakers, how do you make that a teaching moment?
2. When Sarah tells you at 9:45 p.m. that she needs poster board for a project due the next morning, how do you make the most of this teaching opportunity?
3. When Josh stands in front of a well-stocked refrigerator and says there is nothing to eat, how do you capitalize on that moment?
4. When Pete walks in with hair that he has just dyed with lime Jell-O, what truths do you teach?
5. How would you respond to a child who asks, "Why do we have to obey all of these rules?"?
6. How could you respond to the son who says, "I just have to have those shoes! Dad, I need them!"?
7. How could you respond to the son who says, "No one wants to be friends with a kid who has character! All of the popular kids at school, all of the leaders, are jerks. They are the center of attention, they get all the girls, and here I am, a nice guy who can be trusted, and I have no friends! I'd be better off being a jerk! Why be good if nobody notices?"
8. Your daughter says, "If it's the last thing I do, I am going to teach my brother to stay out of my room!" In what areas does she need to learn to trust?
9. In what areas does she need to obey?
10. Give an example of a way a parent might respond self-righteously to his or her teen.
11. When was the last time you went to your children and confessed sin?
12. How can you model for children that there is a Redeemer who forgives, delivers, reconciles, and restores when they are fighting with one another?
13. List two occasions when you shared your struggle with sin to show your children the mercy of Christ.
14. For each of the following examples, write out two ways of handling it.
    In column 1 write a quick, surface solution that ignores the issues of the heart.
    In column 2 write a way to address the problem that develops a heart of Christ-like love.

Example	Column 1	Column 2
A fight over the last drop of milk at breakfast		
A shove in response to an accidental bump in the hallway		
An argument over time spent in the bathroom		
A discussion over borrowed clothes that weren't returned		
Willingness to participate in put-down humor		
A demand for assistance combined with an unwillingness to help others		
A lack of willing participation in household chores		
A debate over who gets the front seat of the car		

5 PARENTS, MEET YOUR TEENAGERS

Core principle We have already concluded that we cannot accept the current cultural definition of our teenagers. It is biologically based and does not recognize the teenager's heart. So we look to Scripture for help in defining our teens. The first several chapters of Proverbs define in practical life terms the typical struggles of youth. In so doing, the Proverbs give us a wonderful, functional definition of the teen years. As we recognize these common struggles, we also begin to recognize that our teenagers' struggles are not far from our own. As we admit this, we realize that, contrary to popular opinion, our teenagers are more like us than unlike us.

Chapter goals The goal is that our interactions with our teenagers would be (1) informed by a biblical understanding of their struggles and (2) infused with gospel hope. We want to become skilled at recognizing the doors of opportunity to lasting heart change that these struggles give us. When we recognize that our primary ministry opportunities come in moments of trouble, God can use us to prepare our teenagers to live responsibly before him, even after they have left our homes. The teenager's lack of hunger for wisdom and correction, tendency toward legalism, lack of wisdom in choice of companions, susceptibility to sexual temptation, lack of eschatological awareness, and lack of heart awareness all provide opportunities to prepare our teens for life by helping them to deal with their own heart issues. The goal is to help parents use the opportunities that are present amid trouble.

Study Questions

1. In Proverbs, the father emphasizes to his son that one thing is of great value and importance. What is it?
2. What can parents do to avoid inflammatory confrontations and verbal power struggles?
3. The author states that giving wisdom is not hitting your teen over the head with words. What is it?
4. What three things does the author do when his teens are being defensive?
5. For what things might a parent need to seek a child's forgiveness?
6. What should you do if you begin to lose it while talking to your teen?
7. How can a parent pursue his or her teens?
8. In what sense do teens tend to be legalists?
9. What kind of teaching should parents do to combat such legalism in their teens?
10. If you point out legalism and remind teens of the true spirit of God's requirements, how can this encourage in them a hunger for Christ?
11. To what does legalism lead?
12. How do teens tend to perceive a parent's rejection of their friends?
13. Rather than attacking their children's friends, how can parents help their teens in this area?
14. What is the key in helping our teens remain sexually pure?
15. What is eschatology?

16. What is meant by the statement that teens don't have an eschatological perspective?
17. How does our culture reinforce the falsehood that life is found in present, earthly, physical treasure and that the successful person is the one with the biggest pile?
18. What does Proverbs describe as the control center of our lives?
19. What higher agenda should parents have as they work with their teens?
20. What approach to discipline can help teens grow in self-awareness?
21. How will parents with a survival mentality of the teen years respond differently from those who see these years as a time of preparation?

Application Questions

1. Do you respond to your teen in ways that make wisdom appealing? How?
2. Do you make correction sweet? How?
3. Teens tend to push parents' buttons. What are some of your buttons?
4. What specific things do you do to pursue your teen?
5. How could you respond to a teen who attempts to avoid correction by pointing out flaws in your parenting?
6. Give two examples of ways you have seen teens emphasize the letter of the law rather than the spirit.
7. What are some biblical principles of friendship that you would want your teen to know and apply?
8. At what age will you bring up the topic of sex with your children? What will you do to keep it "on the table"?
9. What have your children learned from you about the sexual relationship?
10. Do you know if any of your children struggle with lust, fantasy, or masturbation?
11. How do your children view relationships with the opposite sex?
12. What are some of the world's sexual lies? Have your children been exposed to any of these? Have your children adopted any of them?
13. In what situations, locations, and relationships are your teens being tempted?
14. Do your teens feel comfortable discussing sexual issues with you? How do you know?
15. Give two examples of everyday issues your teens face that you can use to teach a focus on eternity.
16. How do you help your child recognize the desires that rule his or her heart?

6 GOALS, GLORY AND GRACE

Core principle The task of parenting a teenager is often exhausting and discouraging. Clearly, it is beyond the wisdom, character, and strength of every parent. It is very easy to give in to defeat, discouragement, and fear. When we do this, our encounters with our teenager are colored by our own hopelessness. Our only hope of loving and consistently doing what we have been called to do is Christ. In his presence and power we find strength to fulfill our calling. We must learn as parents what it means to live out of the rich resources of the gospel, refusing to give way to discouragement and despair and holding onto his promises.

Chapter goals The goal is to have the present benefits of the work of Christ give us hope as we struggle with our children through the teen years. The goal is to look at them and ourselves through the window of the gospel (Eph. 3:20; John 17:20–23; 2 Pet. 1:3–9). The goal is that there would be no struggle so grave as to lead us to give up, since Christ's work for us daily gives us reason to continue. The goal is that we would see the mountain range of the teen years from the vantage point of the majesty of Christ and his grace.

Study Questions

1. What encouragement does God's Word give us when we are weary and feel that we lack the strength to do what we have been called to do?
2. Why do we often miss the experience of God's power?
3. What kind of family unity is possible because Christ gave us his glory?
4. Why, according to 2 Peter 1:3–9, are believers ineffective and unproductive?
5. Why do many Christian parents lack the qualities needed to be effective?
6. Because God has already given us everything we need to do the parenting job he has called us to do, what should we *not* do?
7. What truths can lift us out of weariness and discouragement?

Application Questions

1. How would you characterize the unity in your home? (Circle one the following.)

   1 - Rarely is there any evidence of unity. Our home is characterized by discord and strife.

   2 - The members of our family don't live in discord and strife but each goes his or her own way. Apathy and indifference would describe us better than unity.

    3 - Unity comes and goes in our home. At times we work diligently to be unified but we are easily distracted.

    4 - Our home could be characterized by unity. This doesn't mean our home is perfect, but we are all working to grow in this area and we make a conscious effort to seek God's glory, not our own.

2. What would increase unity in your family?

3. Rate your efforts to grow in the following qualities. (Use the following scale.)

    1 - I rarely exert effort to grow in this quality.

    2 - I occasionally exert effort to grow in this quality.

    3 - I make regular effort to grow in this quality.

Faith	1 2 3
Goodness	1 2 3
Knowledge	1 2 3
Self-control	1 2 3
Perseverance	1 2 3
Godliness	1 2 3
Brotherly kindness	1 2 3
Love	1 2 3

4. Rate yourself: how much does each of the following characterize you when you are at the end of your strength?

    1 - Rarely

    2 - Occasionally

    3 - Regularly

I give in to discouragement.	1 2 3
I quit.	1 2 3
I run away.	1 2 3
I settle for a little bit of faith.	1 2 3
I grow.	1 2 3
I remember God's rich resources.	1 2 3
I seek to do more and better.	1 2 3
I remember I have been forgiven of my past sins.	1 2 3

7 THERE'S A WAR OUT THERE

Core principle Ephesians 6:10–18 provides a much-needed biblical view of life. Paul essentially says that life is war. He is not talking about the fights over situations and relationships that capture our thinking and emotions, but a deeper, more significant war. There is a war for the hearts of our teenagers that takes place in every situation, location, and relationship of daily life. This war is fought on the turf of their hearts. It is fought for control of their souls. Every decision, action, and word of our teenagers reflects this war. It is the great conflict of human life. This war is the reason for all the other wars fought between people. The problem is that our teenagers tend to live in a world that is shockingly physical; that is, they tend to live with little recognition of this great spiritual struggle. Teenagers' lives tend to be dominated by three concerns: appearance, possessions, and acceptance. They need to learn how to understand and participate in the deeper spiritual struggle.

Chapter goals The goal is to help our teenagers recognize the spiritual struggles beneath the seemingly mundane problems of daily life. In these moments, their hearts are progressively being given over to service of Christ or subtly being enslaved to the world. The goal is to teach our children to see how their words and behavior reflect the war that is going on in their hearts. Finally, we want to encourage them to take on the qualities of a successful spiritual warrior.

Study Questions

1. To keep difficult situations from driving a wedge of distance and anger between parents and teens, how should parents view the situations?
2. Why do parents need a concrete set of goals *before* they face difficult moments?
3. What goal should parents avoid?
4. If the parents' goal is control, how will they begin to function?
5. How might a parent try to motivate a child with guilt?
6. How might a parent try to motivate a child with fear?
7. How might a parent try to motivate a child by manipulation?
8. When we seek to inflict guilt, instill fear, and manipulate our children, how does it show that we are trying to do God's job?
9. Why will a rules-and-regulations approach fail?
10. How does a "pastoral" model of parenting differ from a rules-and-regulations approach?
11. What are some "heart-disclosing" questions parents could ask when their teens do wrong?
12. What attitudes should parents have in their encounters with their teens?

13. What two deadly lies do teens tend to believe?
14. What is the difference between a peacetime mentality and a war mentality?
15. What two things keep us from teaching our children to face and fight the spiritual battle?
16. Give an example of how parents might show a greater concern for what is seen than for the unseen.
17. What will result if parents are more concerned about the physical, seen world than the unseen, spiritual world?
18. What five qualities will be present in teens who understand and participate in the spiritual struggle?
19. What does it mean to have a fear of God?
20. Should we expect and accept rebellion in our teens? Why or why not?
21. If I reject God's authority, what, in fact, am I doing?
22. Evaluate this statement: If a teen is going to live a God-honoring life, he needs to acquire biblical knowledge.
23. What does it mean to be biblically self-aware?

Application Questions

1. Give two examples of times when you may have tried to motivate with guilt.
2. Give two examples of times when you may have tried to motivate with fear.
3. Give two examples of times when you may have tried to motivate by manipulation.
4. To what extent do you see yourself trying to motivate by guilt? (Circle one.)
   1 - This would be very uncharacteristic of me.
   2 - I do this occasionally but not habitually.
   3 - I do this habitually.
   If you gave yourself a 3, take the following steps. Put a check beside each step once completed.
   1. Seek God's forgiveness and your teen's forgiveness.
   2. Ask your teen and spouse to alert you when they see you functioning this way.
   3. When alerted, stop, seek forgiveness, and redo it the right way.
5. To what extent do you see yourself trying to motivate by fear? (Circle one.)
   1 - This would be very uncharacteristic of me.
   2 - I do this occasionally but not habitually.
   3 - I do this habitually.

If you gave yourself a 3, take the following steps. Put a check beside each step once completed.

1. Seek God's forgiveness and your teen's forgiveness.
2. Ask your teen and spouse to alert you when they see you functioning this way.
3. When alerted, stop, seek forgiveness, and redo it the right way.

6. To what extent do you see yourself trying to motivate by manipulation? (Circle one.)

   1 - This would be very uncharacteristic of me.

   2 - I do this occasionally but not habitually.

   3 - I do this habitually.

   If you gave yourself a 3, take the following steps. Put a check beside each step once completed.

   1. Seek God's forgiveness and your teen's forgiveness.
   2. Ask your teen and spouse to alert you when they see you functioning this way.
   3. When alerted, stop, seek forgiveness, and redo it the right way.

7. Think of a time when you had a conflict with your child and you asked questions to get to the heart. What specific questions did you ask?

8. With each of your children, evaluate their three best friends in terms of the following characteristics of biblical friends.

   1. My friend is fully devoted to God; he or she has a deep and meaningful relationship with God.
   2. My friend is loving.
   3. My friend is joyful.
   4. My friend is not quarrelsome.
   5. My friend is patient.
   6. My friend is gentle.
   7. My friend is generous, willing to share.
   8. My friend is dependable.
   9. My friend is kind.
   10. My friend is self-controlled, disciplined.
   11. My friend is honest.
   12. My friend is respected and valued by his or her family.
   13. My friend is devoted and loyal to his or her family.
   14. My friend is sensitive.

15. My friend fulfills God-given responsibilities.
16. My friend is friendly.
17. My friend builds up his or her family; my friend is an encourager.
18. My friend is devoted to ministering to others.
19. My friend is consistent and steadfast in doing right.
20. My friend is an industrious, hard worker.
21. My friend is unselfish.
22. My friend is more concerned about internal beauty than external beauty.
23. My friend takes care of him/herself physically; my friend is concerned about his or her appearance, but not excessively so.
24. My friend is not overly intense or serious; my friend is a fun person to be with.
25. My friend is content and satisfied; my friend desires growth, progress, and biblical change but is not overbearing about it.
26. My friend is a good listener.
27. My friend is thoughtful of others, putting them at ease, communicating respect and concern for them.
28. My friend's speech is constructive and wholesome.
29. My friend seeks to grow in wisdom, to sharpen him/herself intellectually.
30. My friend exercises foresight; my friend plans ahead.
31. My friend handles money wisely; my friend practices good stewardship.
32. My friend is grateful.
33. My friend is considerate.
34. My friend does not complain.
35. My friend takes care of problems quickly.
36. My friend is forgiving.
37. My friend is not stubborn.
38. My friend is not pushy.
39. My friend is submissive to authority.
40. My friend is willing to be vulnerable.

9. With each of your children, evaluate their ability to be a biblical friend in terms of the above list of characteristics.

10. Where are your children susceptible to temptation? How can you hold the mirror of God's Word before them in these areas? How can you help them anticipate temptation and teach them how to avoid it?

8 CONVICTIONS AND WISDOM

Core principle Often parents are so busy making decisions for their children that they do not impart to them the critical biblical thinking skills that will enable them to make sound choices after they have left the home. We need to be looking for opportunities to teach our children how to use the commands, themes, principles, and perspectives of Scripture to make sense out of life. To equip teenagers to determine how God would have them respond to the diverse situations of life, we need to teach them two things. First, they need internalized biblical convictions and applicable biblical wisdom. It is not enough to say "yes" and "no" to particular questions. We must show our children how we have arrived at the critical decisions that are so important to biblical living.

Chapter goals The goal is to help your teenager differentiate between boundary issues (issue of conviction where Scripture gives them a clear "thus says the Lord") and wisdom issues (places where there is no clear command, but many biblical principles that apply). We want to assist our children as they internalize biblical convictions, and we want to help them learn how to apply the wisdom of the Word to the everyday life decisions. To do this, it is not always best to say a quick "yes" or "no" to a moral question. It may be better to see the specific circumstance that prompted the question as a God-given opportunity to help the teenager to develop his internal convictions and apply them to his situation.

Study Questions

1. What are "clear boundary" issues?
2. What does a teen need to handle situations involving clear boundary issues?
3. For each of the following, indicate whether it is characteristic of a conviction or a preference.

   Based on truth.   Constant.
   Based on personal desire.   Demands faith.
   Changes with desire.   Relies on the emotions of the moment.
4. What are six characteristics of biblical conviction?
5. List six things you can do to help develop a sensitive conscience and a wise heart.

Application Questions

1. Describe a time in your life when you took a stand on something that was a clear boundary issue. Why did you do it? What was the outcome? What was your response to the outcome?

2. List at least eight biblical principles that would apply to the following situation: Your daughter has been nominated as homecoming queen at the local public high school.

3. List at least eight biblical principles that would apply to the following situation: Your son has been given a four-year athletic scholarship to a secular university.

9 LIFE IN THE REAL WORLD

Core principle Teenagers never live in a vacuum. They are always in contact with culture. Human beings made in the image of God interact with God's world and culture is what results. Culture is all the relationships, customs, institutions, structures, media, beliefs, arts, and values of any society of people. There is no way to escape the cultural struggle. We are always living under culture's powerful influence.

The Christian family has tended to respond to culture in two ways. Some seek to solve the problem of culture by attempting to live in isolation from it. This is a defective choice because the only way to escape human culture is to cease being a human being! (Where people go, there is culture.) This choice also ignores the Bible's call for the people of God to function as salt and light. Others make the choice to assimilate into the culture, thereby losing their distinctive place as ambassadors of Christ. We must teach our teenagers a third way, and show them how to participate in their culture in a way that is redemptive.

Chapter goals We want to teach our children to do five things:

- We want them to understand the power of culture to shape our beliefs, relationships, and decisions.
- We want to help them recognize the influence of the surrounding culture on them personally.
- We want to help them develop biblical analytical and decision-making skills.
- We want to help them to recognize the idol themes of the surrounding culture.
- We want to teach them how to influence their culture in a way that is wise, alert, and redemptive.

Study Questions

1. What does the philosophy, "Evil is in the thing, so avoid the thing" mean?
2. What dangers exist in separating oneself from the world?

3. If evil is not an organic presence within certain things, what is it? Why is this important?
4. What is the assimilation philosophy?
5. What dangers are associated with the assimilation philosophy?
6. What is culture?
7. Is there any way to escape culture? Why or why not?
8. Match the following themes with the correct definition (pp.148–149).

____ Relativism	A. No sense of innate, natural responsibility to a higher authority than self. No functional recognition of the existence of God and the call to live to his glory.
____ Individualism	B. Focus on the present; living for the moment. Focus on present personal happiness. No sense of delayed gratification, investment.
____ Emotionalism	C. No higher goal than my happiness and pleasure. No higher purpose than meeting my own needs, wants, rights, and desires.
____ Presentism	D. No sense of personal responsibility for actions. Belief that I am what my experience has made me. My defects are the result of people and situations outside my control.
____ Materialism	E. No absolute standard for life. Each person determines what is right for him. Right changes with the situation.
____ Autonomy	F. No recognition of the spiritual world. Goal of life is experiencing physical pleasure and possessing material goods. Focus on what is seen.
____ Victimism	G. Feelings are the most influential, important indicator of what is right and best. Feelings as personal guidance system.

9. Match the following themes with the fruit seen in individuals (pp.148–149).

___ Relativism	A. No consistency of lifestyle or conviction. No internal restraint. Susceptibility to influence of others. Dislike of rules.
___ Individualism	B. Regular patterns of blameshifting. Excusing, rationalizing bad behavior; defensiveness. Lack of confession. No sense of need for personal change.
___ Emotionalism	C. Selfishness, self-centeredness, "rights" focus. Lack of commitment to others. Laziness, irresponsibility. Grumbling, complaining.
___ Presentism	D. Tendency toward rebellion to authority. No real Godward focus in life. Authority and correction seen as negative.
___ Materialism	E. Teen moved by what feels right; good feelings focus. Seldom acts against feelings. Sensitive to approval or disapproval of others.
___ Autonomy	F. No independent pursuit of the things of the Lord. No focus on character and attitude. Focus on clothing, beauty, friends, and things.
___ Victimism	G. A "got to have it now" mentality. No focus on long-term investment. No sense of consequences. Impulsive decisions.

10. Match the following themes with the biblical alternative (pp.148–149).

____ Relativism	A. Creaturehood: Life guided by a recognition of the Creator and lived to his glory.
____ Individualism	B. Spirituality: A life shaped by a seriousness about heart issues and one's relationship with God.
____ Emotionalism	C. Two Great Commands: Life shaped by practical commitment to love God and to love neighbor.
____ Presentism	D. Sin: Humble recognition of struggle with sin within and temptation without. Thankfulness for the forgiving grace of Christ.
____ Materialism	E. Biblical Faith: Commitment to test everything by the truths of Scripture.
____ Autonomy	F. Truth: Willing submission and obedience to the commands and principles of Scripture.
____ Victimism	G. Eternity: A personal commitment to do everything with an eye toward the reality of eternity.

11. What error do we tend to make in dealing with culture's vehicles?
12. What strategies does the author suggest for talking to your teens about culture?
13. In what four ways does the author indicate culture influences our lives?
14. What is the alternative to isolation and assimilation?
15. Why is it important to interact with the culture?
16. What are the fundamental objectives of the redemptive interaction strategy?
17. What are five ways you can prepare your teens to interact redemptively with their culture?
18. What is involved in each of the above strategies?

Application Questions

1. Do you personally tend toward rejection or assimilation in your approach to culture? What are you doing to avoid the dangers listed by the author?

2. Which view of culture do you believe each of your children has adopted?

3. Using Figure 1 on pp. 148–149, evaluate yourself and your children in regard to which idols are the biggest danger. Explain why you answered as you did.

4. After studying Phil. 1:12–18, answer the following questions:
   - What does this passage teach us about God, his character, and his plan?
   - What do we learn about ourselves, our nature, our struggle, and the purpose of our lives?
   - What does this passage teach us about right and wrong, good and bad, and true and false?
   - What instruction does it offer about relationships, love, authority, etc.?
   - What does this passage teach us about life's meaning and purpose?
   - What does this passage teach us about the inner man, the heart and how it functions?
   - What have we learned from this passage that would guide the way we live and make decisions?
   - How does this passage help us understand and critique our culture?

5. After studying Gen. 50:15–21, answer the following questions:
   - What does this passage teach us about God, his character, and his plan?
   - What do we learn about ourselves, our nature, our struggle, and the purpose of our lives?
   - What does this passage teach us about right and wrong, good and bad, and true and false?
   - What instruction does it offer about relationships, love, authority, etc.?
   - What does this passage teach us about life's meaning and purpose?
   - What does this passage teach us about the inner man, the heart and how it functions?
   - What have we learned from this passage that would guide the way we live and make decisions?
   - How does this passage help us understand and critique our culture?

6. After studying Jeremiah 17:5–10, answer the following questions:
   - What does this passage teach us about God, his character, and his plan?
   - What do we learn about ourselves, our nature, our struggle, and the purpose of our lives?
   - What does this passage teach us about right and wrong, good and bad, and true and false?

- What instruction does it offer about relationships, love, authority, etc.?
- What does this passage teach us about life's meaning and purpose?
- What does this passage teach us about the inner man, the heart and how it functions?
- What have we learned from this passage that would guide the way we live and make decisions?
- How does this passage help us understand and critique our culture?

7. After studying Rom. 1:18–32, answer the following questions:
   - What does this passage teach us about God, his character, and his plan?
   - What do we learn about ourselves, our nature, our struggle, and the purpose of our lives?
   - What does this passage teach us about right and wrong, good and bad, and true and false?
   - What instruction does it offer about relationships, love, authority, etc.?
   - What does this passage teach us about life's meaning and purpose?
   - What does this passage teach us about the inner man, the heart, and how it functions?
   - What have we learned from this passage that would guide the way we live and make decisions?
   - How does this passage help us understand and critique our culture?

8. Watch the evening news on TV. Choose three news stories and critique them biblically as follows: What view of life is expressed? What is right and wrong with this view? What is the common ground with which we can identify?

10 A HEART FOR GOD

Core principle It is no exaggeration to say that this is the ultimate goal of parenting. It is the fundamental motivation for doing everything else we do. It is the reason for all the talking, praying, instructing, correcting, saying "no" and "yes." We do all of these things with the hope that God would use us to produce teenagers who love and serve God above all else. Our prayer is that there would be a vertical (Godward) focus to everything the teenager says and does. This is the thing that must rule the teenager's heart if she is ever going to live a godly life in this fallen world. We must hold onto this goal. We cannot settle for anything less.

A heart for God must be distinguished from a Pharisaical performance of external Christian duty. This is more about the praise of people and temporal benefits than it is about pleasing God. No, a heart for God is a deep, sincere, and abiding hunger to know, love, and honor God even at the expense of other desirable things in life. We must not give in to the cynicism that would make us think it is ridiculous to expect this quality to grow in the heart of a teenager.

Chapter goals The first goal of this chapter is to help parents consider whether this goal is the fundamental motivator in their relationship with their teenagers. Is this goal more important than other, culturally dictated goals? Have they tended to see this goal as unrealistic? The Bible reminds us that a person who only lives for the physical things of this world is a fool. The second goal is to give parents a functional understanding of what a heart for God looks like. The final goal is to teach parents what they can do to encourage a personal pursuit of God in their children.

Study Questions

1. What should we most want for our children?
2. What is one reason this goal may seem unrealistically high for our children?
3. Why is it so common that, although children do not consciously deny God, other things replace his functional rule over their lives?
4. What might parents have to do to create opportunities to communicate redemptive awe to their children?
5. What is the central characteristic of a heart for God?
6. What signs might a parent expect to see in a teen with a heart for God?
7. What practical things can encourage a heart for God in our teens?

Application Questions

1. What changes do you need to make in your lifestyle to become a better shepherd and discipler of your children?
2. To what extent do you think you have taken Christ and your relationship with him for granted?
3. When you look at yourself and at your children, do you see signs of a pursuit of God? Use the following scale for evaluation.

    1 - Rarely

    2 - Occasionally

    3 - Regularly/habitually

I spend time reading the Bible.   1 2 3

I spend time praying.   1 2 3

I look forward to attending church.   1 2 3

I seek out instruction.   1 2 3

I choose friends who are known to be wise men and women.   1 2 3

I have cultivated friendships with people who are willing to confront me.   1 2 3

I am open and willing to listen to God's Word.   1 2 3

I introduce spiritual things into my conversations with others.   1 2 3

I seek biblical direction for my decisions.   1 2 3

I resist making impulsive, emotional decisions.   1 2 3

I ask myself what would please God in the daily situations I face.   1 2 3

4. What practical things do you do to develop a heart for God in your children?

5. Do you have family worship? What do you do to make it engaging?

6. List three ways in which you pointed your teen to God during the last week.

7. Ask your spouse and each of your children to recall the last time you sought forgiveness. Would they say you regularly seek forgiveness when you fail?

8. Do you invite your family members to hold you accountable for change? For what things are they currently holding you accountable?

9. How would you rate the importance of prayer in your family life? Base your rating on what you actually do, not on what you think would be good to do.

10. Do you hunger after God and does your family see it?

11 LEAVING HOME

Core principle It has often been said that the goal of parenting is to work yourself out of a job. Although that moment of emancipation is painful for parents and often filled with "Not yets" and " I regrets," it is the goal we have been working toward since the child's birth. It is also true that one of the great problems of all cultures is that we are sending generations of children out into the world who are essentially unprepared. Our goal is to reach that point of emancipation with children who are mature, and therefore prepared to face life on their own. This means they will be able to deal wisely with the catalog of circumstances, problems, relationships, concerns, and temptations that they will encounter in the world. Our definition of maturity must take progressive sanctification as its model. Our teenagers will not leave our homes as finished products. Our hope is that we will see seeds of maturity that can then continue to grow after the teen has left our home.

Chapter goal Four primary goals need to be our focus here:
- To help our teenagers develop a biblical definition of maturity that would become a useful tool of self-evaluation.
- To teach our teenagers how to recognize the fruit of maturity in their lives.
- To be used of God to help them grow in areas where growth is necessary.
- To participate with them in an honest evaluation of their readiness to be emancipated from the home.

Study Questions
1. According to the author, few teens who want to leave home desire to do so because of the rules. Why do they want to leave?
2. What four verbs can set the agenda for parents who want to model Christ with their teens? Explain.
3. What six characteristics does the author include in his definition of maturity?
4. What does functional godliness mean?
5. Describe the practical fruit of biblical maturity.

Application Questions
1. How effectively are you modeling Christ? Use the following scale.

    1 - Rarely

    2 - Occasionally

    3 - Regularly/habitually

I greet the sin of others with the accepting grace of Christ.	1 2 3
I hold God's standard high without compromising it.	1 2 3
I refrain from condemning, rejecting, and being judgmental.	1 2 3
I reveal Christ's love to others.	1 2 3
I reveal Christ's patience to others.	1 2 3
I reveal Christ's gentleness to others.	1 2 3
I reveal Christ's kindness to others.	1 2 3
I reveal Christ's forgiveness to others.	1 2 3
I identify with those facing harsh realities.	1 2 3
I identify with those facing temptations.	1 2 3
I recognize my vulnerability to the struggles others might have.	1 2 3
I spend as much time asking good questions and listening as I do speaking.	1 2 3
I know what situations my family members face every day.	1 2 3
I know the pressures my family members are facing.	1 2 3

2. Evaluate the maturity of your family members using the following scale.

   1 - Rarely

   2 - Occasionally

   3 - Regularly/habitually

My family member has a knowledge of God's will in the varied situations of life.	1 2 3
My family member knows how the principles of Scripture apply to everyday life.	1 2 3
My family member desires to please the Lord in everything he or she does.	1 2 3
My family member is teachable.	1 2 3
I see growth in the life of my family member.	1 2 3
My family member refrains from giving up, running away, or quitting in the face of trouble.	1 2 3
My family member endures.	1 2 3
My family member appreciates the great privilege of being born into the family of faith.	1 2 3
My family member does not take our spiritual heritage for granted.	1 2 3
My family member prizes being an heir of God's grace.	1 2 3
My family member pursues God's desires rather than his or her own.	1 2 3

3. Rate your family members on the fruit of maturity you observe in their lives. Use the following continuum.

My family member accepts and finds satisfaction in his or her responsibilities.	1 2 3 4	My family member acts as if life is supposed to be fun and enjoyable all the time.
My family member has a reputation for being trustworthy.	1 2 3 4	My family member frequently excuses irresponsibility with statements such as, "Oh, I'm sorry, I forgot," "I didn't know I was supposed to . . ." or "I guess I misunderstood what you said."

My family member acts responsibly even when no one is watching.	1 2 3 4	My family member must be coerced into doing what he or she is supposed to do.
My family member pursues Bible teaching, personal worship, and ministry on his or her own.	1 2 3 4	My family member's communion with the Lord occurs only when it is initiated or controlled by others.
My family member maintains healthy, productive, God-glorifying relationships with others.	1 2 3 4	My family member requires constant intervention from others to maintain relationships.
My family member knows how to solve problems with others.	1 2 3 4	My family member doesn't understand how he or she creates problems with others.
My family member finds joy and meaning in work.	1 2 3 4	My family member considers work a necessary evil and avoids it whenever possible.
Employers and others indicate my family member is a willing worker.	1 2 3 4	My family member grumbles and complains about work.
My family member erects moral boundaries.	1 2 3 4	My family member likes to see how close he or she can come to the edge of the moral cliff.
My family member can be trusted to make good choices even when others aren't watching.	1 2 3 4	My family member is not responsible or trustworthy even for very small things.
My family member is open and transparent.	1 2 3 4	My family member is intolerant of conversations about what he or she is doing.

My family member seeks out good advice.	1 2 3 4	My family member gets defensive when his or her choices are questioned.
My family member is approachable.	1 2 3 4	I feel like I am walking on eggshells with my family member.
I can lovingly challenge my family member's thinking, choices, and actions.	1 2 3 4	My family member turns even friendly discussions into unfriendly debates.
My family member has a sense of his or her strengths and weaknesses.	1 2 3 4	My family member responds with a "What are you talking about, I never do that!" attitude when I point out weaknesses.
My family member is thankful for what he or she has.	1 2 3 4	My family member is rarely content and constantly wants something new.
My family member reaches out to those who don't have much.	1 2 3 4	My family member judges people by their looks and clothing.
My family member uses money to serve others and the Lord.	1 2 3 4	My family member uses money to buy more stuff.
My family member's goals for life are to please God and serve him.	1 2 3 4	My family member's life goals center around materialistic achievements.

4. We cannot give our teens what we do not have ourselves. How would you rate yourself in the following areas? Use the following scale.

1 - Rarely
2 - Occasionally
3 - Regularly/habitually

I meet the standard of biblical maturity.	1 2 3
I model a winsome, mature godliness before my family.	1 2 3
I live a responsible life.	1 2 3
I am approachable and teachable.	1 2 3
I live with moral boundaries that shape my decisions and actions.	1 2 3
I have an accurate sense of where I am weak and where I am strong.	1 2 3
I am open to help from others.	1 2 3
I hold physical things in proper balance.	1 2 3

12 THREE STRATEGIES FOR PARENTING TEENS

Core principle God's redemptive work in us is strategic. He knows exactly what he is trying to produce (conformity to Christ) and exactly how he is going to accomplish it (the means of grace). As parents of teenagers, we are called to mirror the work of our Heavenly Father. We do not want our parenting to be aimless, ineffective, and unproductive. We not only want to parent with a sense of direction, we also want to know practically how to get to the destination. This chapter presents three strategies to get us where we want to go in the hearts and lives of our teenagers.

Project parenting. Here we learn to regularly evaluate our teenagers to gain an accurate, current sense of where they are struggling, experiencing temptation, or need to grow. We do this so we can take advantage of the daily opportunities God will give us to go after what is "hot."

Constant conversation. Here we recognize that, like other sinners, our teenagers need daily exhortation, encouragement, and intervention. We also recognize that they probably will not pursue us, so we commit ourselves to seek them out daily, engaging them in conversation, expressing our love, and looking for opportunities to encourage a Godward heart.

Leading your teenager to repentance. We do not want to simply constrain behavior. If that is all we have done, there will be nothing within the teenager to keep him moving towards God when he has left home. It is only when the heart turns that the life will turn. We need to regularly call our teenagers to confession and repentance. Our goal is to tell them over and over again that there is nothing in life more important than turning their hearts toward God.

Chapter goals The goal of focusing on these three strategies is twofold. First, we need to remind ourselves that God always gives his people a means of accomplishing what he has called them to do. He hasn't called us to an unrealistic, undoable life. In his grace he is not only the God of ends, but of means as well. Second, the goal is that in focusing on these strategies, we can function with prepared spontaneity. Although I do not know what a particular day will bring, I am prepared for it and able to spontaneously respond because I have committed myself to concrete goals and to practical strategies for reaching them. So I will regularly be surprised but not caught unprepared.

Study Questions

1. What does the term "project parenting" imply?
2. What two deficiencies in the heart of the wicked are described in Psalm 36?
3. How might these deficiencies show up in teens?
4. Besides clear goals, what else do parents need to accomplish "project parenting"?
5. What two components of personal insight does the author point out?
6. Why do our teens need constant (daily) conversation?
7. What four steps are involved in turning away from God?
8. What four steps does the author suggest to lead teens to repentance and reconciliation?

Application Questions

1. For each family member, ask yourself, "What important struggles are present in his or her life that we need to pursue?" How does your family member currently view these areas? Where does he or she tend to minimize or rationalize sin?
2. In which of the three strategies presented in this chapter are you strongest? Weakest? What can and will you do to strengthen any weaknesses?

13 SMALL STEPS TO BIG CHANGE

Core principle God's goals are high. What he wants for us is much grander than anything we would ever want for ourselves. What he calls us to do is higher, better, and more important than what we would have decided to do if left to ourselves. This is true of parenting as well. It would be very easy to get to the end of a book like this and be overwhelmed as you look at the huge mountain of parental responsibility placed before you. But we must remember that our God is a God of little steps. The radical work of change that God works in and through you is rarely accomplished through a single event. It is a process. He calls us to climb mountains with small steps. These steps, although small, are not unimportant. Each little step is significant because it gets us closer to the God-assigned goal.

This chapter is about recognizing the small things that must be done regularly to function as God's instrument of change in the life of your teenager.

Chapter goals The first goal of this chapter is to see that God's work in our teenagers' lives is incremental. We do not have to feel pressured to accomplish something in a single encounter when it actually takes years. The second goal is to learn the little things that contribute to big change in a teenager's life. This chapter offers a list of constructive small steps. The third goal is to determine which of those steps would be particularly helpful for your teenager.

Study Questions
1. List the twenty steps the author suggests to bring about change.

Application Questions
Summarize the things that have been helpful to you from this book.

Paul David Tripp (M.Div., Philadelphia Theological Seminary; D.Min., Westminster Theological Seminary) is the president of Paul Tripp Ministries, a nonprofit organization whose mission statement is "Connecting the transforming power of Jesus Christ to everyday life." This mission leads Paul to weekly speaking engagements around the world. From 2007 to 2011, Paul was also on the pastoral staff at Tenth Presbyterian Church in Philadelphia, Pennsylvania, where he preached on Sunday evenings and led the Ministry to Center City. Paul is also the Professor of Pastoral Life and Care at Redeemer Seminary in Dallas, Texas, and the Executive Director of the Center for Pastoral Life and Care in Fort Worth, Texas, and has taught at respected institutions worldwide. As an author, Paul has written ten books on Christian living that are read and distributed internationally. He has been married for many years to Luella, and they have four grown children. For speaking engagements and other information see www.paultrippministries.org.

RESOURCES FOR CHANGING LIVES

Addictions—A Banquet in the Grave: Finding Hope in the Power of the Gospel. Edward T. Welch shows how addictions result from a worship disorder—idolatry—and how they are overcome by the power of the gospel. *978-0-87552-606-5*

Age of Opportunity: A Biblical Guide to Parenting Teens, 2d ed. Paul David Tripp uncovers the heart issues affecting parents' relationship with their teenagers. *978-0-87552-605-8*

Blame It on the Brain? Distinguishing Chemical Imbalances, Brain Disorders, and Disobedience. Edward T. Welch compares the roles of the brain and the heart in problems such as alcoholism, depression, ADD, and homosexuality. *978-0-87552-602-7*

Instruments in the Redeemer's Hands: People in Need of Change Helping People in Need of Change. Paul David Tripp demonstrates how God uses his people, who need change themselves, as tools of change in the lives of others. *978-0–87552–607–2*

Seeing with New Eyes: Counseling and the Human Condition through the Lens of Scripture. David Powlison embraces, probes, and unravels counseling and the problems of daily life with a biblical perspective. *978-0-87552-608-9*

Step by Step: Divine Guidance for Ordinary Christians. James C. Petty sifts through approaches to knowing God's will and illustrates how to make biblically wise decisions. *978-0-87552-603-4*

War of Words: Getting to the Heart of Your Communication Struggles. Paul David Tripp takes us beyond superficial solutions in the struggle to control our tongues. *978-0-87552-604-1*

When People Are Big and God Is Small: Overcoming Peer Pressure, Codependency, and the Fear of Man. Edward T. Welch exposes the spiritual dimensions of pride, defensiveness, people-pleasing, needing approval, "self-esteem," etc. *978-0-87552-600-3*

Booklet Series: *A.D.D.; Anger; Angry at God?; Bad Memories; Depression; Domestic Abuse; Forgiveness; God's Love; Guidance; Homosexuality; "Just One More"; Marriage; Motives; OCD; Pornography; Pre-Engagement; Priorities; Procrastination; Self-Injury; Sexual Sin; Stress; Suffering; Suicide; Teens and Sex; Thankfulness; Why Me?; Worry*

FOR FURTHER INFORMATION

Speaking engagements with authors in this series may be arranged by calling The Christian Counseling and Educational Foundation at (215) 884-7676.

Videotapes and audio cassettes by authors in this series may be ordered through Resources for Changing Lives at (800) 318-2186.

For a complete catalog of titles from P&R Publishing, call (800) 631-0094.